CHARLES TALBOT

DUKE OF SHREWSBURY

T0371200

CHARLES TALBOT, DUKE OF SHREWSBURY

From the portrait in the National Portrait Gallery

CHARLES TALBOT
DUKE OF SHREWSBURY

BY

T. C. NICHOLSON, M.A.
New College, Oxford

AND

A. S. TURBERVILLE, M.A., B.LITT.
New College, Oxford
Professor of Modern History in the University of Leeds

CAMBRIDGE
AT THE UNIVERSITY PRESS
1930

CAMBRIDGE
UNIVERSITY PRESS

University Printing House, Cambridge CB2 8BS, United Kingdom

Cambridge University Press is part of the University of Cambridge.

It furthers the University's mission by disseminating knowledge in the pursuit of education, learning and research at the highest international levels of excellence.

www.cambridge.org
Information on this title: www.cambridge.org/9781107475311

© Cambridge University Press 1930

First published 1930
First paperback edition 2014

A catalogue record for this publication is available from the British Library

ISBN 978-1-107-47531-1 Paperback

CONTENTS

PREFATORY NOTE . . . . p. vii

CHAPTER I *Ancestry and Early Life* . . . 1

II *The Revolution* 23

III *In Opposition* 50

IV *Second Secretaryship of State* . . 75

V *The Fenwick Case* 108

VI *The Aftermath of the Fenwick Case* . 131

VII *Travels Abroad, 1700–1705* . . . 143

VIII *Alliance with the Tories* . . . 162

IX *The Paris Embassy, and the Irish Lord-Lieutenancy* 182

X *The Hanoverian Succession* . . . 206

XI *Conclusion* 222

BIBLIOGRAPHY 236

INDEX 242

ILLUSTRATIONS

Charles Talbot, Duke of Shrewsbury . . *frontispiece*
From the portrait in the National Portrait Gallery

Charles Talbot, Duke of Shrewsbury . *facing page* 102
From the portrait by Sir Peter Lely in the Charterhouse

PREFATORY NOTE

A number of years ago Mr Nicholson began a Life of the Duke of Shrewsbury on a much more elaborate scale than that of the present volume. He had accumulated a great quantity of material and had finished the text as far as the early part of Chapter VI, when, unfortunately, the pressure of other work compelled him to relinquish the undertaking. Professor Turberville's contribution has been the revision and abridgement of the original portion written by Mr Nicholson and the completion of the biography on the reduced scale which seemed desirable, with the addition of bibliography and index.

14 *July* 1930

CHARLES TALBOT
DUKE OF SHREWSBURY

CHAPTER I

Ancestry and Early Life

Among the statesmen of the Revolution period and the age of Anne few present a more interesting character study than the man who in 1668 succeeded to the dignities of the ancient house of Talbot, which with a pedigree dating back in the male line to the Norman Conquest rivalled even the De Veres of Oxford in antiquity. Edward III had summoned one of its members to sit in Parliament as Baron Talbot. The dignities of Valence and Montchesny and of Strange of Blackmere had fallen to descendants of his, and a subsequent marriage to the heiress of the Furnivals had brought to the Talbots the baronies of Verdon and Lovetot and large estates in and around Sheffield. The twelfth Baron Talbot, who acted for some time as Lieutenant of Ireland and fought with distinction in the French wars of Henry VI, was in 1442 created Earl of Shrewsbury and in 1446 Earl of Waterford and Wexford and Lord of Dungarvan in the peerage of Ireland. He fell in the battle of Châtillon; his son, the second Earl, having thrown in his lot with the Lancastrian party, was killed at the battle of Northampton.[1]

It was from a younger son of this, the second Earl, that Charles Talbot, the twelfth holder of the title, was descended. The elder branch of the family became extinct in 1618 on the

[1] J. Hunter, *History of Hallamshire* (ed. Gatty, 1869), pp. 61–101; A. Collins, *Complete Peerage* (ed. Sir E. Brydges, 9 vols. 1812), vol. III, pp. 1–39; J. E. Doyle, *Official Baronage of England* (3 vols. 1806), vol. III, pp. 309–24.

death of the eighth Earl, the son of the custodian of Mary Queen of Scots during her confinement in Sheffield Castle, and their estates in Hallamshire passed to the house of Howard. The Irish estates of the family had been forfeited by Henry VII's Statute of Absentees. These were restored by Charles II, but the Irish peers refused to recognise the original patent of 1446. The new branch of the family under a grant of Henry VII had become possessed of the manor of Grafton with its dependencies, which served in some slight degree to counterbalance the loss of estates on the failure of the direct line. After passing to the nephew of the ninth Earl, the title devolved in 1654 upon his son Francis Talbot, who, his first wife having died without issue, married as his second wife, Anna Maria, daughter of Lord Brudenell, afterwards second Earl of Cardigan. Two sons were born of this marriage.

But the union was far from happy. The Countess, one of the beauties of the Court of Charles II, figures prominently in Grammont's *chronique scandaleuse* of Whitehall. While satire was busy at the expense of Lady Castlemaine, he tells us, duels were fought every day for the favours of Lady Shrewsbury, who thought it her greatest merit to be more of a coquette than her rivals. No one could boast of monopolising her good graces, and no one could complain of having met with a bad reception from her.[1] Among the most conspicuous of her numerous lovers was Killigrew the actor, who had "nothing better to do"; but he was before long supplanted by a more distinguished admirer in George Villiers, Duke of Buckingham, who seems to have been inspired to meddle by Killigrew's incessant boasting of his relations with the Countess.[2]

The intrigue began when Buckingham was entertaining Lord and Lady Cardigan and the Earl and Countess of

---

[1] *Mémoires du Comte de Grammont*, par le Comte Antoine Hamilton (La Haye, 1741), pp. 107, 124–7.
[2] *Ibid.* pp. 373–5.

Shrewsbury at York in June 1666. "The days were spent in visits and play, and all sorts of diversions that place could afford; and the nights in dancing sometimes till day the next morning: only the two Earls, not being men for these sports, went to bed something early." Reresby, who narrates the story of this month's sojourn in York, adds: "I sent at this time for my wife to wait on the Duchess of Buckingham, who, good woman, perceived nothing at that time of the intrigue that was carrying on between her husband and the Countess of Shrewsbury; but her stay there was short, it being no good school for a young wife". Late one night Lady Shrewsbury's brother was summoned to try to compose "a great quarrel of jealousy concerning the Duke, and yet the Countess had so great a power with her Lord that he stayed some time after that".[1]

As Reresby truly remarked it was "no good school for a young wife". But Shrewsbury seems to have been fascinated by the Countess, and he was the most patient and long-suffering of husbands. Having succeeded in capturing higher game, Lady Shrewsbury promptly threw over Killigrew, who in his anger not only publicly upbraided her for her faithlessness but also cast reflections upon her personal appearance. He was, however, afraid of Buckingham and after an encounter with hired ruffians, who left him for dead, he fled abroad, feeling that it would be useless to remonstrate and unsafe to remain.[2] Besides, there were reports that the infuriated Countess, who found him an intolerable nuisance, was resolved to have him killed. Presently she also ran away —some said in order to slay Harry Killigrew with her own hands, others to enter into a monastery. The Earl sent to Dover and Deal to stop her.[3] Whether he was successful or

[1] *Memoirs of Sir John Reresby* (ed. J. Cartwright, 1875), p. 67.
[2] *Grammont*, pp. 375–6.
[3] *Savile Correspondence* (ed. W. D. Cooper, Camden Soc. 1858), p. 22.

not is uncertain. At any rate the much-injured husband had now reached the limit of his notorious forbearance. "Being too honourable a man to complain to his wife", he sent a challenge to Buckingham.[1] It was accepted, and the duel took place on January 16, 1667/8. Each principal was accompanied by two seconds, who also engaged—a proceeding common on the Continent, but rare in England. That the duel was "all about my Lady Shrewsbury" was perfectly well known.[2] "They met yesterday in a close near Barne-Elmes", Pepys records, "and there fought: and my Lord Shrewsbury is run through the body, from the right breast through the shoulder: and Sir John Talbot all along up one of his arms; and Jenkins killed upon the place....It is said that my Lord Shrewsbury's case is to be feared, that he may die too; and that may make it much the worse for the Duke of Buckingham".[3] Eleven days after the encounter the Duke succeeded in obtaining a full pardon, and this was followed by a similar grant to his antagonist.[4] The duel was the talk of London, more especially as a story was soon bruited about that the Countess of Shrewsbury had been present disguised as a page, holding the Duke's horse, and that she had embraced her lover while he was still stained with her husband's blood, ready, had the latter proved victorious, to shoot both herself and him.[5]

The Earl of Shrewsbury lingered for a couple of months and died on March 16, not apparently of the wound itself, which had perfectly healed, but of a malady occasioned by it. In his *Diary* for May 15, Pepys writes: "I am told...that

[1] *Grammont*, p. 376.

[2] *Pepys' Diary* (ed. H. B. Wheatley, 9 vols. 1893–9), Jan. 17, 1667/8, vol. VII, pp. 283–4.

[3] *Ibid.* p. 284.

[4] *C.S.P.* (*Dom.*), 1667–8, pp. 192–3.

[5] Lady Burghclere is inclined to reject the story on the ground that the Duke stated in 1674 that the Countess was in a convent at the time and that this statement was accepted by the Peers by whom

the Countess of Shrewsbury is brought home by the Duke of Buckingham to his house, where his Duchess saying it was not for her and the other to live together in a house, he answered, 'Why, Madam, I did think so, and, therefore, have ordered your coach to be ready, to carry you to your father's', which was a devilish speech, but they say true, and my Lady Shrewsbury is there, it seems".¹ And with Buckingham "this famous Helen"² remained. Scandal followed scandal. On May 18, 1669, at night, while going in a hackney coach from the park to his house at Turnham Green, Killigrew was attacked on the high road and wounded in nine places. His assailants were said to be in Lady Shrewsbury's employ. Her coach apparently stood by the while, and the French am bassador writes that she hounded on the ruffians, shouting "kill the villain", and that she did not proceed on her way till Killigrew was believed to be dead. Though badly wounded he was not dead, however, and he swore an information against his assailants. "You may fancy the noise the attempt to murder him causes, and the worry and anxiety of the Duke of Buckingham who is still passionately in love with his virago", wrote the French ambassador, Colbert de Croissy.³ James, Duke of York, was gratified to think that this new outrage would seriously damage the influence of his enemy Buckingham,⁴ but the matter was allowed to drop, and the Countess continued to live with the Duke. There was even

he was being tried, though they were not predisposed in his favour. *Life of Buckingham* (1903), pp. 194–5.

¹ *Pepys' Diary*, May 15, 1668, vol. VIII, pp. 17–18.
² *Grammont*, p. 370.
³ Colbert to Lionne, May 20, 1669, in T. Longueville, *Rochester and other Literary Rakes* (1902), p. 93; *Pepys' Diary*, May 19, 1669, vol. VIII, p. 326.
⁴ *Pepys' Diary*, vol. VIII, p. 327. Charles II's sympathies seem throughout to have been with Buckingham against Killigrew. Cf. his letter to the Duchess of Orleans, Oct. 17, 1668, in Julia Cartwright's *Madame* (1900), pp. 273–4.

a report that the latter's chaplain had been induced to go through the farce of a marriage service.[1]

When a son was born to the couple, the father's conduct astounded even those who had had ample experience of his effrontery. The King was asked to stand godfather to the child, whom Buckingham chose, without any authorisation, to style Earl of Coventry, and when the infant died it was with that title that it was interred. In the burial register, however, the non-committal entry appears: "A young male child was laid in the Duke of Buckingham's vault, being related to that family".[2] A few months later (October 1671), Evelyn speaks of the Duke as being "in mighty favour". He finds him and "that impudent woman, the Countess of Shrewsbury" at Newmarket among a number of "jolly blades raceing, dauncing, feasting, and revelling, more resembling a luxurious and abandon'd rout, than a Christian Court".[3] By that time the influence exerted over her paramour by Lady Shrewsbury had become so notorious that she was taken into the pay of the French Government as a means of securing French influence at the English Court, and she received a pension of 10,000 livres in November.[4]

During the existence of the so-called Cabal Administration Buckingham continued powerful, but by the end of 1673 the political situation had greatly altered and he was in disgrace; the opportunity for which his enemies had long been waiting had at last arrived. On January 7, 1673/4, a petition against him and the Countess was presented by Lord Brudenell and five relatives of the late Earl on behalf of the latter's eldest

[1] *Rochester and other Literary Rakes*, pp. 92–3.
[2] *Westminster Abbey Registers* (ed. J. L. Chester for Harleian Soc. 1876), vol. VIII, p. 173.
[3] *Evelyn's Diary* (ed. W. Bray, 1827), Oct. 21, 1671, vol. II, p. 355.
[4] Dispatch from Colbert, Nov. 9, 1671, in Sir J. Dalrymple's *Memoirs of Great Britain and Ireland* (3 vols. 1776–88), vol. II, app. p. 82.

son.[1] It set forth "the killing of the late Earle of Shrewsbury, their open and scandalous way of living together, and the publick interment of their bastard child in Westminster as Earl of Coventree".[2] The Duke was ordered to file his reply within a week. Lady Shrewsbury promptly fled on receipt of a summons to appear under pain of "being proceeded against as to banishment and loss of her joynture".[3] Sobered by his fall, Buckingham publicly revealed himself as a "greate converte" by going to church on Sunday with the Duchess, and he and Lord Shaftesbury, to whom he had become reconciled, laboured "to gett him fairely quitt of my Lady Shrewsbury's businesse".[4] He even confessed, and begged pardon of the House of Lords, requesting that all mention of the affair might be erased from the records. When the Peers refused this request he withdrew the confession, "having ownde more than ye Petitions against him could prove";[5] but a week later he "made a very submissive recantation", acknowledged the "miserable and lewd life he had led", and expressed his thankfulness that the displeasure of the House had opened his eyes to the foulness of his past life, which he was now resolved to amend. On his promising to break with Lady Shrewsbury the House absolved him, and ordered that they should both enter into bonds of £10,000.[6] In the autumn the Countess retired to the Continent, accompanied by the Earl of Cardigan.[7]

Such was the mother of Charles Talbot, twelfth Earl and

---

[1] *Lords Journals*, Jan. 7, 1673/4, vol. XII, p. 599; *MSS. of the Duke of Somerset* (H.M.C. Rept. XV, app. pt vii), p. 104; *Letters to Sir Joseph Williamson* (ed. W. D. Christie, Camden Soc. 1874), vol. II, p. 120.

[2] *Essex Papers* (ed. O. Airy, Camden Soc. 1890), vol. I, p. 160.

[3] *Letters to Williamson*, vol. II, p. 120.

[4] *Essex Papers*, vol. I, p. 167.

[5] *Ibid.* p. 170.

[6] *Ibid.* pp. 173–4, *L.J.* vol. XII, p. 628.

[7] *C.S.P. (Dom.)*, 1673–5, p. 369.

only Duke of Shrewsbury, and such were the circumstances under which his early years were spent. Born on July 24, 1660, he was the first child for whom Charles II acted as god-father after his Restoration.[1] Through the tragic death of his father on March 16, 1667/8, he became head of his house before he had completed his eighth year.[2] With his grand-father the Earl of Cardigan and his uncle Sir John Talbot as his principal guardians, he was brought up in the Roman Catholic faith of both his father's and his mother's families. Shortly after the conclusion of the proceedings in the House of Lords on the petition against the Duke of Buckingham his guardians decided to send him abroad to complete his edu-cation, in accordance with the custom of the time among the upper classes, especially those who still adhered to the old religion. The boy, not yet fourteen, took much interest in the preparations for the expedition, and especially in the sartorial arrangements. He must have a handsome riding suit, and if the periwig-maker does not make a very good periwig he will not have it.[3]

In May 1674 the young Earl came up to London and obtained a pass "to travel beyond the seas for seven years",[4] and soon after he set out accompanied by a tutor or governor named James Morgan. Embarking somewhere on the Thames, they crossed over to Dieppe, and after the Earl had spent two days in Rouen, "in visiting what that town could afford worth his curiosity", they reached Paris and took lodgings in the Faubourg St Germain. The tutor reported

[1] *The Life and Character of Charles, Duke of Shrewsbury* (1718), p. 3.

[2] He now became Earl of Shrewsbury, Wexford and Waterford; Baron Talbot, Strange of Blackmere, Furnival, Verdon, Lovetot, Giffard of Brimsfield, Comyn de Badenoch, Valence and Mont-chesny, and Hereditary High Steward of Ireland.

[3] *Buccleuch MSS. at Montagu House* (H.M.C.), vol. II, pt i, p. 17.

[4] *C.S.P.* (*Dom.*), 1673–5, p. 246.

their safe arrival to the Earl's guardians. His young charge had undergone the difficulties of their journey beyond expectation; the stay in Rouen had not been made for the purpose of recovering from the sea voyage, during which "his Lordship was so well in health, that one may believe he was rather designed to become an admiral at sea, than to be esteemed a passenger the first time he ever was on shipboard".[1] It was intended to establish the boy as a pupil in Navarre College, the splendid fourteenth-century foundation of Joanna, Queen of Navarre and of Philip IV of France.[2] However, when he was taken on a tour of inspection to the College, the tutor did not "find his Lordship inclined to shut himself up in the walls of it".[3]

Shrewsbury had not been many months in Paris before he fell a victim to small-pox. The attack was, however, only a mild one. The tutor, treating the illness much as we should nowadays treat an attack of measles, expressed his gratification that the Earl had "cancelled a debt most men are solvable for". He had enjoyed the services of an able doctor and "a careful and experienced nurse-keeper".[4] In less than a month Shrewsbury had recovered; he was not in the least disfigured, and a wish was expressed that his brother were "as well past the danger".[5] Possibly it was in part because of this illness that his mother and his grandfather crossed over to France in September. In the following spring the three went to Pontoise and they remained there during the month of May. Lady Shrewsbury shewed a decorum, which, as her son quaintly expressed it, "gave good content" to his friends;

[1] *Buccleuch MSS.* vol. II, pt i, pp. 17–18.
[2] H. Rashdall, *Universities of Europe in the Middle Ages* (2 vols. in 3, 1895), vol. I, pp. 491, 494.
[3] *Buccleuch MSS.* vol. II, pt i, pp. 17–18.
[4] Morgan to Sir J. Talbot, Oct. 17, 1674, in *Buccleuch MSS.* vol. II, pt i, pp. 18–19.
[5] Cardigan and Shrewsbury to Talbot, Nov. 7, 1674, in *MSS. of Lord E. Talbot* (H.M.C. Various Collections, vol. II), p. 312.

she paid a visit to the Lady Abbess of Maubuisson, near Pontoise, who was Prince Rupert's sister, and saw "the virtuous lady's austere way of living, which did work very much upon her".[1]

On their return to Paris the Countess stayed a week with her son in his lodgings. During this time they were taken to see the palace and grounds of Versailles by one of the most remarkable of English residents in France, Walter Montagu, second son of the first Earl of Manchester.[2] Employed on diplomatic missions in France under Charles I, he had then adopted Roman Catholicism. During the Civil War he had acted as an intermediary for the royalists till he was arrested and thrown into the Tower by their opponents. Being banished in 1649 he had returned to France, where he was at one time or another influential with Mazarin, Anne of Austria, Henrietta Maria, and the Duchess of Orleans. He had been successively Abbot of the Benedictine Monastery of Nanteuil near Metz and of St Martin near Pontoise. While he had by this time resigned the latter dignity in favour of Cardinal Bouillon, he still received its large emoluments.

After her brief visit to her son in Paris the Countess retired to the convent at Pontoise. But she was not content to remain in retirement, and the following January Abbot Montagu solicited Shrewsbury's help in endeavouring to obtain his mother's readmission to Court, the Queen having stated that she would not receive her back without the consent of the Talbot family. Montagu urged that the Countess, "was the only lady of her quality that was restrained from paying her duty to her Majesty; that she had no intention to become a Courtier, and that her design of going to Court was only

---

[1] Louise Hollandina, sixth child of Frederick V, Elector Palatine, and the Princess Elizabeth. She was Abbess of Maubuisson from 1664 till her death in 1709.

[2] See *D.N.B.* (1909), vol. XIII, pp. 717–19.

to wash out the particular blot that lay upon her; that it was her intention and would be more to her honour to have the power of going to Court, and yet use it but seldom". Shrewsbury noted with some amusement the eagerness and simplicity of Montagu in pressing the matter. "Abbot Montagu," he wrote to his uncle, "good man, believing there was no other difficulty in the business than in penning the letter I was to write to my Lord Arlington, took that pains upon himself, and brought it me to copy over, and told me it was very convenient it should be so, and that I must write it against the next post, and he would come and call for it."[1] Shrewsbury had to point out that the Queen's undertaking had been given to the whole Talbot family and that his consent as its head would not suffice. He, however, interested himself in the matter, and apparently prevailed upon his relatives to agree. At all events after prolonged negotiations the Countess was in the following December "admitted to kiss the Queen's hand". Evidently Charles II's personal intervention was necessary to overcome the Queen's reluctance. In a letter written a few days after the reception it is stated that "Lady Shrewsbury hath bin by the King's absolute command received by the Queene, who did beg itt of her to gratifie, as he said, the long reitterated request of her son and father".[2]

Meanwhile another important negotiation had been opened. Although Shrewsbury was not yet sixteen, his guardians were considering the question of his marriage, and in February 1675/6 he was informed that an alliance with the daughter of Lord Northampton was under discussion. His uncle suggested his coming over to England for a short while in the spring, but Shrewsbury shewed no eagerness. The proposed visit, he said, would involve too

[1] Shrewsbury to Talbot, Jan. 12/22, 1675/6, in *Buccleuch MSS*. vol. II, pt i, pp. 19–20.
[2] Lady Chaworth to Lord Roos, Dec. 19, 1676, in *Rutland MSS*. (H.M.C.), vol. II, p. 33; same to same, Dec. 25, in *ibid*. p. 34.

much expense and too great an interruption of his studies.[1] His reply produced a peremptory letter from Sir John Talbot, demanding compliance with his wishes. The fifteen year old boy was prepared to obey, but first addressed to his uncle a long and spirited remonstrance. He pointed out that in his first letter Sir John had asked him whether he would like to come, when he would like to come, and how long he would like to stay; whereas now he commanded him to come forthwith and spoke of only a month's visit, "as if you designed me nothing but the drudgery of a troublesome journey to and fro". He agreed that it was necessary he

should have a view of the young lady, yet I cannot see the necessity of this particular time, or at least how you should not necessarily have foreseen it, and so be able to have given me timely notice, that I might not have been forced upon the disorder I am now in to prepare myself upon such a troublesome journey as I must expect from a Lenten accommodation, and such a distraction as I must necessarily receive in the Holy Week, a time far differently employed by other countries and other beliefs, than that you live in. It is an easy thing to give orders; those that comply only find the inconveniences that attend them. If you had reflected on that maxim, may be you would have concluded after Easter had been as proper a time to travel as Lent; a competency to have prepared in, much easier than precipitation; a yacht more commodious than a nasty packet-boat. But by a good fireside, in a handsome room, and good company, none of these unpleasant circumstances have admittance; and as it was resolved I was to come over in ten or twelve days' time, though the impossibility of my compliance is sufficiently grounded upon the contradiction of your own orders; for you would have me bring over two suits of clothes, two suits of linen, periwigs, belts, hats, gloves, shoes, boots, etc. (for all must be new, nay, even my lacqueys' liveries too, having delayed from time to time both the clothing them and myself in expectation of this journey); and to prepare all this tackling you allow me bare two or three days' time, whereas under ten or twelve Chedreux will not undertake to make a periwig, and it is a great favour if he keeps his word.

[1] Shrewsbury to Talbot, Feb. 16/26, 1675/6, in *Buccleuch MSS.* vol. II, pt i, p. 21.

A month's stay was "very short to enjoy my mother [and] my sister, and wait upon the rest of my friends, especially since this journey will not prove so much an interruption of my studies as a conclusion of them". However, he would come as soon as was possible. He hoped it would be possible for things to be contrived "so that I may have a view of the young lady without the world's taking notice of it". He concluded by expressing the esteem which he had felt and always would feel for his uncle.[1]

Whether Shrewsbury was unfavourably impressed by his "view of the young lady" or whatever else may be the explanation, nothing came of this visit and in October he was back in Paris preparing for his entrance into the Academy, which served as a sort of finishing school for the sons of the aristocracy, riding, fencing, and the use of arms holding the chief place in the curriculum, but dancing, music, drawing, mathematics, and "many other things befitting persons of quality" being included.[2] For his "exercise" at the Academy, Shrewsbury required a coach and livery. What would be the "cheapest and honorablest way of doing it"? He and Morgan decided that it would be cheapest and most serviceable to hire a coach by the month, "since they would run no risk of killing a horse", which was a "very dear commodity" in Paris, or of "being forced to stay at home for the lameness or sickness of one of them". But would such a proceeding be in keeping with his dignity? "The question is whether this coach (though it be new and has my crown and arms, if I please, and the coachman wears my livery) be so honourable as my own, which if it is not, I would rather undergo the charge than do a thing below myself."[3]

[1] Shrewsbury to Talbot, March 4/14, 1675/6, in *Buccleuch MSS.* vol. II, pt i, pp. 21–3.

[2] *Mémoires de Dumont de Bostaquet* (ed. C. Read and F. Waddington, Paris 1864), pp. 6–8 and n.

[3] Shrewsbury to Talbot, Oct. 18/28, 1676, in *Buccleuch MSS.* vol. II, pt i, p. 23.

The eventual decision was in favour of purchasing coach and horses.

Shrewsbury was very conscious of his own dignity, as another anecdote shews. The Duke of Somerset had been to call on Berkeley, the English ambassador, who received him sitting and wearing his hat. On leaving he encountered Shrewsbury, who was on his way to call on Berkeley also, and informed him of the character of his reception. The Earl said he would be even with Berkeley, and finding that he was received in exactly the same manner as the Duke he drew up a seat for himself and deliberately put on his hat. The ambassador was furious, but Shrewsbury coolly informed him that he knew how to treat him both in his public and in his private state, and that Berkeley ought to be aware that at home he was a better man than himself.[1]

The fact that Shrewsbury had been over in England to meet Lord Northampton's daughter seems to have been kept secret, for there is no mention of it even in the letters of the busy matchmakers who circulated numerous reports of his being most advantageously engaged.[2] Meanwhile his mother had been received at Court. Shortly afterwards she secretly married George Rodney Bridges, for whom in the following year she purchased a Bedchamber appointment for £4500.[3] Her acknowledgment of her second marriage led to a violent quarrel with her parents, followed by her abrupt departure from Cardigan House. She concealed her intentions even from her son, and in February 1677/8 Shrewsbury complained to his uncle that for ten or eleven months past he had received no communication whatever from his mother save for one letter which in three words informed him of her

---

[1] *MSS. of Sir H. Verney* (H.M.C. Rept. VII, app.), p. 493.
[2] Cf. *Hatton Corr.* (2 vols. ed. Sir E. Maunde Thompson, Camden Soc. 1878), vol. I, p. 134; *Rutland MSS.* vol. II, pp. 45, 50; *Verney MSS.* pp. 467, 472.
[3] *Hatton Corr.* vol. I, p. 52.

marriage, "and that not till six months after she owned it in Town".[1]

Early in 1678 Shrewsbury received from his uncle a communication which abruptly terminated his residence in France. In the previous November the Duke of York's elder daughter Mary had married William of Orange. Before William returned to Holland, it was arranged that Charles II should offer mediation between France and the United Provinces, who were then at war. Louis XIV peremptorily refused to conclude peace on the terms suggested, whereupon Charles signed an agreement with the Dutch to enforce their acceptance and ordered preparations for war. James, who was to lead the troops sent to Flanders, commanded Shrewsbury's attendance in his suite. Shrewsbury embraced the prospect "with as much joy and content as can be". He did not apparently at first realise that James had issued an "express order", and was apprehensive lest his grandfather should refuse his sanction. He feared that his entering the army was least in Cardigan's thoughts, and that the latter designed for him "an idle life in England as secure from danger as honour".[2] Once more the young Earl was much exercised in mind about his coach and horses. Should he sell them or bring them over to England? The horses would fetch "a pretty good price". Not so the coach, which it might be better to retain. "It is not extreme fine, neither has it the lustre of a new coach, but it is yet neat enough for anybody to ride in."[3] There was also the difficult but

[1] *Savile Corr.* p. 62; *Buccleuch MSS.* vol. II, pt i, p. 24. The Countess's reception at Court and her second marriage did not "wash out the particular blot that lay upon her". She figures in a scurrilous poem of 1679 written against the King's mistresses.— *Poems on Affairs of State* (2 vols. 1716), vol. I, p. 133.

[2] Shrewsbury to Talbot, Feb. 20/Mar. 2, Feb. 27/Mar. 9, 1677/8, in *Buccleuch MSS.* vol. II, pt i, pp. 24, 26.

[3] *Ibid.* pp. 25, 27. Besides, it would be "infinitely inconvenient and chargeable" to be without a coach of his own if peace were to be signed.

attractive problem of choosing liveries. He left the choice of the lace and embroidery to his uncle, but he selected blue as the colour. "The reason why I most incline to blue, is first because red is too near the King; and besides it is in France, and I believe in all other countries, the common livery everybody gives, which made me, since my last coming to France, give blue. Pink is not so common, but it does not wear well nor last long handsome." He requested his uncle to examine his tenants' leases, both old and new, to see if there were any who lay under an obligation to provide money or men on occasion of war, since "I must look not to run myself too much in debt, for I perceive by the last post you will allow us no employments, but honour as volunteers to stop bullets, and so try both our active and passive valour".[1]

Shrewsbury saw but little of military service. Charles II was as usual playing double, and Louis was doing his utmost to prevent English interference on the Continent by offers of bribes to the King and to the leaders of the Opposition. The Earl crossed over to England in April[2] and soon after proceeded to Flanders. Life in the army evidently appealed to him, for he writes to his uncle, "Were I not afraid of appearing too much a soldier in your peaceable country, I would declare my inclination, being much more charmed with this sort of curiosity than I expected, and the little I have seen serves only to make me more inquisitive, though not much more knowing". He spent some time before Luxemburg, and then in the middle of June was on his way to join the army of Schomberg, where he expected to find news of a peace or of "some considerable siege".[3] Beyond this there is no record of his part in the campaign, which was cut short by the conclusion of the peace, for which Louis had been

[1] Shrewsbury to Talbot, in *Buccleuch MSS.* vol. II, pt i, p. 26.
[2] *Rutland MSS.* vol. II, p. 50.
[3] *Buccleuch MSS.* vol. II, pt i, p. 28.

working, at the end of July, and Shrewsbury then returned to England.

He had now reached the age of eighteen, and his education was regarded as complete. Endowed by nature with considerable abilities, he had taken pains to improve them and he soon came to be regarded as one of the finest gentlemen of his time and one of the most cultured. Although when he visited Italy later on he complained of "the want of speaking the language", although he understood it, that difficulty soon disappeared, and he is said to have spoken both French and Italian as well as he spoke English.[1] He read widely and "his learning is proved by notes which are still extant in his handwriting in books in almost every department of literature".[2]

A year after his return to England Shrewsbury took the important step of seceding from the Church of Rome and joining the Anglican communion, a proceeding which owing to his rank and to the religious situation in the country aroused a great deal of attention and speculation, and it is not surprising that it was attributed by not a few to interested motives. It was a period of great religious ferment. During his sojourn in France, Shrewsbury's attention must have been aroused by Louis XIV's quarrel with the Papacy over the question of the *régale* and the liberties of the Gallican Church and to his persecuting policy towards the Huguenots which eventually culminated in the revocation of the Edict of Nantes. In England religion had been a dominating issue in politics, particularly since the Duke of York's conversion to Roman Catholicism and the passing of the Test Act in 1673, while but recently the fanaticism aroused by the "Popish

---

[1] Add. MSS. 7121, f. 65; *Memoirs of John Macky* (ed. 1733), p. 39.

[2] Macaulay, *History of England* (ed. Firth, 6 vols. 1913–15), vol. II, p. 970. As Macaulay puts it, "He spoke French like a gentleman of Louis's bedchamber and Italian like a citizen of Florence".

Plot" had led to the Parliamentary Test Act of 1678 which excluded Roman Catholic peers from the House of Lords. It was shortly after this that Shrewsbury procured from his grandfather and other prominent co-religionists written statements of their reasons for adhering to the Church of Rome. These he submitted to Tillotson, then Dean of Canterbury, for whom he seems to have conceived a profound respect and admiration. The Dean produced a reply to these; the others made a rejoinder. Shrewsbury pondered these documents for some time, and then decided upon abjuring the faith of his ancestors. His conversion was advertised to the world by his attendance at public worship in the chapel of Lincoln's Inn, where Tillotson was officiating, on May 4, 1679.

It is not surprising that Shrewsbury's action was attributed to the great unpopularity under which Roman Catholics were labouring at the time and to their disabilities under the Test Acts, which debarred them from any public career either civil or military. Some, too, scoffed at a conversion which was not accompanied by an improvement in his moral conduct, which had not altogether escaped contagion from the vicious atmosphere in which he had been brought up. Tillotson told him he was more concerned that he should be "a virtuous and good man, than become a protestant", and referred to stories which had "afflicted him very sensibly" of a connection which Shrewsbury had formed, "dangerous both to your reputation and virtue, two of the tenderest and dearest things in the world".[1]

There is, on the other hand, some evidence in favour of Shrewsbury's sincerity in making the change, though perhaps there was more in it of aversion to the Church of Rome than of attachment to the Church of England. This at least was

[1] Thomas Birch, *Life of Tillotson* (2nd ed. 1753), pp. 58–60. His moral delinquencies attracted the attention of some of the satirists of the time. Cf. *Poems on Affairs of State*, vol. II, pp. 137, 145.

the opinion of Burnet, who wrote in the earlier version of his *History*:

The earl of Shrewsbury...had been bred a papist; but had for-saken the church of Rome upon a very critical and anxious inquiry into matters of controversy. He certainly forsook popery with all his heart; but it is not so easy for me to affirm that he became a hearty protestant; I am afraid he is too sceptical in matters of religion; but as to all other things, he is the worthiest man I know.[1]

After all, the best argument in favour of Shrewsbury's sincerity is his subsequent conduct. In the reign of the popish James II, when every inducement was offered to converts to the Roman faith and it was generally predicted that Shrewsbury would be among the first to return,[2] he not only did not do so but was one of the foremost leaders in the Protestant Revolution.

Being now qualified to take his seat in the House of Lords, Shrewsbury, although not yet of age, received on October 19, 1680, a writ of summons to the Parliament which met at Oxford two days later, and when the Peers assembled he attended and took the oaths and his seat. Soon after the dramatic dissolution of the Oxford Parliament he attained his majority, and in the following September he was appointed to the first of the numerous lord-lieutenancies which he held at different periods of his career, that of Staffordshire.[3] Two years later, on the death of the Earl of Manchester, he was

[1] H. C. Foxcroft, *Supplement to Burnet's History of his Own Time* (1902), p. 288. The published version is less favourable to Shrews-bury and blunter on the question of his religious views. "Some thought"—which probably means Burnet thought—"that though he had forsaken popery he was too sceptical, and too little fixed in the points of religion."—*History of his Own Time* (2 vols. 1723–34), vol. I, p. 762, and Swift's note. The folio references are also given in the 1823 (7 vols.) and 1833 (6 vols.) editions.
[2] Foxcroft's *Supplement to Burnet*, p. 220.
[3] Doyle, *Official Baronage*, vol. III, p. 324.

nominated a Gentleman of the Bedchamber Extraordinary.[1] Ere this he had contracted a disease of the eyes, resulting in the permanent loss of one, while the other was for some time in danger. "My Lord Shrewsbury has so great a blemish of one eye, that 'tis offensive to look upon it", writes the Dowager Countess of Sunderland in January 1679/80,[2] and four months later, "My Lord Shrewsbury's eye is out, and with great deformity yet and the other in danger".[3] Fortunately he escaped with the loss of one eye only.

In February 1684/5 died Charles II, and the accession of his brother brought to the throne a Roman Catholic sovereign who was not only a bigot but an active proselytiser for his faith, whose zeal and energy were greatly encouraged by the failure of Monmouth's rebellion. That insurrection gave an excuse for the raising of additional troops, and Shrewsbury, who had been confirmed in the Lieutenancy of Staffordshire, was among those to whom the King assigned commissions for the purpose. On June 20, 1685, he was appointed Captain of a troop of horse which he had raised at Lichfield,[4] and a month later, on July 29, he was promoted to be Colonel of the second Regiment of Horse.[5] In the following year, James began his practice of dispensing with the penal laws against Roman Catholics in order to introduce his co-religionists into the army and also started his attempt to undermine the Anglican monopoly of the universities. In April 1687, a Declaration of Indulgence was issued, completely suspending the penal laws. Meanwhile "the Court was much set on making converts".[6]

[1] Doyle, *Official Baronage*, vol. III, p. 324.
[2] Dowager Countess of Sunderland to Sidney, in *Diary of Henry Sidney* (ed. R. W. Blencowe, 2 vols. 1843), vol. I, p. 239.
[3] *Ibid.* vol. II, p. 62.
[4] *Talbot MSS.* p. 312; C. Dalton, *English Army Lists and Commission Registers, 1661–1714* (6 vols. 1892–1904), vol. II, pp. 8 n., 15.
[5] Dalton, p. 8; and *List of King James' Army on Hounslow Heath*, dated June 30, 1886, *ibid.* p. 89.   [6] Burnet, vol. I, p. 683.

All the nobility was tried if they could be engaged to change their religion, so that popery might begin to make a better figure in the nation. The firmness which the duke of Norfolk, the earl of Shrewsbury, and the lord Lumley shewed, surprised many. They had changed their religion during the late heats that had been against popery, so that it was generally believed that they would be the first that would return; but they, on the contrary, declared that they had forsaken popery upon a full intention not to return ...and that, as they had been the last that had left it, so they would be the last that would return to it.[1]

Shrewsbury's firmness cost him his position in the army. There was no place among James's officers for any one who was not prepared to comply with his wishes. For two months the threat of dismissal was held over his head, and, as he still refused to yield, he was practically forced by the King to resign in January 1686/7; at least it was generally believed that his retirement was not voluntary.[2] At the end of June the King decided to try what could be done with a new parliament, and on July 2 he dissolved the existing one, which, docile to the verge of supineness in all other matters, had been doggedly opposed to the abrogation of the penal laws. James had every reason to believe that he could manipulate the borough constituencies in such a way as to secure a majority of members from them in favour of his

---

[1] Foxcroft, *Supplement to Burnet*, p. 220. Cf. *Advice to the Test holders* and *A Warning to the Protestant Peers from their best of friends the Jesuits*, both of 1687, printed in a *Third Collection of Poems etc. relating to the Times* (1689), pp. 21, 29.

> "For N...ke, S...ke, L...ley, S...bury,
> They were our men and so shall be again,
> If Shrewsbury, whom once we had so fast,
> With stile of Heretick his name will blast,
> As hee's the first, so shall he be the last."

[2] Cf. Narcissus Luttrell, *Historical Relation of State Affairs* (6 vols. 1857), Jan. 24, 1686/7, vol. I, p. 393; *Autobiography of Sir J. Bramston* (ed. Lord Braybrook, Camden Soc. 1845), p. 267; Van Citters' dispatch, Feb. 4, 1686/7, in Add. MSS. 17,677, vol. H.H. f. 18.

policy of religious indulgence. With the counties it would be more difficult, but he hoped to accomplish something through the agency of the lord-lieutenants. He desired them to put a series of questions to their deputies and to the justices of the peace. "The first was, whether, in case they should be chosen to serve in parliament, they would consent to repeal the penal laws and those for the tests. The second was, whether they would give their vote for choosing such men as would engage to do that. And the third was, whether they would maintain the king's declaration."[1] On making inquiries James discovered that nine of his intended instruments, including Shrewsbury, had no intention of allowing themselves to be used as the King's tools. Early in August they were all dismissed from their posts,[2] and Shrewsbury's breach with the Court was complete.

[1] Burnet, vol. 1, p. 719.
[2] Luttrell, vol. 1, p. 413; *Ellis Corr.* (ed. G. A. Ellis, 2 vols. 1829), vol. 1, p. 339.

CHAPTER II

The Revolution

In the decisive events of 1688 Shrewsbury played an active and determined part, of which nothing in his previous career had given any foreshadowing. Indeed of late the charge of cowardice had been brought against him by the gossips of the day because of his neglect to avenge the death of his younger brother, who was killed in a duel with the Duke of Grafton fought on February 2, 1685/6.[1] But if by temperament he was averse to the conventional code of honour which substituted private revenge for public justice, he was not prepared to submit to public wrongs. Two months before Shrewsbury was deprived of his lieutenancy, a confidential agent of the Prince of Orange returned to Holland, having fulfilled a mission which was ostensibly to the King, but in reality to the leaders of the opposition to the royal policy, whose views he was commissioned to ascertain. Among the

---

[1] Luttrell, Feb. 2, 1685/6, vol. I, p. 370: "This morninge Jake Talbot, the Earle of Shroosberry's brother, was kilde at a diwell by the Dwke of Croftone: his Grace is gone out of the way for some time". *Buccleuch MSS. at Drumlanrig* (H.M.C.), vol. II, p. 97; *Buccleuch MSS. at Montagu House*, vol. I, p. 345; Dalrymple, vol. II, app. pt i, p. 163. See also *Poems on Affairs of State*, vol. III, p. 230:

> "In Shrewsbury we find
> A gen'rous mind
> So kindly to live with his mother,
> And never try yet
> To revenge the sad fate
> Of his father and only brother.
> Thus fighting we see,
> With some folks won't agree
> . . . ."

collection of letters which he took back with him to William was one from Shrewsbury, at whose house most of the meetings between the agent and the magnates of the Opposition had taken place. The Earl wrote as follows:

I fear you will think this an unpardonable presumption in one that is so inconsiderable, and so much a stranger to your Highness; but I was unwilling to let pass the occasion, without assuring you that tho' I hope you have a great many servants and friends in this place, yet there is not one more entirely and faithfully so than myself. It is so much every honest man's interest, not only to say, but to be so, that I hope you will the easier believe what I speak is not a compliment but the truth of my heart. The great, and only consolation that we have left is, that you are so generous to countenance us in our misfortunes, Sir, at the same time we know you approve we here are in the right. Your commands is the rule I have set myself to conduct the rest of my life; and whenever I shall be so happy as to receive them, they shall be obeyed with that duty that becomes, Sir, your Highness's most humble and most obedient servant.[1]

This letter was soon followed—at the end of August, after his dismissal—by a personal visit of Shrewsbury to The Hague. He carried with him a letter of introduction from the Marquis of Halifax, who spoke of him in the most flattering terms, as "without competition the most considerable man of quality that is growing up amongst us", who had "right thoughts for the public and a most particular veneration for your Highness". He felt sure that "upon the first discourse" the Prince would be "encouraged to treat him without any manner of reserve".[2] Nor was Halifax' confidence misplaced, for

the Prince found not only that he had interests and reputation enough among the principal men in England, but found in a little

[1] Shrewsbury to the Prince of Orange, May 30, 1687, in Dalrymple, vol. II, app. pt i, p. 198.
[2] Halifax to the Prince of Orange, Aug. 25 and Sept. 1, 1687, in *ibid.* pp. 207–9.

time by conversing with him, that he had a temper and genius equal to the design, and sufficient to recommend him to such a confidence; that he was master of himself, had the gift of retention, was wise, faithful, sagacious, and had a judgment season'd by just observations, and experience above his years; not easie to be imposed upon, and not confused in the most apparent hurry of thought; a head clear and sedate, a strong imagination, capable of the most important resolutions and building them upon right conclusions from the circumstances of the time.[1]

This description of the impression produced by Shrewsbury upon the Prince is highly coloured and really represents an opinion based on maturer knowledge, but William seems to have liked Shrewsbury from the first and to have found him a pleasant change from Charles, Viscount Mordaunt, who had paid him a visit the previous year, as "his gentleness and modesty suited better with the Prince's temper than Mordaunt's fire and fierceness".[2]

How long Shrewsbury remained abroad on this occasion is not clear, but the visit was probably of the briefest. In the following May we find him writing to William to express his regret that he will be unable to come over again in the summer.[3] Nevertheless, Shrewsbury did visit The Hague again before the summer weather of that year was over, so fast had events moved in England in the meanwhile. On April 27, James issued his second Declaration of Indulgence; a week later an Order in Council appeared directing the clergy to read it in their churches and chapels on two successive Sundays specified in the Order. On May 18 the famous seven bishops presented their petition against the Order, and after appearing before the King in his Council on June 8 they were committed to the Tower upon a charge of seditious libel. Two

---

[1] *Memoirs of Public Transactions in the Life and Ministry of his Grace the Duke of Shrewsbury* (printed for T. Warner at the Black Boy, 1718), p. 20. This work has been attributed to Defoe.

[2] Foxcroft, *Supplement to Burnet*, p. 288.

[3] Shrewsbury to the Prince of Orange, May 14, 1688, in Dalrymple, vol. II, app. pt i, pp. 225–6.

days later the Queen gave birth to a son. For Shrewsbury, as for many other members of the opposition, the birth of the Prince of Wales must have seemed decisive. Hitherto the continuance of the present hated régime had been limited to the lifetime of the existing sovereign who was already fifty-five, and his successor was the Protestant Princess Mary, wife of William of Orange; now with the appearance of a Roman Catholic heir to the throne its continuance had become quite indefinite.

Whether Shrewsbury had previously entertained any serious thoughts of armed intervention is at least very doubtful, while the Prince of Orange at their meeting at The Hague had not gone "further than to give general assurances".[1] But an entirely new situation had now been created, and it was clear that if anything was to be done at all it must be done quickly. The Prince had informed his supporters through the intermediacy of Edward Russell, the future admiral, that no intervention on his part was to be expected unless he received a written invitation signed by "a considerable number of men, that might be supposed to understand the sense of the nation".[2] Shrewsbury, now reckoned as one of William's "principal friends",[3] determined to act upon it at once. Several meetings of the leaders of the opposition were held, probably at his house, as in the previous January, and on June 30, as the result of their deliberations, the formal invitation was drawn up and signed.[4] The date was auspicious, for it coincided with the acquittal of the seven bishops.[5]

[1] Foxcroft, *Supplement to Burnet*, p. 288.
[2] Burnet, vol. I, p. 763; Foxcroft, *Supplement to Burnet*, p. 290.
[3] Sidney to the Prince of Orange, June 18, 1688, in Dalrymple, vol. II, app. pt i, p. 227.
[4] The invitation is printed, *ibid.* pp. 228–31.
[5] Shrewsbury had attended in court together with twenty other Peers ready to provide bail if necessary, when Sancroft and his suffragans were brought up on a writ of habeas corpus. Van Citters' dispatch, June 25, in Add. MSS. 17,677, vol. H.H. f. 444.

For two months longer Shrewsbury remained in England, while the plans of the conspirators were being matured in concert with Zuylestein (afterwards Earl of Rochford), who had been sent on an official mission of congratulation on the birth of the Prince of Wales. The latter event had proved a blessing in disguise, for the majority of the population, furious at the unexpected and unwelcome advent of a popish heir to the throne, refused to believe that the infant was the Queen's child, and all the King's efforts to counteract this convenient supposition by the production of direct evidence were futile. The Government lost ground rapidly, and when Zuylestein returned to The Hague, Shrewsbury wrote to the Prince: "If the violence of my wishes do not deceive me, I flatter myself you never had more friends in England than now".[1] By the middle of September arrangements were complete, and Shrewsbury and Russell, having hired a small vessel, secretly sailed for Holland, being entrusted with "a full scheme of advices, together with the heads of a Declaration, all of which were chiefly penned by Lord Danby".[2] Shrewsbury also took with him a sum of £12,000, which he had raised by mortgaging his estates, and lodged it in the Bank of Amsterdam as his contribution to the expenses of the expedition.[3] So secret had his flight been kept that,

[1] Shrewsbury to the Prince of Orange, July 28, 1688, in Dalrymple, vol. II, app. pt i, p. 239.

[2] Burnet, vol. I, p. 766. There is a copy of a proposed Declaration (probably the one referred to) in *Buccleuch MSS.* vol. II, pt i, pp. 33–5.

[3] *Memoirs of Public Transactions*, p. 18. According to White Kennett (*Complete History of England*, 3 vols. 1719, vol. III, p. 518) the amount which Shrewsbury borrowed was £40,000. Dr A. W. Ward in his article on Shrewsbury in the *D.N.B.* suggests that he actually raised the larger sum and applied £12,000 to the cost of the expedition, and quite gratuitously cites Macaulay as his authority. If the suggestion is correct, Shrewsbury probably raised the larger sum by way of precaution against the failure of the expedition, which would certainly have involved the confiscation of his estates and exile if he escaped capture.

although rumours were current that he had gone to Holland, there was still some uncertainty as to his movements as late as October.[1]

Once out of James's reach he "declared openly for the laws and liberties of his country".[2] His action was ascribed by the ever loyal Ailesbury to pique at being turned out of his regiment of horse;[3] by James to "a factious temper", he having "no personal pretence of disgust".[4] On the principles of Locke, who had been living in exile in Holland since 1683, the despotic government of James II fully justified his action and absolved him from his allegiance.

By the time Shrewsbury arrived at The Hague William's preparations for the expedition had been practically completed. On October 10, the Declaration which was to be published on landing in England was signed and sealed. A subsequent attempt to alter it by inserting ill-advised references to Charles II was defeated through the representations of Shrewsbury and others as to the impolicy of such a proceeding.[5] Nine days later there was a lull in the "Papist wind", which had previously prevented the expedition from starting, and the fleet set sail, only to be sent back by a westerly gale in the North Sea. It was not till the beginning of November that the "Protestant wind" again began to blow. On the 5th, after successfully evading the English fleet under Dartmouth, the expedition landed at Torbay. From Torbay the invaders advanced to Exeter. William had expected an instant rush to his banners, and when several days elapsed without any sign of a rising in his favour he was inclined to think himself betrayed. Shrewsbury endeavoured

[1] Cf. *Ellis Corr.* vol. II, pp. 227–8; *Hatton Corr.* vol. II, p. 92; *Lindsey MSS.* (H.M.C.), p. 448.

[2] *Life and Character*, p. 5.

[3] *Memoirs of Thomas Bruce, Earl of Ailesbury* (Roxburghe Club, 2 vols. 1890), vol. I, p. 129.

[4] *Life of James II* (ed. J. S. Clarke, 2 vols. 1816), vol. II, p. 204.

[5] Burnet, vol. I, pp. 776, 780.

to allay his anger by saying that "he believed the great difficulty...was who should run the hazard of being the first; but if the ice were once broken, they would be as much afraid of being the last". His confidence was soon justified. A week after the landing adherents of rank began to drift in, and with Shrewsbury's warm approval an association of the Prince's supporters was formed, a document being drawn up by Burnet and signed by those who had already run the hazard of being the first.[1]

Encouraged by the now rapid influx of adherents, the Prince continued his march. Shrewsbury accompanied the main body as far as Sherborne, and then branched off to the north with a regiment of horse and 500 foot and dragoons, under the command of Sir John Guise, to occupy Bristol and Gloucester on William's behalf, and with the latter's authority to act as temporary Governor of Bristol and to take any steps he might deem necessary or advisable in his interests.[2] The result of his mission was a foregone conclusion. The neighbourhood he was bound for had vivid recollections of the Bloody Circuit, of "Kirke's Lambs" and the ruthless suppression of Monmouth's rebellion, and nowhere was James less beloved. When Shrewsbury reached Bristol, therefore, on December 1, he was received "with all possible joy".[3] He was able to report that the occupation had been effected without difficulty, and he received the Prince's congratulations and the warm commendation of Trelawney, the Bishop of Bristol, who wrote to William that they were "all extremely pleased" with his emissary's conduct.[4]

[1] Burnet, vol. 1, pp. 790, 792–3, and Dartmouth's note.

[2] Foxcroft, *Supplement to Burnet*, p. 531.

[3] *Ibid.* p. 533. Shrewsbury delivered to the Mayor a letter from the Prince, for which see *Portland MSS.* (H.M.C.), vol. II, p. 53.

[4] Diary of the March from Exeter to London in *Marchmont Papers* (ed. Sir G. H. Rose, 3 vols. 1831), vol. III, p. 100; *Denbigh MSS.* (H.M.C. Rept. VII), p. 227; *Buccleuch MSS.* vol. II, pt i, p. 35; Dalrymple, vol. II, pt i, pp. 335–6.

The situation in this part of the country being so obviously favourable, Shrewsbury was content to send Guise to occupy Gloucester, while he himself rejoined the Prince at Hungerford. He arrived just in time to take part in a conference which was held in the largest room in the inn on December 8, between the Prince's chief adherents and commissioners from James, headed by Halifax, who had been sent to try to arrange a *modus vivendi* by a King who was already despairing of the situation. The principal subject discussed was the summoning of a new Parliament. It was proposed that the King should be requested to cancel writs which had been already issued for a new Parliament. The proposal was supported by the Whigs who had little hope of members of their party being elected so long as the boroughs remained in James's control, but it was strongly opposed by the Tories present and also by Shrewsbury, who possibly was already aware of the Prince's views on the subject. At all events when a reply to be handed over to James's representatives was drafted and was submitted to William for his approval he ordered the clause relating to the cancelling of the writs to be struck out. The formal reply, as amended, was delivered to the King's commissioners by three of the Prince's supporters specially nominated by William, of whom Shrewsbury may have been one.[1]

The invaders had at first intended to proceed from Hungerford to Oxford, but on receiving an invitation from the authorities of the City of London, they made straight for Windsor, where they were greeted by the unwelcome news of the failure of James's attempted flight from the country.

[1] According to Burnet (vol. I, pp. 794–5) the three commissioners were Oxford, Clarendon, and Shrewsbury, but Clarendon himself substitutes the name of Schomberg for Shrewsbury. *Clarendon's Diary*, Dec. 8, 9, 1688, in *Corr. of Clarendon and Rochester* (ed. S. W. Singer, 2 vols. 1828), vol. II, p. 221. Possibly Burnet confuses this occasion with Shrewsbury's subsequent embassy to Whitehall.

On December 17 a meeting of all the peers who were at Windsor was summoned to discuss the situation, Halifax, who had now joined the Prince, being in the chair. It was decided to request the King to withdraw to Ham, and William nominated Halifax, Shrewsbury, and Delamere to carry the message. Discussion then turned upon the question of a guard for the King while he remained at Ham. The suggestion being made that instructions should be delivered to the commander of the guard as to what steps he ought to take in the event of James's again attempting to escape, Shrewsbury moved and carried a proposal that the debate be adjourned, no doubt with the object of shelving this proposal altogether. Anything that tended to facilitate James's retreat tended towards the solution of what must otherwise prove a most difficult problem and strengthened the position of the Prince of Orange.[1]

Shrewsbury and his colleagues set out immediately and arrived at Whitehall shortly after one o'clock the following morning. The King was in bed asleep, half-dazed with the disasters which had befallen him, but the three insisted upon seeing him at once. They were ushered in by the Earl of Middleton,[2] who had roused his master, and delivered the message with which they were charged. James at once raised objections to being sent to Ham. The house, which belonged to the Duchess of Lauderdale, who was away in Scotland, would be empty, cold, and damp. Rochester was proposed as an alternative. The three peers said they had no authority to make any alteration, but they dispatched a courier to William, who, appreciating the greater facilities for escape which James would enjoy at Rochester, readily consented.

[1] *Clarendon's Diary*, Dec. 17, 1688, pp. 229-30; Burnet, vol. 1, p. 800.

[2] Charles, Earl of Middleton in the Peerage of Scotland, later Secretary of State to James in France. See A. C. Biscoe, *The Earls of Middleton* (1876).

On the morning of December 18 James left his palace for the last time. The character of the day harmonised with the occasion: it was dull and gloomy, and rain was falling heavily. Shrewsbury and his colleagues escorted the King to White-hall Stairs, where the royal barge was waiting to convey him as far as Rochester. There was a marked difference between the behaviours of the two senior commissioners. Halifax had opposed James's request to be allowed to travel by water to Gravesend and was not inclined to shew any kindness to his fallen Sovereign. Shrewsbury, on the other hand, did his best to comply with the King's wishes as far as possible and to console him in his misfortunes, and his courtesy earned him the gratitude of James. As Ailesbury afterwards wrote: "The Earl had a soft and genteel way of speaking and was so in his ways, and the King told me he treated him gentlemanlike".[1]

Within a few hours of the King's departure for Rochester the Prince of Orange arrived at St James's, and was soon surrounded by those who came to pay their court to the winning side. Four days later he was informed that James had taken advantage of the intentional laxity with which he was guarded and had crossed the Channel to seek shelter and support from Louis XIV. The realm being thus deprived of its Sovereign, an assembly of some seventy Peers assembled at Westminster asked the Prince to summon a Convention and in the meantime to carry on the executive government. William agreed, and the Convention was summoned to meet on January 22, 1688/9.

Shrewsbury no doubt attended these meetings of Peers at

---

[1] *Ailesbury's Memoirs*, vol. I, pp. 217–18; Clarke, *Life of James II*, vol. II, p. 267; J. Macpherson, *Original Papers* (2 vols. 1775), vol. I, pp. 167–8; Burnet, vol. I, p. 801; *Ellis Corr.* vol. II, pp. 372–3; *Lindsey MSS.* p. 455; *Life and Times of Anthony Wood* (5 vols. Oxford 1817), vol. III, pp. 289–90; *Works of John Sheffield, Duke of Buckinghamshire* (2 vols. 1729), vol. II, pp. 80–1.

Westminster, but there is no record of the part he took in their deliberations. When the Convention met to determine the future government of the country, it had a choice of various courses before it, including the two extremes of the unconditional recall of the King on the one side and the establishment of a republic on the other. The most practical Tory scheme was that of a regency; the Whigs were divided between the proclamation of Mary as Queen and that of Mary and William as joint Sovereigns. The principal debates between the Lords, who were predominantly Tory, and the Commons, where there was a large Whig majority, turned upon the latter's proposition that James had by his flight "abdicated the government" and that "the throne is thereby vacant". On January 31 the motion to agree with the Commons was lost in the Upper House by forty-one to fifty-five. Thirty-six of the minority signed a protest. Shrewsbury's name is not among these,[1] but when the matter once more arose on February 4, he was teller for the Whigs, who were this time in a minority of only one (fifty-three to fifty-four), and he with thirty-eight others entered a protest.[2] Possibly his adoption of a more decided attitude on the second occasion may have been due to his learning what the views of the Prince of Orange were, for it was somewhere between January 31 and February 6 that the Prince sent for Shrewsbury and a few other leading politicians "on whom he relied most"[3] and gave them to understand that in no circumstances would he accept the position of his wife's lacquey and that unless he became King with full sovereign powers he would return to Holland. Now "Danby, Shrewsbury, Sidney, and all the other moderate church of England men were for putting both in the throne". On February 6 the Tories

---

[1] *L.J.* Jan. 31, 1688/9, vol. XIV, pp. 112–13.
[2] *L.J.* Feb. 4, vol. XIV, pp. 115–16; *H.L. MSS.* 1689–90 (H.M.C.), p. 17.
[3] Foxcroft, *Supplement to Burnet*, p. 308.

gave way and both Houses agreed that the throne should be declared vacant, and the crown offered to the Prince and Princess of Orange jointly.

On the day following the formal proclamation of the new Sovereigns, Shrewsbury was sworn of the Privy Council and nominated Lord-Lieutenant of the county of Worcester. He was also appointed Secretary of State for the Northern Province[1]—apparently at Halifax's suggestion and in spite of some hesitation on the part of William,[2] who seems to have demurred on the ground of his youth and lack of experience.[3] Certainly at so critical a time in the nation's history he was undertaking a task onerous and difficult for one who was only in his twenty-ninth year. But Shrewsbury shewed himself capable of filling the post with credit to himself and advantage to the Government. No doubt his success was largely due to his exceptional charm of manner, which was admitted by political opponents as well as by his political friends. "Shrewsbury", wrote Burnet, "was the best beloved of the whole ministry, and deserved to be so; there lay no prejudice against him, but that of his youth which was soon overcome by his great application and wonderful temper".[4]

Enemies indeed there were who asserted that he was neither zealous nor competent. Such was the garrulous Jacobite the Earl of Ailesbury, who asserts that Shrewsbury only took office to recoup himself for the money he had spent in support of William's enterprise, and that "he pitched on the only one capable of that, viz. First Secretary of State, the profits of which are immense on a King's coming to the Crown by reason that all patents, commissions and in fine, all to which the King puts his signet, the Secretary of State hath five

[1] Luttrell, Feb. 14, 1688/9, vol. I, p. 502; *C.S.P. (Dom.)*, 1689–90, p. 17.
[2] "Mdm. Hee made a good deal of objection to the making Ld. Shrewsbury Secretary, when I moved him to him" (Foxcroft, *Life of Halifax* (2 vols. 1898), vol. II, p. 204).
[3] *Ibid.* pp. 250–1.   [4] Foxcroft, *Supplement to Burnet*, p. 313.

guineas, and all was countersigned by him only, so within that year it was computed that he had reimbursed himself". Ailesbury also has a story of calling at Shrewsbury's office to take him out of town to Weybridge, when great quantities of letters came in. Ailesbury supposed the Secretary would not now be able to accompany him. Shrewsbury smilingly inquired what was to hinder him; he never read or wrote a letter. The principal official in the office did that and "reported to him the material contents, on which he drew what answers were requisite, and then he set his name to them, and in ending, 'That is all I do'".[1]

Ailesbury need not be taken seriously. He was biassed, had a bad memory (as he sometimes admits),[2] and was frequently inaccurate. To assert that Shrewsbury chose the office of Secretary of State because it was lucrative is palpably absurd; he was not given a choice. To suggest that a minister of state in leaving his letter-bag to be opened and its contents first perused by a subordinate is neglectful of his duties is equally ridiculous. No minister who acted otherwise could properly carry out his duties. It is, however, perfectly true that Shrewsbury had no love for the routine duties of his office, and he confessed to William that diligence and industry were talents that naturally he never had.[3] That the King was nevertheless fully satisfied with Shrewsbury's work is obvious from his anxiety to retain him in his post even against the Secretary's own wishes. Shrewsbury was indeed from the first one of his ministers in whom William had the greatest confidence, Halifax, Danby, and Sidney being his chief competitors for the royal favour, although William's

[1] *Ailesbury's Memoirs*, vol. I, pp. 239, 245–7.
[2] *E.g. ibid.* p. 256, where in discussing Shrewsbury's resignation in 1690 he adds: "There was such chopping and changing at Court that I have really forgot who had the Northern Province, perhaps Mr John Trenchard".
[3] Shrewsbury to William, Aug. 27/Sept. 6, 1689, in *Correspondence of the Duke of Shrewsbury* (ed. W. Coxe, 1821), p. 7.

fellow-countryman Bentinck had more influence than the others put together.[1]

As Secretary for the so-called Northern Province Shrewsbury was responsible, not only for England, but also for Ireland and the countries of northern Europe generally, but his position with regard to foreign affairs was anomalous. Much business was transacted upon which his advice was not asked and of which he was not infrequently kept in partial or even complete ignorance. Among living Englishmen the only one whose experience at all qualified him to control foreign policy was Sir William Temple, and he refused to accept office. By a tacit understanding the guidance of foreign affairs was left to the King by his English ministers, who could not but feel their inferiority in this department to the man who was recognised alike by friend and foe as one of the ablest and most tenacious diplomatists in Europe.

But if William could, and did, undertake the direction of foreign policy, he was without knowledge of the internal affairs of his new kingdom and he was consequently dependent, so far as they were concerned, upon his English advisers, and the situation in England and Ireland in the uncertain conditions of 1689 put a sufficiently heavy burden on the Secretary of State. In England there was always the risk of a Jacobite rising with intent to effect a second Stuart restoration, and it was consequently unsafe to ignore any information that reached the Secretary's office, however improbable it might seem;[2] while Ireland was in the hands

---

[1] Burnet, vol. II, pp. 3, 5. Cf. dispatch of Terriesi, the Tuscan ambassador at St James's, Mar. 18, 1688/9, in Add. MSS. 25,377, f. 400.

[2] *E.g.* in July an unsigned letter came in to Shrewsbury "signifying that there was a design going on for destroying the King and Queen, firing the Citty and seizing the Tower". The troops were placed under arms and other precautions were taken. "This mightily alarmed the town but there was no mischeif done." (Luttrell, July 21, 1689, vol. I, p. 561.)

of the Earl of Tyrconnel and the Roman Catholic natives, who were quick to seize the opportunity of taking vengeance on their Protestant oppressors and soon had their former masters shut up in Londonderry and Enniskillen. When six months after William's landing a state of war came into existence between England and France it was a virtual certainty that Louis XIV would utilise the possibilities of the Irish situation in the interests of his royal refugee.

The position of affairs would have been difficult enough even if the Ministry had been united; but the composite body of ministers which William had drawn from both parties in the State had no coherence. The party conflict was also embittered in Parliament. An Indemnity Bill had to be dropped because of the endless disputes in the Commons as to its scope; the same fate befel the Bill of Rights because the Lower House would not accept an amendment unanimously accepted by the Peers adding the Electress Sophia of Hanover and her heirs to the entail of the Crown. Thus the practical difficulties of trying to maintain an equipoise between the two fiercely hostile parties were early made manifest to the new King. He began to consider the desirability of giving a preponderating influence to one side or the other. In that case which should he choose? William soon found that if there was greater loyalty among the Whigs, there was greater administrative experience among the Tories. The Tories, moreover, supported the royal prerogative, while the Whigs stood for the limitation of the powers of the Crown, and the more advanced of them had leanings towards republicanism. Thus, to their intense indignation, the Whigs, who chose to regard the Revolution as peculiarly their work and themselves as entitled to the largest share of the King's confidence, if not a monopoly of it, saw the King incline more and more to their opponents. Meantime Mordaunt, now Earl of Monmouth, and Delamere, now Earl of Warrington, "were infusing jealousies of the king into their party, with the same industry that the earl of Nottingham was, at the same time, instilling into the king jealousies of them; and both acted with too much success; which put matters out of joint".[1]

The party strife made things very difficult for Shrewsbury. He could not but see that the Whigs were giving the King only too much justification for his growing aversion. With the aid of Devonshire he did all he could "to stop the progress and effects of those suspicions, with which the whigs were possessed", but to his disgust he found "they had not credit enough to do it".[2] Still more troublesome was the problem of his own relations with his Tory colleague in the Secretary-ship, the Earl of Nottingham. His efforts to counteract Nottingham's attempts to instil into the King dislike of the Whigs led to constant disputes between them, and to his disgust he found that his colleague's advice was preferred to his own, and that "though he had more of the king's favour, yet he had not strength to resist the earl of Nottingham's pompous and tragical declamations".[3] The irritation which he felt was revealed not only at the Council Board, but in unceasing wrangles between the two Secretaries in the House of Lords often over the most trivial matters.[4]

At first on his appointment Shrewsbury attended assidu-ously to the duties of his office,[5] as Burnet bears witness and as the record of his attendance at committee meetings shews, but before long, as the King's alienation from the Whigs grew and the ill-success of his own rivalry with Nottingham be-came more manifest, he began to lose heart, or to lose temper.

[1] Burnet, vol. II, p. 15.
[2] *Ibid.*
[3] *Ibid.*
[4] Cf. A. Cunningham, *History of Great Britain* (2 vols. 1787), vol. I, p. 117.
[5] In May Shrewsbury was appointed a Governor of the Charter-house, an honour confined to a few of the leading Peers, in place of Sunderland who had failed to take the oaths.

His nervous depression brought on an illness which was rather mental than physical, and he contemplated resignation. On August 27 he wrote to the King a long letter, fretful, miserable, importunate. He had hoped, he said, to have been able to wait upon his Majesty in person, but he could not leave his bed. How long he would have to remain there God alone could tell, but it would probably be so long that he would be wanting to the King, his country and himself, "if I did not now lay before you, your own interest, as well as my condition". The King's affairs demanded the attention of someone of more vigorous health. Everything was at a standstill; there was a ruinous lethargy in public business. His indispositions of late had been so frequent, and he had so comfortless a prospect of ill health in the future that he was very sensible how incapable he was of filling a position in which diligence and industry were absolutely requisite. "They are talents", he continued, "that naturally I never had, and have now more reason than ever to despair of obtaining, since ill health, as well as a lazy temper, join to oppose it. Sir, there are a thousand faults I see in myself, and more than a thousand that, without question, others see, which make me sensible of my own unfitness for the employment I am now in." While he would ever feel all the "gratitude imaginable" for the King's choice of him, he did now "with the same sincerity, affirm in the presence of God, that I think it would be for your majesty's interest, to permit me to retire from a situation that, through my incapacities, I am unable to discharge as I ought". He had, he said, as his Majesty would remember, never sought for the employment of Secretary of State, but rather accepted it "with fear and trembling", being all his life sensible of his own inabilities. Nothing but rest could repair his health, the consciousness of his obligation to be at work "puts my mind upon the rack at the same time with my body". He continued: "The importunities of some people, private business, with my own fears of neglecting the public, make my whole life one continual disquiet; and at the same time I thus torment myself, I also prejudice your majesty's affairs, which are neglected by me, whilst they might be effectually done by many others". He besought the King not to interpret his letter "as the melancholy whimsy of a sick man"; he was in earnest in putting forward this "instant prayer of a faithful servant".[1]

This pitiful and unmanly epistle with its dismal reiterations of hopelessness and incapacity must have disgusted a Sovereign, who although a lifelong invalid suffering from just the same trouble as Shrewsbury, in spite of failures and disappointments stuck doggedly to his task, prepared "to die in the last ditch". William at once replied that the Earl's resignation at that particular time would be highly prejudicial to his service, as well as to the kingdom, that in the meantime the matter must be mentioned to no one, and that he would send Bentinck (now Earl of Portland) the following day "with the view to explain clearly his sentiments" on the subject.[2]

Shrewsbury had a long interview with the King's confidant, as the result of which he agreed to allow himself to be disposed of as the King pleased, though his disgust seems even to have been increased as the result of the conversation. For Portland mentioned that suspicions were entertained in several quarters of the loyalty of his Under-Secretary, James Vernon, and also of Dr Wynne, another of his subordinates. That the King shared this distrust is shewn by Halifax's journals, and in the case of Vernon at any rate he had spoken of them to Shrewsbury already.[3] Although he had promised Portland to place himself unreservedly in the King's hands, the existence of these suspicions so much wrought upon his

[1] Shrewsbury to William, Aug. 27/Sept. 6, 1689, in Coxe, pp. 6–9.
[2] William to Shrewsbury, in Coxe, pp. 9–10.
[3] Foxcroft, *Life of Halifax*, vol. II, pp. 225–6; Burnet, vol. II, p. 18.

mind that he forthwith made another earnest appeal to be released. "My incapacity to go through with a place of so much toil and trust", he wrote, "does every day grow more apparent, as my health and strength decay." The distrust felt for his subordinates made matters far worse. "I must either employ those that are believed to betray your majesty, or, in the condition I am in, take the whole drudgery upon myself—a hardship I hope your majesty will not impose upon me." Since he had seen Portland he said he had been making inquiries for suitable men, but he could not "find one with whose ability and integrity I can satisfy myself. It is no wonder I should have acquaintance with none, for business was a thing I had always so little to do with, or inclination for, that the men of that trade were ever strangers to me". Again he lamented his ill-health and his uselessness.

I am not the same man I was six months since; neither my memory, my application, nor my judgment is, or I believe ever will be, the same...I have yet, God be thanked, just enough understanding to know that I am now fit for nothing: if you are not enough convinced already, it would be better to trust me than to find it by your own experience; that would cost both your majesty and me too dear....I never pass three hours of the day, nor night, without violent torment, of which my mind has its share as well as my body. Nothing but rest from business and retirement can ever make me a reasonable creature again.[1]

To this letter the King made no answer. Thereupon Shrewsbury wrote to Portland asking him to intercede for him.[2] William then replied:

I entreat you to relinquish at present your intention of resigning the seals, as it would be greatly prejudicial to my service, and to the welfare of my kingdom. I will use all my endeavours to render your post as little troublesome to you as possible....I likewise assure you, that no man can feel more friendship for you than I do,

[1] Shrewsbury to William, Sept. 1/11, 1689, in Coxe, pp. 10–13.
[2] Shrewsbury to Portland, Sept. 4, 1689, in *ibid.* p. 13.

of which I will strive on all occasions to give you the most convincing proofs.[1]

To the Sovereign's personal appeal with its expressions of high regard Shrewsbury was bound to respond. Sorely against his own wishes he retained his post. The difficulty about his subordinates was solved by the cashiering of Dr Wynne[2] and the confirmation in his post as Under-Secretary to Vernon, who soon overcame the suspicions entertained of his fidelity and developed into a trusted and important member of the Administration.

But if Shrewsbury consented to continue in office, the causes of his dislike of it remained as pronounced as ever. When Parliament reassembled on October 19 after the recess, the Whig majority in the Lower House were as strident as ever, loud in their complaints against the Government, especially against its management of affairs in Ireland, and bitter in their attacks upon prominent supporters of James II and upon the Marquis of Halifax. To Shrewsbury such conduct, and especially the refusal of the Whigs to agree to a Bill of Indemnity, was doubly irritating. It offended his ingrained dislike of extreme courses, and he recognised only too clearly that it was bound to alienate the King. He remonstrated with his followers, but to no purpose; on the other hand, as a leading member of the party, he must bear some of the responsibility. At the same time he lost the assistance of Halifax, who, deeming it prudent to bow to the storm in Parliament, resigned his position as Speaker in the House of Lords during the recess and withdrew from all participation in the Government, though he retained the Privy Seal for some time. The "English Junto", as a Scotsman termed the principal members of the Administration,[3]

[1] William to Shrewsbury, Sept. 5, 1689, in Coxe, p. 14.
[2] Luttrell, vol. I, p. 579.
[3] D. Forbes to Sir Patrick Hume, Aug. 22, 1689, in *Marchmont MSS*. (H.M.C. Rept. xiv, pt iii), p. 118.

was thus reduced to Carmarthen, Nottingham, and Shrewsbury—two Tories and one Whig. Thus Shrewsbury had to contend single-handed with the two ablest Tories in the country.

Before long Shrewsbury had a serious difference of opinion with the King over the question of the prorogation of Parliament. William's desire to be rid of the exasperating Whig majority in the Lower House was greatly increased when he found that his sister-in-law, the Princess Anne, at the instigation of Lord and Lady Marlborough and without consulting either the Queen or himself, was canvassing Members of Parliament with a view to securing the settlement of a large independent revenue upon herself. The Princess, however, asked for more than the Commons were prepared to give, and in Committee her friends were defeated. On the following day Shrewsbury was sent to her by the King to endeavour to effect a settlement of her claim privately. He was ordered to inform her that if she would cease her present manœuvres, her brother-in-law would pay her debts and allow her £50,000 for that year, and would undertake to secure her an annuity of that amount when his own revenue was settled. Shrewsbury mentioned his commission to Marlborough, who assured him his wife "would by no means hear of it but was like a mad woman". And indeed the Secretary's interviews, first with the Countess, then with her mistress, proved entirely futile, the latter telling him that "she had met with so little encouragement from the King that she could expect no kindness from him, and therefore would stick to her friends".[1]

---

[1] *Memoirs of Mary, Queen of England* (ed. R. Doebner, Leipzig and London, 1886), pp. 13, 18; *Account of the Conduct of the Duchess of Marlborough* (1742), pp. 33, 34. Scurrilous writers accused Shrewsbury of having been a lover of the Countess. See *The Secret History of Queen Zarah and the Zarazians, being a looking-glass for— in the Kingdom of Albigion* (1705), pp. 74–5, in which Shrewsbury figures under the nickname of Salopius. Macaulay accepts these

This rebuff decided William to accept the advice of his Tory ministers that he should prorogue Parliament with a view to a dissolution and a fresh election, and almost immediately after the failure of Shrewsbury's mission the King wrote to him requesting his advice on the subject and suggesting a prorogation till the middle of January. The Secretary replied in a long letter in which he endeavoured to dissuade him from taking this step. He was convinced, he said, that so long an adjournment would be not advantageous but prejudicial to the King's business, "for the nation will reasonably conclude, either that you part with your parliament in anger...or else that you have not that pressing occasion for money, which you and your friends have often represented to them, since you defer the consideration of it for three weeks, without any apparent good reason". He spoke sharply about the question of party, while professing to be able to take an unbiassed view.

"I wish", he wrote, "you could have established your party upon the moderate and honest principled men of both factions; but as there be a necessity of declaring, I shall make no difficulty to own my sense, that your majesty and the government are much more safe depending upon the whigs, whose designs, if any against, are improbable and remoter than with the tories, who, many of them, questionless, would bring in king James, and the very best of them, I doubt, have a regency still in their heads; for though I agree them to be the properest instruments to carry the prerogative high, yet I fear they have so unreasonable a veneration for monarchy, as not altogether to approve the foundation yours is built upon."[1]

Shrewsbury's remonstrance was so successful that the project was dropped, but the prorogation was only postponed for a month. For the parliamentary situation grew worse and worse. When a Bill was introduced into the Commons with

charges as founded on fact, but there is a complete refutation of them in J. Paget, *Paradoxes and Puzzles, Historical, Judicial and Literary* (Edinburgh, 1874), p. 10 n.

[1] Shrewsbury to William, Dec. 22, 1689, in Coxe, pp. 14–16.

the laudable purpose of restoring their charters to the corporations which had surrendered them to Charles II and James II, the Whigs in the committee stage introduced amendments to render those who had been responsible for the surrender of the charters—Tories to a man— incapable of holding municipal office for seven years and in the event of contravention of this regulation to a fine and permanent exclusion. The Tories succeeded in defeating this attempt, but when they in turn endeavoured to push on the neglected Bill of Indemnity the Whigs instantly converted it into a Bill of Pains and Penalties.

William had another motive for desiring to dissolve Parliament. He wished, after an absence of fourteen months from his own country, to return to Holland in order to mature plans for the forthcoming campaign. When he announced his intention to his ministers they were thunderstruck at the prospect of being left to their own resources, and both Carmarthen and Shrewsbury besought him to abandon the idea. He eventually decided to take charge of the campaign in Ireland instead of going to Holland,[1] but from this resolve he would not withdraw. When this design became known there was a great outcry among the Whigs, who began to draw up a remonstrance to be presented by the House of Commons. This was the last straw. As soon as the King heard of the manœuvre he was determined to forestall it and hastily prorogued Parliament. The prorogation was followed by a dissolution and writs were issued for the new Parliament to meet on March 20.[2] The Whigs had overreached themselves and their policy of proscribing their opponents recoiled upon their own heads.

"There was a great struggle all England over in elections," writes Burnet, "but the corporation bill did so highly provoke

[1] Burnet, vol. II, p. 40; Foxcroft, *Supplement to Burnet*, pp. 338-9.
[2] William to Portland, Jan. 14/24, 21/31, Jan. 24/Feb. 3, Jan. 28/ Feb. 7, 1689-90, in Add. MSS. 34,514, ff. 58-60.

all those whom it was to have disgraced, that the tories were by far the greater number in the new parliament."[1] One significant result of the Tory victory at the polls was that the Tories, who since the Revolution had been entirely excluded from the lord-lieutenancies of the counties, were now admitted. When Carmarthen and Nottingham, who had been responsible for drawing up the new commission, submitted it to the King for his approval, it met with vain opposition on the part of Shrewsbury, "who was much troubled at the ill-conduct of the whigs, but much more at this great change in the king's government".[2] The Earl's attempted resignation at the beginning of September had been kept a secret, but that he was not in agreement with the Government's policy was now becoming known,[3] while William, although still as anxious as ever to retain his services, realised that his dissatisfaction had increased rather than abated during the last eight months.[4] A complete rupture took place during the brief session prior to William's departure for Ireland.

The Whigs introduced a Bill in the Lower House requiring every holder of office, whether civil, ecclesiastical, or military, to abjure James II on pain of instant dismissal. They also proposed that justices of the peace should be empowered to tender the oath of abjuration to any subject whatever at their discretion, with imprisonment as the penalty of refusal. The Tories, who disliked the measure intensely, as it placed them in the awkward dilemma of either abjuring their principles or incurring the charge of disloyalty to the existing régime, appealed to William, who came to their rescue when he let

[1] Burnet, vol. II, p. 40.
[2] *Ibid.* pp. 40–1.
[3] Foxcroft, *Supplement to Burnet*, p. 340.
[4] Foxcroft, *Life of Halifax*, vol. II, p. 246: "[The King] said hee believed Ld. Shrewsbury had in his own mind more inclination to live out of business. Commended him very much".

it be known to the Commons that "he desired they would let that debate fall, and go to other matters, that were more pressing".[1] The Bill was rejected.

Shrewsbury was furious at this interference as he "was at the head of those who pressed the abjuration most". He was now quite resolved to resign on the instant.[2] Burnet met him "in some heat", on his way to deliver up the seals, and with difficulty dissuaded him from insisting upon an audience with the King that same night. He feared "that Shrewsbury might have said such things to him, as should have provoked him too much".[3] Burnet might well have added that the eve of his departure for the campaign in Ireland was a singularly inconvenient time for the King to be faced with the loss of one of the ministers in whom he chiefly trusted. Burnet's intervention secured only the briefest of postponements. On April 29, Shrewsbury went to Kensington with the seals, fully determined to leave them there. But William, inflexible as ever, refused to accept the Secretary's resignation,[4] and in the hope of avoiding a repetition of the scene, he sent Tillotson and "all those who had most credit with the earl" to induce him to change his mind.[5] Seldom, if ever, have more earnest or more persistent efforts been made to persuade a minister to retain his portfolio against his will.

The Whigs in the meantime had not abandoned their project of embarrassing their foes, and on May 1 a new Abjuration Bill was introduced, this time in the House of Lords. Next day the second reading was carried after a long debate which the King attended. So far all had gone well

[1] Burnet, vol. II, pp. 44, 45.

[2] *Ibid.* Burnet also says: "The credit that the marquis of Carmarthen had gained was not easy to him; so he resolved to deliver up the seals".

[3] *Ibid.* p. 45.

[4] *Clarendon's Diary*, April 29, 1690, in *Corr. of Clarendon and Rochester*, vol. II, p. 311.

[5] Burnet, vol. II, p. 45.

and Shrewsbury, who had not been present on either of the two previous occasions,[1] made his appearance at the committee stage as the Whig leader. But now fortune changed. The Tories employed very effective obstructionist tactics and eventually secured the rejection of the whole clause containing the Declaration of Abjuration by thirty-eight to thirty-five. Shrewsbury was too much disheartened to continue the struggle, and when the House reassembled he was not in his place.[2] Instead he retired to his country house near Newmarket, accompanied by Lord Wharton, "both somewhat disgusted",[3] which they might well be, since the Bill had been so altered as to be practically useless from a Whig point of view. Shrewsbury left the seals behind in his office.

His health was once more impaired. He had been frequently ill since the beginning of the year; he was now prostrated by fever, which nearly cost him his life.[4] Recounting these events at a later date, he wrote: "I was seized with so violent a fever, that nobody thought I could live, and when the king went for Ireland, was too weak even to turn myself in bed, and, of a month after, could not walk the length of my chamber".[5] The state of his health was now generally known. Rumours of his impending resignation had been current since the middle of April, if not earlier,[6] and there was much speculation as to its causes.[7] It was not, however, until the day before the King left London for Ireland that it actually took place. William had as a last resource pressed

[1] L.J. May 1, 2, 1690, vol. XIV, pp. 480, 481.
[2] Ibid. May 5–12, 1690, vol. XIV, pp. 483–5.
[3] Luttrell, vol. II, p. 38.
[4] Burnet, vol. II, p. 45.
[5] Shrewsbury to Somers, Sept. 22/Oct. 2, 1697, in Coxe, p. 497.
[6] Luttrell, vol. II, p. 35; Life and Times of Anthony Wood, vol. III, p. 330.
[7] E.g. by the Tuscan Ambassador. See Terriesi's dispatches of May 6/16, 13/23, 16/26, and May 23/June 2, 1690, in Add. MSS. 25,380, ff. 83, 98, 100, 114.

him to retain his position, even if he performed none of its duties, until his return from the Irish campaign, "but he could not be prevailed upon".[1] On June 3, being still in bed with fever and dreading another personal interview with the King, Shrewsbury sent the seals to him by the hands of Russell. With a feeling that further expostulation was useless, and not without considerable resentment at the Earl's obduracy, William accepted them.[2]

So ended Shrewsbury's first period of office, the story of which is a sorry appendage to that of his vigorous and decisive action in the Revolution—a story of miserable weakness of health, of nerves, and of will, of discontent and self-distrust. It is clear that though he boasted that he was unbiassed by faction he was mainly actuated by party animus against the Tories and personal jealousy of Nottingham and Carmarthen. His zeal for his royal master was more than matched by his unwillingness to continue in his service. The great forbearance shewn by William, his extraordinary reluctance[3] to part with his Secretary in these circumstances, form an eloquent proof of the remarkable charm of personality of which Shrewsbury was, according to universal testimony, possessed.

[1] Burnet, vol. II, p. 45.
[2] *Clarendon's Diary*, June 3, 1690, in *Corr. of Clarendon and Rochester*, vol. II, p. 316.
[3] After Burnet had dissuaded Shrewsbury from incontinently giving up the seals he took the precaution of warning the King of the step which the Earl was meditating. He writes: "It troubled him more than I thought a thing of that kind could have done: he loved the earl of Shrewsbury; and apprehended that his leaving his service at that time might alienate the whigs more entirely from him" (vol. II, p. 45). Here clearly was one of William's chief motives for trying to retain him.

CHAPTER III

In Opposition

"Shrewsbury's conduct", wrote Clarendon on the day of his resignation, "is to many yet a mystery."[1] William ascribed it entirely to pique against the Tory members of the Administration. While his letters to Shrewsbury himself are full of forbearance, his natural annoyance was expressed to Halifax, whom he told that he was ill-satisfied with him, and particularly with the reason he gave for his desire to retire. "Lord Shrewsbury did not consider how kind he had been to him." He had a good understanding but he was very young and new in his place.[2]

By another King (James II) Shrewsbury's resignation was attributed to a zeal for the Jacobite cause, his discontent with William's government being construed as indicating a desire for the restoration of the exiled monarch. Indeed James assured Louis XIV that the resignation was due to his instructions. Shrewsbury's mother was now engaged in the congenial task of helping to stir up trouble for the new Government and was employed by the exiled court as one of the channels of communication with its friends, real and professed, in England. There is no evidence to shew precisely what steps, if any, were taken by the Jacobites to win Shrewsbury to their side, but it seems that, perceiving his discontent, they endeavoured through the medium of his mother to induce him to resign the seals and to throw in his lot with them. That his mother, desiring a Jacobite restoration, would naturally be anxious to win over her son to the

---

[1] *Clarendon's Diary*, June 3, 1690, in *Corr. of Clarendon and Rochester*, vol. II, p. 316.
[2] Foxcroft's *Life of Halifax*, vol. II, pp. 250, 251.

cause, is true; it is true also that Shrewsbury was nearly related to Middleton and to other well-known Jacobites and that he associated with Ailesbury and other malcontents of more or less pronounced Jacobite leanings. On the other hand, the Countess's past conduct was not such as to have given her any authority over him, and Shrewsbury's association with his relative the Earl of Middleton and his friendship with Ailesbury do not necessarily imply that he shared their political views. Such evidence as exists in favour of the theory that he had leanings towards Jacobitism comes entirely from Jacobite sources and is of doubtful validity, even if it be not the work of deliberate forgery perpetrated by James's admirers at St Germain to give greater plausibility to their appeals for assistance from Louis XIV.[1] The *prima facie* evidence is against the accusation of disloyalty to William. If there was any member of the Whig party who had reason to dread a second May 29, it was assuredly Shrewsbury. He had abandoned the religion for which James had sacrificed his crown; he was one of those who had signed the invitation to William of Orange; he had conspired at The Hague and returned with the invading army; he had taken a prominent part on the side of the Prince in the proceedings which culminated in the flight and deposition of the King, and he had accepted high office under the usurper. Promises

[1] See "James Macpherson and the Nairne Papers", by Col. the Hon. A. Parnell, in *E.H.R.* April, 1897. In support of his view the writer quotes Ailesbury's significant remark about forged documents, *Memoirs*, vol. II, p. 391. On the other hand see Ranke, *History of England* (6 vols. Oxford 1875), vol. VI, pp. 34–5, and Godfrey Davies, "James Macpherson and the Nairne Papers", *E.H.R.* 1920, pp. 367–76. The latter makes out a strong case for the authenticity of the Nairne Papers.

The accusation of Jacobitism brought against Shrewsbury is based upon documents printed by Macpherson in his *Original Papers* (2 vols. 1775), vol. I, pp. 435, 456–8, 481. The originals are among the Nairne Papers preserved among the *Carte MSS.* in the Bodleian, vol. CLXXXI, pp. 496–504, 540, 568–71, and vol. CCIX, pp. 100, 101.

of immunity and of favour had little value from a bigoted Roman Catholic such as James II, who, once re-seated on the throne, would have been in a position to indulge in a repetition of the Western Circuit of 1685, presided over by another Judge Jeffreys. Shrewsbury must have been far indeed from possessing the "true exactness of judgment" attributed to him by Burnet if he had allowed himself to be duped by specious promises from the Court of St Germain.

Shrewsbury's resignation on the eve of William's departure for Ireland, left William no time in which to consider the question of a successor, and Nottingham was therefore entrusted with the seals of the Northern Province and ordered to act as sole Secretary of State until the King's return from the Irish campaign.[1] William was obliged to leave the administration in the inexperienced hands of the Queen, assisted by a council whose members were both personally and politically at variance with one another. It had been intended to include Shrewsbury in this inner Council, and the King had specially recommended him to her as one whom she might specially trust, as indeed "almost the only one he could entirely rely on". Mary was dismayed when she heard of Shrewsbury's resignation. It "surprised me extremely and gave me a very melancholy prospect of things", wrote the Queen in her diary, "I saw myself going to be left in many difficulties not knowing whom to trust. This man for whose person the King had a great kindness...he leaves him in a humour at a time when it must be very prejudicial to his affairs, what could I then expect from others?"[2]

Mary and her Council were soon faced by the crisis occasioned by the naval defeat off Beachy Head. There was a serious threat of invasion, and although the tension was considerably relieved by the announcement of the victory of the Boyne, the situation remained disquieting. After his

[1] Luttrell, vol. II, p. 53.   [2] *Memoirs of Mary*, pp. 27–8.

resignation Shrewsbury had retired to Epsom to try to drive away the recollection of the harassments of the past six months; but as soon as he heard of the naval disaster he hurried back to Whitehall and waited upon the Queen to offer his services to the Government should they be required.[1] After consultation with the leading members of both parties, including Marlborough, Godolphin, and Wharton, it was arranged that Marlborough on Shrewsbury's behalf should offer to raise 1200 men at their joint expense, merely stipulating that they should be reimbursed at a future date convenient to the Government, and that when the offer was brought before the Council no names should be mentioned. Mary at once declared the latter condition to be inadmissible; indeed she did not like the scheme at all, and when Marlborough admitted that the troops could not be ready for six weeks she rejected it on the reasonable ground that they would come too late to be useful.[2]

Shrewsbury now left London for Southborough, "a place that had as much the air of real solitude as the most romantic grove you ever read of". But on his way he encountered a large number of Dutch seamen making their way inland from the shattered remnants of their fleet, and this suggested to him another scheme which he hoped might meet with a more favourable reception than his last proposal. On July 12 he wrote to Carmarthen once more offering his services to the Government in case they decided to replace Torrington in command of the fleet by a commission composed of a Peer and two professional seamen. The letter was couched in Shrewsbury's habitual terms of self-depreciation. Carmarthen was not to mention the offer unless he considered it "neither too vain nor too foolish", but he had heard from several sources that there was "too great a backwardness in

[1] Mary to William, July 3/13, 1690, in Dalrymple, vol. II, app. pt ii, p. 128.
[2] Mary to William, July 10/20, in *ibid.* p. 138.

every body to undertake the regaining this lost game ", and if the need were so great that he could be serviceable, "which is hardly credible", he would do his best,

if joined with two able mettled seamen, which I am sure are the only people can recover this disgrace. I cannot help being so ridiculous as to be mightily piqued at the affront the nation has suffered, and think it so much concerns the interest as well as reputation of every man that calls himself an Englishman not to suffer this domineering fleet to go home without a revenge, and call themselves ever after sovereigns of the sea, that I am very solicitous to hear good men are named for this command....[1]

At first it seemed possible that this second proposal might be accepted as the idea of some such commission as he had suggested found general favour. Russell approved the idea and hoped that if Lord Pembroke did not desire the post of chief member of the commission Shrewsbury would be chosen.[2] The selection of Haddock and Ashby as the two seamen disgusted Russell, but he still continued to press for Shrewsbury's nomination. The Queen hoped that her husband would approve and wrote to him informing him of the proposal.[3] But the scheme fell through. William no doubt objected to entrusting with another responsible post, for which he had no special aptitude, a statesman who had recently insisted, against his wishes, on relinquishing the one he already held.

Six weeks later the King returned from Ireland and on October 2 he summoned Parliament. Shrewsbury had been

[1] Shrewsbury to Carmarthen, July 12, 1690, in Dalrymple, vol. II, app. pt ii, pp. 172–3. In *C.S.P. (Dom.)*, 1690–1, p. 31, this letter appears as one from Shrewsbury to the King and is misdated *June* 12.

[2] The restless Earl of Monmouth also appears to have been gratuitously busying himself with a design to restore Shrewsbury to office. See Dalrymple, vol. II, app. pt ii, p. 141, Mary to William, July 15/25, 1690.

[3] Same to same, July 22/Aug. 1, July 24/Aug. 3, 1690, in *ibid*. pp. 144, 147–9.

left to brood in solitude over the rejection of his offers of assistance and to watch his rival Carmarthen occupying the chief place in the Royal Council.[1] The re-opening of Parliament afforded a possible opportunity of ousting the Marquis from his predominant position, and Shrewsbury threw himself vigorously into the task of stirring up opposition to the Lord President. The parliamentary atmosphere did not at first seem conducive to the efforts of mischief-makers, and the Government had reason for satisfaction with the legislators. The Commons voted with alacrity the sums, large beyond precedent, which the King demanded for the prosecution of the war. But if the Ministry was fairly secure, the Lord President was not. As Burnet expressed it, he "was again falling under an universal hatred". His enemies initiated a debate in the House of Lords upon the old question whether impeachments could continue from one Parliament to the next in order to pave the way for a revival of the case against him, and they revived the argument that a royal pardon was no bar to an impeachment. They were answered that there was no precedent for the continuation of an impeachment from one Parliament to another save by special order, and that whatever doubts there might be as to the validity of a royal pardon there could be none as to the efficacy of the Act of Grace passed by Parliament in the previous session. Judged by Burnet's account of the debate Shrewsbury and his friends had the worst of the argument. Nor did the attack meet with any better success in the House of Commons, while Carmarthen's prestige was actually increased owing to the fact that he was instrumental in procuring the arrest of the plotters inculpated in a serious conspiracy which was discovered in the following December.[2]

In the autumn Sidney (now a Viscount), who had acted with indifferent success as one of the three Lord Justices to

---

[1] See Burnet, vol. II, p. 69.   [2] *Ibid.* pp. 69–70.

whom William had entrusted the government of Ireland, was recalled from Dublin "like a footman at a play, to keep a place till his better came",[1] to take charge of the seals resigned by Shrewsbury. Carmarthen suggested to the King that the latter might take Sidney's place,[2] but if he entertained any hopes that his rival might be shunted to Ireland they were at once disappointed. William was resolute not to employ Shrewsbury again after his conduct as Secretary. The Earl's star was indeed at this time in complete eclipse. It was noticed that he had lost the honour of discussing affairs of state with the Queen and that he remained outside the door of the Council Chamber while his less illustrious successor was influential within.[3] He remained assiduous in his attendance at the Palace, but it was noticed that he paid more court to the Princess Anne than to the Queen, and that meant intimacy with the disaffected Marlboroughs,[4] while he was renewing his efforts to oust Carmarthen. In the next session of Parliament the prospects were more promising. It was well known that there were dissensions in the Cabinet between Carmarthen, Nottingham and Godolphin. It was noticed that Godolphin had now formed an intimate association with Shrewsbury, Marlborough, and Lord Montagu, and that the four were acting together in the Upper House.[5] "It appeared that a party was avowedly formed against the government."[6]

[1] Carmarthen's sarcastic comment. See Dartmouth's note to Burnet, vol. II, p. 5.

[2] Carmarthen to William, Feb. 20, 1690/1, in Dalrymple, vol. II, app. pt ii, p. 178.

[3] Newsletter from Blancard to Dykvelt, June 30/July 10, in Denbigh MSS. (H.M.C. Rept. VII), p. 200. See also Bonet's report, Nov. 24/Dec. 4, 1691, in Ranke, vol. VI, p. 169.

[4] See Denbigh MSS. (H.M.C. Rept. VIII), p. 202, July 14/24, 1691.

[5] Ibid. p. 208, Blancard to Dykvelt, Nov. 24/Dec. 4, Dec. 1/11, 1691.

[6] Burnet, vol. II, p. 85.

The connection with Marlborough just at this time was most unfortunate for Shrewsbury. There was evidence that the former was in correspondence with the Jacobite Court and that he was plotting against the King and against the Dutch. At any rate the King felt he had sufficient justification for dismissing Marlborough from all his employments and forbidding him to come to Court, as he did on January 20, 1691/2. Since the Princess Anne refused to dismiss Lady Marlborough from her household, the Earl's disgrace was speedily followed by an open rupture between her and the King and Queen.[1] His dismissal only encouraged Marlborough to embarrass the Court the more, and he was particularly anxious to secure the ejection of all foreigners who held commissions in the English Army. He succeeded in persuading the House of Lords to appoint a committee to draw up an address to the Crown on this subject. The committee accomplished nothing, and its meetings were effectively terminated by the prorogation on February 24, but it is worth noting that Shrewsbury was among its members.[2] For the time being he received no positive proof of William's displeasure at his conduct in associating himself with the schemes of the disgraced Marlborough, and, if Dartmouth is to be believed, he complied with the royal order forbidding attendance upon the Princess of Denmark.[3]

The spring of 1692 brought revelations of supposed Jacobite plots. One which came from a certain William Fuller, who had previously been employed as a spy by Shrewsbury when he was in office,[4] was discovered to be spurious. It was at a critical period, when invasion was once again threatened, just before the fears of it were dispelled by

---

[1] Luttrell, Jan. 21, 1691/2, vol. II, p. 342; Burnet, vol. II, p. 90.
[2] *H.L. MSS.* 1692–3, p. 186.
[3] Note to Burnet, vol. II, p. 92. But cf. *Ailesbury's Memoirs*, vol. I, p. 308.
[4] *Memoirs of Public Transactions*, p. 29.

the victory of La Hogue, that on May 29 another informer named Robert Young forged an association for the restoration of James II, purporting to be signed by Marlborough, Sancroft and others. Marlborough was promptly consigned to the Tower, but the fraud was soon discovered, and those who had been imprisoned in consequence of it were released on bail, Shrewsbury being one of Marlborough's sureties.[1] Ten days later the Queen—her husband being absent abroad —ordered the names of Marlborough, Halifax, and Shrewsbury to be struck off the list of Privy Councillors. The reason officially assigned for the removal of the two latter was that "they had foreborne to come to Council for some time past",[2] but the real cause, unquestionably, was their recent association with Marlborough.

The new parliamentary session which opened on November 4 was one of the most active and important in Shrewsbury's career. In both Houses the Government was subjected to constant bitter attacks, but "the ill-humour prevailed most in the house of lords, where a strong opposition was made to everything that was proposed for the government". The leaders of the Opposition there were Halifax and Mulgrave, assisted by Shrewsbury, who was now extremely irritated by the recent treatment of his friend Marlborough, and also by the more personal rebuff which he had recently experienced in his removal from the list of Privy Councillors.[3] Their conduct assured them the support of such questionable allies as the extreme (republican) wing of the Whigs and the Jacobites.

Advantage was taken of a clause in the King's Speech in which he asked for the advice and assistance of Parliament, to move for the appointment of a committee of both Houses

[1] *Hatton Corr.* vol. II, p. 180.
[2] Luttrell, June 25, 1692, vol. II, p. 494; *Ancaster MSS.* (H.M.C. Rept. XIII, app. pt vi), p. 248.
[3] *Ailesbury's Memoirs*, vol. I, pp. 302, 308; Burnet, vol. II, p. 104.

to consider the state of the nation and the advice which should be given to his Majesty upon it. Shrewsbury was one of those who protested when the motion was lost on December 7 by twelve votes, forty-eight to thirty-six, on the grounds that "in a time of such imminent danger to the nation, by reason of so many mis-carriages as are supposed generally to be committed, the closest and strictest union of both Houses is absolutely necessary to redeem us from all that ruin, which, we have too much cause to fear, is coming upon us ".[1] A new Abjuration Bill had to be abandoned owing to the strength of the resistance made by the Ministerial party.[2] Much time was spent in stormy debates on the Government's shortcomings in their conduct of the naval war, but despite their great persistence the Opposition failed completely in securing their main object, the disgrace of Nottingham.[3]

If the Opposition hoped to recommend themselves to the King and to gain their own return to office, they certainly were not taking the right course, as Blancard the Dutch agent remarked.[4] Their attempts to interfere with the granting of supplies were particularly ill-advised. When the Land Tax Bill came up to the Lords from the Commons, a determined attempt was made to secure the insertion of a clause enabling the Peers to appoint commissioners of their own to value their estates for the purposes of the Bill. The Commons rejected this amendment. Halifax and Mulgrave did their utmost to induce the House to insist upon its retention, but they were defeated and had to content themselves with entering two protests against the decision of the

---

[1] *L.J.* Dec. 7, 1692, vol. xv, pp. 136–7; J. E. Thorold Rogers, *Complete Protests of the Lords* (3 vols. Oxford 1875), vol. I, pp. 105–6.

[2] *H.L. MSS.* 1692–3, pp. 304–5; Burnet, vol. II, p. 103; Foxcroft, *Supplement to Burnet*, p. 380.

[3] Burnet, vol. II, pp. 103–4.

[4] *Denbigh MSS.* p. 211.

House. Amongst the signatories to these protests appears the name of the Earl of Shrewsbury.[1] But whilst he acted with the Opposition in this instance, he does not seem to have been altogether satisfied with their policy, for it was observed that he was more moderate than the rest.[2]

It was clear to Shrewsbury that little progress could be made against Nottingham so long as the present Parliament continued to exist, and that his right policy was to endeavour to enforce a dissolution. A basis for attack was soon forthcoming in the shape of a statute of Edward III long fallen into abeyance providing for the holding of annual Parliaments. On January 12, 1692/3, Shrewsbury, with the support of Halifax and Mulgrave brought in a Bill "for the frequent meeting of Parliament", similar in its stringent methods to enforce the summoning of Parliament to the Triennial Act of 1641. In future, writs were to be issued for the meeting of Parliament on a date to be fixed by the Houses. In the event of the Crown neglecting to issue them, the writs were to be issued by the Lord Chancellor, Lord Keeper, or Commissioners of the Great Seal. Any one of these officials failing to carry out the duties imposed on him by the Bill was to forfeit his office and was rendered liable to such penalties as the next or any succeeding Parliament should think fit to inflict "for a crime tending to the subversion of the whole government".[3] The King disliked the projected measure intensely, first because it trenched upon his prerogative, secondly because it involved the early dissolution of the present Parliament, which from his point of view was proving eminently satisfactory.[4]

[1] *L.J.* Jan. 19, 1692/3, vol. xv, p. 190.
[2] Bonet's report of Jan. 20/30, 1692/3, in Ranke, vol. vi, p. 207. Shrewsbury took little or no part in the debates on the Place Bill and abstained from signing the protest which followed its rejection on Jan. 3, 1692/3. (*L.J.* vol. xv, p. 172.)
[3] *H.L. MSS.* 1692–3, p. 299.
[4] Bonet's report, Jan. 13/23, 1692/3, in Ranke, vol. ii, p. 204.

Shrewsbury and his friends had no difficulty in inducing the Peers to agree to the second reading, and the Bill was then referred to a committee of the whole House. At this stage its whole character was altered. It was resolved that Parliament should sit every year, that a new one should be summoned every third year, and that a definite date should be fixed for the dissolution of the existing Parliament; it was also resolved that the compulsory clause should be deleted. When the House was resumed, the committee's report was agreed to, and a select committee was appointed to draft a clause in accordance with its recommendations, with the assistance of the judges. From the committee room Shrewsbury went to the Palace and was closeted with the King for more than an hour and a half.[1] If the main object of this audience was to induce Shrewsbury either to withdraw or still further modify his Bill, it was fruitless. The date January 1 was subsequently chosen for the dissolution of the present Parliament, and the Bill in the greatly altered guise in which it emerged from committee was read a third time and passed on January 21. It had a less smooth passage through the Lower House, which was inclined to view with suspicion the fact that the Peers had originated a measure so nearly affecting the individual member's tenure of his seat— a Peer sits permanently, a member of the House of Commons only for the lifetime of a single Parliament. But eventually it was passed with several amendments—including the postponement of the date for the dissolution of the present Parliament from January 1 to March 25—which the Lords accepted. The Bill now, therefore, required only the royal assent at the end of the session. As Burnet says, "the rejecting a bill, though an unquestionable right of the crown, has been so seldom practised, that the two houses are apt to think it a hardship, when there is a bill denied".[2] Neverthe-

---

[1] *Ibid.* p. 206.   [2] Burnet, vol. II, p. 107.

less, when at the prorogation on March 14 the title of the Bill was read out, the reply was: "Le Roy et la Reine s'aviseront". "So", says Burnet, "the session ended in ill humour".[1]

In addition to his having introduced the most important Bill of the Session, Shrewsbury's part in it had been notable for his enlightened attitude towards the censorship of the press, when the question of the continuance of the existing Licensing Act had been raised on March 8. The Earl, who had been paying a short visit to Glamorganshire with the object, as it was rumoured, of arranging a marriage with a rich grand-daughter of Lord Wharton,[2] had just returned to London and took an outstanding part in the proceedings. Two amendments were proposed—the first the insertion of a new clause protecting the houses of Peers from the search for offending publications, a purely selfish suggestion of no advantage to the public welfare, but the second of a very different character—to the effect that no license should be required for any book if the names of author and printer appeared in it. Both amendments were negatived,[3] and the Licensing Act was continued for another couple of years. Shrewsbury, who had acted as teller for both the amendments, and ten of his supporters, including Halifax and Mulgrave, at once signed a protest.

"We conceive", they wrote, "that the benefit which may accrue to the public by the continuance [of the Act], will not countervail the prejudice there may be in many respects by rejecting the aforesaid clauses which we offered as amendments....Because it subjects all learning and true information to the arbitrary will and

[1] Burnet, vol. II, p. 107.
[2] Luttrell, Feb. 25, 28, 1692/3, vol. III, pp. 44–5. It was afterwards said that the marriage did not take place because the lady was too young (*Dispatches of L'Hermitage*, Aug. 31/Sept. 10, 1694, in Add. MSS. 17,677, vol. O.O. f. 334). It appears, however, that Lord Wharton for some reason or other objected to the match. See Shrewsbury to Wharton, Aug. 15, 1693, in *Carte MSS*. (Bodl.), vol. CCXXXIII, ff. 246–7.
[3] The latter by eighteen to twenty-six.

pleasure of a mercenary, and, perhaps, ignorant licenser, destroys the properties of authors in their copies, and sets up many monopolies."[1]

Though Shrewsbury and his supporters failed at this time their influence was not without effect, for when the two years for which the Act was renewed had expired, it was finally allowed to lapse altogether.

Shortly after the prorogation, in order, according to Burnet,[2] to soften the distaste that his rejection of the Triennial Bill had given, the King made two important Whig appointments, that of Somers as Lord Keeper and that of Sir John Trenchard[3] to the Secretaryship left vacant by Sidney's appointment as Lord-Lieutenant of Ireland. There was a general belief that Shrewsbury could now return to his former post if he chose.[4] Nottingham remained the stumbling-block, and the King was not prepared to dismiss him as the price of Shrewsbury's return to office at the bidding of the Whigs.[5] But although the expectation of Shrewsbury's return to office was not fulfilled at the time, events later on in the year had the effect of inducing the King to turn more and more in a Whig direction. Naval management under the direction of a commission consisting of Admirals Killigrew, Delaval, and Shovell in place of Russell was singularly unsuccessful, and the destruction of the merchant fleet bound for Smyrna was as serious as the loss of a battle. That disaster, together with the defeat which the King sustained in the Flemish campaign at Landen, increased the dissatisfaction which the Tories felt with a war which they believed was being fought more in Dutch than

[1] *H.L. MSS.* 1692–3, pp. 379–81; *L.J.* Mar. 8, 1692/3; T. Rogers, *Protests of the Lords*, vol. I, pp. 109–10.
[2] Burnet, vol. II, p. 107.
[3] See *D.N.B.* vol. XIX, pp. 1123–5.
[4] Blancard to Dykvelt, Mar. 31/April 10, 1693, in *Denbigh MSS.* p. 213.
[5] Bonet's report, Jan. 17/27, 1692/3, in Ranke, vol. VI, p. 206.

in English interests. Their doctrine that England should concentrate her resources upon the war at sea did not commend itself to William, to whom the Continental campaign appeared of paramount importance. By the time he returned to England in the autumn, he was convinced of the necessity of further changes, and was prepared to listen to the advice of the Earl of Sunderland,[1] that he should give the Whigs a preponderating position in the Ministry. Whether Sunderland had been acting with the knowledge and approval of William or not, he had in fact been in communication with Shrewsbury, Russell, and other leaders of the party for some time past.[2]

The King reached London on October 30. A week later he sent to Nottingham for the seals of his office, and when the Secretary had returned them in person, much against his will, at once sent for Shrewsbury in order to offer them to him. Now that Nottingham had gone, William did not anticipate that Shrewsbury would make any difficulties; it was, therefore, to his great surprise and annoyance that he found him, though perfectly courteous, bent on driving a bargain. The price asked for his acceptance of the seals was the King's acceptance of the Triennial Bill. He had, Shrewsbury said, supported it actively in the House, and he believed so strongly that it was for the good of the King and of the nation that he felt bound to continue to support it, "and if his Majesty did not like it, he should not serve him agreeably". William's reply was that "he did not think fit to purchase any man's friendship and service so dear as at the expense of passing that Bill", and the interview came to an abrupt conclusion. On November 9, Trenchard, who with Somers

[1] Burnet, vol. II, pp. 123–4.
[2] Luttrell, Aug. 24, 1693, vol. III, pp. 167–8. There was also a vague report current at the time that Shrewsbury was to be Lord Privy Seal. See Baden's dispatch, Aug. 25/Sept. 4, 1693, in Add. MSS. 17,677, vol. N.N. f. 221.

and Russell was now regarded as one of the "governing men", removed his papers to the office vacated by Nottingham. Shrewsbury thus lost the opportunity of taking precedence of Trenchard, and it was not supposed that he would be willing to accept the junior position.[1] His reason for declining the King's offer was generally believed to be the same as that which had been given for his resignation in 1690—the presence in the Ministry of some with whom he did not agree—and by neutral observers as well as by friends this was regarded as quite inadequate. The Whigs, indeed, were said to be "greatly annoyed" with him, for conduct which to them seemed to be merely unreasonable obstinacy. Contemporary reports do not allude to the Triennial Bill, and that Shrewsbury's reason for refusal might be a matter of principle does not seem to have occurred to them.[2]

There was much speculation as to what William would do next. Some thought that Trenchard would continue to act as sole Secretary for some time, while the King waited to see whether the Whigs could be won over and would be strong enough to carry on the Government alone, ready, if this should prove not to be the case, to fall back upon a Tory Secretary again.[3] Though mortified by his failure, the King had by no means abandoned his wish to reinstate Shrewsbury. He had quite made up his mind that if he must form a predominantly Whig Ministry—and this seemed inevitable—

[1] Luttrell, Nov. 7, 9, 1693, vol. III, pp. 221, 222; *Hatton Corr.* vol. II, pp. 186-7-198; *Dispatches of L'Hermitage*, Nov. 7/17 and 10/20, 1693, in Add. MSS. 17,677, vol. N.N. ff. 338, 346; Burnet, vol. II, p. 123; Bonet's dispatch, Nov. 10/20, 1693, in Ranke, vol. VI, p. 218.

[2] Cf. Bonet's report, Nov. 10/20, 1693, in Ranke, vol. VI, p. 218, and Blancard to Dykvelt, in *Denbigh MSS.* p. 214. The former writes that his refusal is attributed "en partie à ce qu'il aime l'aise, et en partie à ce que les causes qui la luy firent quitter, assavoir quelques personnes qui sont encore dans le Ministère, subsistent encore".

[3] Luttrell, Nov. 9, vol. III, p. 222; Bonet's report, Nov. 7/17, 1693, in Ranke, vol. VI, p. 217.

the Earl should fill one of the chief places in it. His own efforts having in the meantime failed, he decided to try what could be done through the agency of his mistress, Mrs Villiers, the future Countess of Orkney.[1] Mrs Villiers employed as a go-between Mrs Lundy (or Lundee), a daughter of the late Governor of Londonderry, who was a personal friend of Shrewsbury. Through Mrs Lundy's agency an interview was arranged between Shrewsbury and Mrs Villiers. She failed to induce him to change his mind. The Earl, knowing the King's persistence of old, suspected that renewed efforts would be made, and, in the hope of escaping further importunities, he retired to his country seat at Eyford in Gloucestershire.

His hope was speedily disappointed. He was bombarded with letters from Mrs Villiers and her friend. The former wrote and told him that his flight was proof to her, as she was sure it was to him, that he was in the wrong.[2] He did not even escape the personal interviews he had felt confident of avoiding. Mrs Villiers wrote a second letter the very same evening by the King's orders, "to assure him that he desired him to come back to serve him and the nation", and sent it to Mrs Lundy, who was to add her personal solicitations to those which the letter contained.[3] She could not think, she said, that he would refuse to comply with the King's wishes. Nevertheless, courteously but firmly, he once again declined.

"It is impossible", he said, "to be more highly sensible than I am of the favourable thoughts the king has been pleased to express concerning me, nor be more convinced of the obligations I have to you, madam, for your part in this matter. It challenges all the duty and gratitude in my power, both to the king and to yourself; and could I be persuaded that my service would be of any use

[1] Mrs Villiers to Mrs Lundee, Mrs Lundee to Shrewsbury, both undated, in *Buccleuch MSS.* vol. II, pt i, pp. 56, 58.
[2] *Buccleuch MSS.* vol. II, pt i, p. 57.
[3] Mrs Villiers to Mrs Lundy, in Coxe, pp. 19–20; *Buccleuch MSS.* vol. II, pt i, p. 58.

to his majesty, or to the public, there are no difficulties of any kind should hinder me from begging I might be employed, with the same earnestness I now beg I may be excused, because of the unfitness of my own temper for the present circumstance of affairs; and this, upon my word, is my true reason to decline what otherwise would be my interest to take."[1]

These grandiloquent nothings tell us very little and probably told the King not much more.

With this answer Mrs Lundy had perforce to be content and had to leave Shrewsbury in the country to the diversion of "drinking strong ale with the parson".[2] His secret agents having failed to accomplish anything, the King now turned to the Earl's political friends, and bade Wharton, now Controller of the Royal Household, use his influence. In a letter to Shrewsbury, which was shewn to William before it was sent, Wharton informed him that his Majesty "is more convinced every day that it is for his interest, and that of the public, to pursue such measures in the management of his affairs, as he knows will be agreeable to you; and that if you will be prevailed upon in it, he is most confident that you shall not disagree in anything material, and doth promise to order it so, that you shall have no sort of reason to repent your entering into his service".[3]

The Controller's appeal was supported by fresh letters from Mrs Villiers and Mrs Lundy[4] and one from Russell, who told Shrewsbury that his acceptance of the seals would be "a great satisfaction to the sober party".[5] But Shrewsbury was still not to be won over. The Triennial Parliaments Bill still remained an obstacle. During Shrewsbury's absence at Eyford the matter had been brought up again, and another

[1] Shrewsbury to Mrs Villiers, Nov. 24, 1693, in Coxe, p. 21. See also *Buccleuch MSS.* vol. II, pt i, pp. 57–8.
[2] *Buccleuch MSS.* vol. II, pt i, p. 59.
[3] Wharton to Shrewsbury, Dec. 1, 1693, in Coxe, p. 23.
[4] *Ibid.* pp. 24–9.
[5] *Ibid.* p. 24.

Bill introduced, this time in the Lower House. It passed successfully through all its stages until the last was reached on November 28, when it was unexpectedly defeated.[1] The Whigs were wavering in their support of the measure. Mulgrave was reported to have said that if the King still persisted in his objection to it, it should be dropped,[2] and his unwillingness to press the scheme was no doubt shared by other members of the party whose reforming zeal was, as usual, considerably cooled by the prospect of office. But such counsels did not appeal to Shrewsbury, who had not changed his opinion as to the virtues of the measure and did not believe in bartering his convictions for the sake of assisting his own or his party's return to power.

Some others of the Whigs were still in favour of persistence, and on the same day on which Wharton's letter was written Monmouth introduced a new Triennial Bill in the House of Lords with the same terms as that which the King had rejected the previous session.[3] Whether Shrewsbury knew of Monmouth's action when he replied to Wharton is not clear, but in any case he seems to have been thoroughly disheartened by the loss of the previous Bill in the House of Commons, and the idea of accepting office seemed more distasteful than ever now that he felt he would not have a united party to support him. In his replies to Wharton and Mrs Villiers there is apparent, not only all his old self-distrust and shrinking from office, but also suspicion of his party. He wrote to Wharton on December 2:

I have now had more time, and some opportunities to observe how unfit I am for a court. I doubt whether I am skilful enough to agree, even with those of whose party I am reckoned, in several notions they now seem to have of things; and if that should prove

[1] *C.J.* Nov. 14, 16, 18, 21, 25, 28, 1693; Bonet's report, Nov. 28/ Dec. 8, 1693, in Ranke, vol. VI, pp. 222–3. There seems to have been some talk of turning the Bill into one for biennial parliaments. See *Hatton Corr.* vol. II, p. 199.
[2] *Denbigh MSS.* p. 215.   [3] *Ibid.* pp. 216–17.

so, joined with the many defects which make me improper for a place of so much industry and application, I beg the king would have the justice to consider how useless I should be to his affairs, and how inconsiderable I shall appear in them.[1]

He apparently contemplated going abroad and, with the King's permission, travelling in Spain—or so he pretended—but actually he lingered until nearly the beginning of December at Eyford. In his absence Monmouth's Triennial Bill was rapidly passed by the Lords after a five hours' debate in committee and sent down to the Commons. There after much discussion it finally shared the fate of its predecessor, being rejected after the third reading by 197 votes to 127.[2] That Shrewsbury chose to remain in the seclusion of his country house in Gloucestershire while his favourite triennial scheme was being revived at Westminster must presumably be taken as an index of the keenness of his anxiety to keep out of reach of the King. He reappeared in the House of Lords on December 12.[3] No further attempt had been made in the meantime to induce him to accept office, and he may have come to the conclusion that there was no longer any reason to apprehend a renewal of it. He did not present himself at Kensington, being anxious (as he subsequently told Mrs Lundy) not to give any signs of "coquetting". On the 17th, however, he went to Whitehall to "pay his duty to the King".[4]

This visit may have been due solely to a wish not to give cause for comment by his absence from Court, but his present proceedings were interpreted as a sign of wavering.

[1] Coxe, pp. 25–6.
[2] *Denbigh MSS.* p. 217; *H.L. MSS.* 1693–5, pp. 51–2; *L.J.* Dec. 1, 4, 6, 8; *C.J.* Dec. 9–22, 1693.
[3] *L.J.* vol. xv, p. 320, Dec. 12, 1693.
[4] *Buccleuch MSS.* p. 59. The King was apparently irritated with those who had led him to expect that Shrewsbury would accept office, the Earl's refusal having put him "out of all his measures". See *Letters of Humphrey Prideaux to John Ellis* (ed. E. M. Thompson, Camden Soc. 1875), p. 162.

His replies to Mrs Lundy had not been regarded as final and it was hoped that at a personal interview with the King his scruples would be overcome. No sooner, then, had he appeared at Whitehall than he received a communication from Mrs Lundy that Mrs Villiers desired to see him the following day. Shrewsbury replied that he was "infinitely surprised that there must never be an end of this matter. Could I have thought it possible, I would have buried myself yonder this winter in the snow". He excused himself from attending on Mrs Villiers on the morrow on account of a big dinner party that he was giving and the uncertainty of parliamentary hours, and he requested a postponement of the interview.[1] In reply, Mrs Villiers merely sent a verbal message that the King wished to see him. Realising that if he saw the King he would almost certainly receive a renewed offer of the seals, and being apparently as firmly resolved as ever not to accept them, although to quote Mrs Lundy "his devilish party were very angry already",[2] Shrewsbury replied to Mrs Villiers, "I have such a dread, from what happened the last time, that though it is an honour I must not refuse, yet I cannot help receiving it with great apprehension". He repeated his customary assertions of incapacity, and expressed himself as "obstinate in a thing of such consequence".[3] In the absence of evidence it is safe to assume that the proposed interview did not take place. For a space of six weeks the matter was allowed to rest.

But William did not abandon his purpose. Trenchard continued to act as sole Secretary of State; there still remained the vacancy for Shrewsbury to fill could he be prevailed upon to do so. In the words of a later Jacobite writer the King "was forced to set several engines to work to per-

[1] Shrewsbury to Mrs Lundy, Dec. 18, 1693, in Coxe, pp. 27–8.
[2] Mrs Lundy to Shrewsbury, n.d., in *ibid.* pp. 28–9. See also *Buccleuch MSS.* p. 60.
[3] Shrewsbury to Mrs Villiers, Dec. 25, 1693, in Coxe, pp. 29–30.

suade him to it ".[1] His patience was at length rewarded, for by means of those same "engines" (to quote the same authority) "some discoverys were made either of a certain tendency to return to his duty or at least of a dissatisfaction of the ill-success of his former disloyalty".[2] Sir James Montgomery, who had been one of the three commissioners nominated by the Convention Parliament of Scotland to offer the Scottish throne to William, had not been rewarded by the Revolution Government as he considered his services merited, and he was now engaged in plotting to bring about its overthrow.[3] Recently arrested on a charge of libelling the Government, he succeeded in escaping from confinement. Before crossing to France he obtained access to Shrewsbury and apparently talked to him as to a fellow Jacobite deep in the plots then being concocted by the malcontents. He received from the Earl only the most non-committal replies to his advances. Events soon proved Shrewsbury's caution to be eminently wise, for Montgomery appears to have divulged this conversation and the news of it reached William almost immediately.

The King at once sent for Shrewsbury and had an interview of more than an hour with him.[4] He began by reproaching him for his repeated refusals of the seals. Shrewsbury replied that the bad state of his health prevented his accepting office. "That is not the only reason", William retorted. "No, Sir," was Shrewsbury's outspoken answer, "it is not; for you received the crown upon certain conditions which have not been complied with, and I cannot go the same lengths that others will." Ignoring this challenge, the King suddenly asked the Earl when he had last seen Montgomery, and was told that he had seen him often since he brought William the offer of the crown of Scotland; whereupon to

[1] Clarke's *Life of James II*, vol. II, p. 520. [2] *Ibid.*
[3] See *D.N.B.* vol. XIII, pp. 763-4.
[4] Bonet's dispatch, Feb. 9/19, 1693/4, in Ranke, vol. VI, p. 240.

the Earl's complete surprise William revealed that he knew all about the last meeting with Montgomery. Conscious of his rectitude or at least his circumspection in this matter, Shrewsbury countered the King's story by saying that his Majesty would see from it that he had given no encouragement to the man who had sought to tempt him from his loyalty. "No," replied the King, "I know you are a man of honour, and if you undertake it, you will serve me honestly." Before the interview terminated Shrewsbury had agreed to act as Secretary of State, the King readily accepting the stipulation that he should be allowed a few days' grace to go into the country to recuperate his health and to attend to pressing private business.[1] It is possible that there were other more important stipulations, and that William agreed, should a Triennial Bill again pass in the two Houses, he would not withhold the royal assent. On the very same day the commission of Lieutenancy for the City of London, which had been one of the chief sources of the quarrel between the King and Shrewsbury in 1690, was remodelled in favour of his party, forty Tories being replaced by thirty-four Whigs.[2]

Shrewsbury remained for nearly three weeks at his country seat and then returning to London finally verified rumours which had been current ever since his last interview with the King by receiving from him the seals of office as Secretary of State on March 2, to the general satisfaction of his party.[3]

[1] See Clarke's *Life of James II*, vol. II, pp. 520–1.
[2] Bonet's dispatch of Feb. 9/19, in Ranke, vol. VI, p. 240; Luttrell, Feb. 6, 8, 1693/4, vol. III, pp. 265, 266. The list of the new commissioners named in the warrant of Feb. 6 is given in C.S.P. (*Dom.*), 1694/5, p. 21.
[3] Luttrell, Feb. 15, vol. III, p. 269; L'Hermitage, Feb. 27/Mar. 9, in Add. MSS. 17,677, vol. O.O. f. 193; Bonet's dispatch, Mar. 2/12, in Ranke, vol. VI, p. 242; Burnet, vol. II, p. 123; C.S.P. (*Dom.*), 1694–5, pp. 51, 56. According to the author of the *Life and Character* (p. 7), Shrewsbury's final compliance was due to the intervention of the Queen, who wrote "enforcing the reasons of the necessity of his coming in, and granting all his demands of bringing in his own

Meanwhile, as usually happened when one of his supposed adherents was preparing to take office under the usurper, James II was being fervently assured that all was for the best. On February 28, Marlborough wrote to say that it was in the exiled Sovereign's "real interest" that Shrewsbury should be in office again.[1] According to a Jacobite authority Shrewsbury had been intriguing to induce Russell to hand over the fleet to James.[2] At the same time the Countess of Shrewsbury informed an agent from St Germain who paid her a visit that her son had postponed his acceptance of the seals as long as he possibly could in the hope and expectation that there would be a Jacobite invasion headed by James II in person, and that he would in such an event have joined the invaders at once. His motive in asking for a brief postponement even after he had accepted office had been this same expectation of an immediate Jacobite movement. Unfortunately the movement had not taken place and Shrewsbury had felt compelled to his great regret to undertake the Secretary's duties, but in that position he would only serve the rightful Sovereign more effectually.[3] But in what way Shrewsbury's acceptance of office under William III could be of service to James II was not made clear. In 1692, James's minister, the Earl of Melfort, had written with reference to Godolphin and Shrewsbury that "there is not much more clearness here

people with him". The statement may well be true, but it is possibly due to a confusion with the letters of Mrs Villiers.

[1] Clarke's *Life of James II*, vol. II, p. 519.

[2] Cf. also the "instructions" sent out from St Germain on Oct. 16, 1693, through the intermediation of the Countess of Shrewsbury, "Earls Shrewsbury, Danby, Godolphin, Churchill, Russell, etc., that they do, what in prudence they can, to hinder money or retard it and hinder the going out of the fleet, so soon as it might do otherwise", in Macpherson, *Original Papers*, vol. I, p. 459. We do not need to take seriously as incriminating evidence the issue of these orders, which were certainly never executed.

[3] Clarke, *op. cit.* vol. II, pp. 520-1; Macpherson, *Original Papers*, vol. I, pp. 456-7, 481.

than you have there; and therefore I can say nothing of positiv concerning them as yet";[1] and it had always been the same. The Jacobites had never been able to say "anything of positiv" where Shrewsbury was concerned. In later years the compiler of James II's memoirs spoke with the bitterness of disillusion of "the putts off the King met with from these pretended friends, who never did him any essential good or themselves any harm for if they were out of employment, it passed for aversion to the Government and they made a merit of it; and if they found means of being re-admitted, then it was represented as a mighty advantage to the King, their being in a better capacity of serving him".[2]

Long and painful experience was needed before this unpalatable truth was at length impressed upon the minds of James and his adherents; but it must be admitted that the prolonged hesitation of Shrewsbury before his eventual acceptance of office for the second time gave occasion for those who were anxious to discover in Jacobitism the explanation of political conduct, the motives of which were to most observers incomprehensible. Why did Shrewsbury hang back even when William was doing his utmost to make things easy for the Whigs? The importance which Shrewsbury attached to the Triennial Bill does not seem to have been appreciated, nor the disgust produced in him by the willingness of some of his party to compromise on that matter understood. We seem to come to the crux of the situation in a letter he wrote to Mrs Villiers on December 2, 1693:

I find by the votes there is no such a thing left in being as a party of my mind. Either they or I are much changed since last year, and be it one or the other, my figure in that station is likely to be very odd; hated by one side for coming in the room of a man [*i.e.* Nottingham] they reckon a martyr for their cause; and not fully agreeing with the others, in the late notions they seem to have entertained.[3]

[1] Macpherson, *Original Papers*, p. 481.
[2] *Ibid.* p. 420.   [3] Coxe, p. 26.

CHAPTER IV

Second Secretaryship of State

After four years of opposition Shrewsbury now found himself once more in office, and the leading member of the Government in the Upper House. Instead of being a critic of the King's policy, he became its chief advocate, and he rendered valuable services through his influence with the Peers.[1] From William's point of view, this in itself was no small gain, but the results as regards the Earl's followers were even more satisfactory and amply justified the persistence with which he had laboured to secure Shrewsbury's return to office. Encouraged by the appointment of their leader, and also by the alteration made in the commission of Lieutenancy for the City after Nottingham's dismissal, "the whigs expressed new zeal and confidence in the king", the effect of which was soon apparent in the ease with which the all-important business of supply was transacted in the Commons.[2] But the favour of the Whigs could only be secured at the expense of antagonising their opponents, and in proportion as the zeal and confidence of the other party increased, as Burnet remarked, "the Tories began now to grow very backward in the king's business".[3] Nottingham, not without some justification, felt that he had been most unfairly dismissed to make way for his rival, and with the

[1] See, *e.g.*, Bonet's report, April 20/30, 1694, in Ranke, vol. VI, p. 247; L'Hermitage, same date, in Add. MSS. 17,677, vol. O.O. f. 240.
[2] Burnet, vol. II, p. 124; Bonet, Feb. 9/19, 1694, in Ranke, vol. VI, p. 240.
[3] Foxcroft, *Supplement to Burnet*, p. 395.

assistance of Rochester, "obstructed the king's measures...
in the house of lords with a peculiar edge of violence".[1] On
the whole, however, William had no cause to regret his
decision to transfer his favour from the Tories to the Whigs,
for it had been the means of averting the serious crisis which
might have arisen from his rejection of the Place Bill, and of
securing the establishment of the Bank of England. Having
received these proofs of their ability and willingness to
conduct the business of the Government in Parliament, he
felt justified in committing himself more completely to their
side. Consequently, after the prorogation which took place
on April 25, Shrewsbury had the satisfaction of seeing two
of his Whig colleagues promoted. Charles Montagu,[2] to
whom the success of the concluding part of the session was
very largely due, was appointed Chancellor of the Exchequer as a reward for his services, while Russell was made
First Lord of the Admiralty.

If William had no cause to repent of the favour shewn to
the Whigs or to regret the pains he had taken to induce their
leader to return to office, Shrewsbury, on his side, had no
cause to complain of the way in which either he or his party
was treated. Having at length succeeded in securing
Shrewsbury's support by dint of infinite patience and trouble,
the King was determined to run no risk of losing it again,
and, as one of the Earl's biographers said of him, "if he had
been to remain till the King had dismiss'd him by inclination,
'tis very like he had continued so [as Secretary of State] all
that Prince's reign".[3] He was rewarded with the highest
honours which it was in the power of the Sovereign to bestow.
On the day on which Parliament was prorogued a warrant
was signed for his creation as Marquis of Alton and Duke

[1] Burnet, vol. II, p. 125.
[2] See article on Charles Montagu, Earl of Halifax, in *D.N.B.*
vol. XIII, pp. 665–70.
[3] *Memoirs of Public Transactions*, etc., p. 32.

of Shrewsbury,[1] and he was elected and invested a Knight of the Garter in a chapter of the Order held at Whitehall in the place of the Duke of Hamilton.[2] He was also appointed Lord-Lieutenant of the County of Hereford and of North Wales, in addition to the Lieutenancy of Worcestershire which he already held.[3]

There was only one point on which he failed to persuade William to comply with his wishes, and that was the question of Marlborough's restoration to favour. As the exiled King's biographer said, William had not "the same kindness for his person or opinion of his sinceritie" as he had in the case of the Earl's advocate,[4] and he had neither forgotten nor forgiven the conduct which had led to his dismissal two years before. He was adamant in refusing to listen to any suggestion that the disgraced favourite of his sister-in-law should again be given a command in the army.

After being detained for nearly a fortnight by adverse winds, the King crossed over to Holland on May 6. The Government in his absence was, as usual, entrusted to the Queen, assisted by the Cabinet Council. But it was a very different Cabinet Council from that by which she had been assisted in 1693. The only Tories who still retained their places in it were Carmarthen (who had just been created Duke of Leeds) and Godolphin. The influence of the former, however, was not what it had once been. As for Godolphin, he was retained much more in the character of a useful official of the Treasury than as one of the leading members of the Tory party. He was, besides, the intimate friend of Marlborough, and had been drawn towards Shrewsbury by their common antipathy to Leeds. There was, therefore,

---

[1] *C.S.P.* (*Dom.*), 1694–5, p. 116.
[2] Luttrell, June 5, 1694, vol. III, p. 323; L'Hermitage, same date, in Add. MSS. 17,677, vol. O.O. f. 269.
[3] Warrant dated April 28, 1694, in *C.S.P.* (*Dom.*), 1694–5, p. 119.
[4] Clarke, *Life of James II*, vol. II, p. 521.

no particular reason, so far as Shrewsbury was concerned, for ousting him from his place, though the Duke had not always cause to be satisfied with his conduct.[1] Shrewsbury's predominant position in the Council was thus secure, and he had no need to fear a repetition of the rivalries for the chief place in the King's confidence which had marked his first period of office as Secretary of State. His mother, it is true, reported to St Germain that the Queen would "entirely follow the advices" of the Duke of Leeds and her son.[2] But, however much the recollection of his efforts on her behalf in 1689 might tempt Mary to give the Tory minister the first place in her confidence, she was practically compelled to accept his Whig colleague as her chief adviser. He had the support of the other members of the Council, and the full confidence of the King.

But the chief place in the Cabinet Council and the King's confidence was not without its drawbacks, as Shrewsbury soon discovered, for it entailed corresponding responsibilities unpalatable to one of his temperament. Before leaving for the Continent, William had ordered him to communicate to him privately anything that in his judgment ought not to go through the Secretary's office in the ordinary way, and consequently a regular correspondence was kept up between them during the King's absence, in addition to that on routine business through the latter's private secretary, William Blathwayt.[3] The control of foreign relations was entirely in the King's hands as well as the conduct of the war on the Continent.[4] But whilst in this department Shrewsbury

[1] See, *e.g.*, Shrewsbury to William, July 10/20, 1694, complaining of Godolphin's conduct in connection with the appointment of a new Board of Commissioners for the Customs and Excise Department, in Coxe, pp. 51–2.
[2] Macpherson, *Original Papers*, vol. I, p. 483.
[3] Shrewsbury to William, May 11/21, 1694, in Coxe, p. 33.
[4] See, *e.g.*, Shrewsbury's correspondence with Blathwayt, May 1694, in *Buccleuch MSS.* vol. II, pt i, pp. 66–9.

was relieved of responsibility, having merely to act as ordered by the King, and was not always informed by the latter of the negotiations in which he was engaged,[1] he was left with the task of satisfying as far as possible the latter's requirements in the important matter of supplies and of ensuring that Russell and the Admiralty acted in accordance with William's wishes. The former problem was an incessant source of anxiety owing to the constantly increasing financial difficulties with which the Government had to cope, and which, though somewhat lessened by the institution of the Bank of England, were by no means ended by the success of Montagu's scheme.

In naval matters also his position was not free from difficulties, for he was entrusted with the task of supervising the carrying out of plans with which he was not always in complete agreement. The naval campaign of 1694 was marred by the failure of the expedition against Brest and the death of Tollemache, the leader of the attack, to the great chagrin of the King who had been counting on its success to effect a diversion of the attention of his antagonists. Shrewsbury had shared Russell's opinion that it would probably clash with the latter's proposed expedition to the Mediterranean, and whilst doing his best to forward both schemes in accordance with the King's wishes, had not hesitated to express his doubts on the wisdom of the King's plan. "I must own", he wrote to William shortly before the attack took place, "I never had any great opinion [of the scheme], so now less than ever, because of the delays which have been made, and the alarm it has given beyond sea."[2] In reminding him of these forebodings a month later, he took the opportunity afforded by the death of Tollemache once more to recommend the readmission to favour of his friend Marlborough.

[1] See, *e.g.*, his letter to Lexington of June 8, 1694–5, in *Lexington Papers* (ed. H. M. Sutton, 1851), p. 40.
[2] Shrewsbury to William, May 22/June 2, 1694, in Coxe, p. 33.

"Writing upon this subject", he said, "it is impossible to forget what is here become a very general discourse, the probability and conveniency of your majesty receiving my lord Marlborough into your favour. He has been with me since this news, to offer his service, with all the expressions of duty and fidelity imaginable.... It is so unquestionably his interest to be faithful that single argument makes me not doubt it."[1]

This attempt to serve his friend said more for his attachment to Marlborough than for his knowledge of the King's character. William's answer was curt and decisive. "As to what you wrote in your last letter concerning lord Marlborough, I can say no more, than that I do not think it for the good of my service to entrust him with the command of my troops."[2] Fortunately for Marlborough, William knew nothing of the letter which he had sent to St Germain at the end of February giving information of the intended attack on Brest, or his offer of service would have met with something more disconcerting than a simple rejection.[3]

Soon after this, Shrewsbury was compelled to exert his influence to keep the peace between another of his friends and the King. After the disaster before Brest William determined that Russell should spend the winter in the Mediterranean without returning to England. The scheme was novel and did not commend itself to Russell. Shrewsbury himself fully approved of the plan, but he was inclined to think that the Admiral should be allowed to exercise some discretion as to whether to winter at Cadiz or return to England.[4] The

[1] Shrewsbury to William, June 22/July 2, in Coxe, p. 47.
[2] William to Shrewsbury, July 15, in *ibid.* p. 53.
[3] As to Marlborough's alleged responsibility for the failure of the Brest expedition see "Marlborough and the Brest Expedition 1694", by Col. E. M. Lloyd, *E.H.R.* vol. IX, p. 130; Viscount Wolseley's *Life of John Churchill, Duke of Marlborough* (1894), vol. II, pp. 304-19; Col. Hon. Arthur Parnell in "James Macpherson and the Nairne Papers" (*E.H.R.* vol. XII, p. 254); C. T. Atkinson, *Marlborough and the Rise of the British Army* (2nd ed. 1924), pp. 143-7.
[4] Shrewsbury to William, Aug. 3/13, in Coxe, pp. 65-8.

Queen's council shared this opinion and modified Russell's instructions accordingly, so as to allow him to return if he should think it absolutely necessary. In informing the King of this, Shrewsbury expressed the hope that if these orders differed from his instructions, they at least carried out his intentions.[1] But he soon discovered that this was not the case. The King was determined that Russell should spend the winter in the Mediterranean at all costs and at once sent instructions that the orders given to him by the Council should be altered so as to leave him no choice in the matter.[2] Shrewsbury had already done his best to reconcile Russell to the King's plan, and, knowing that his friend was not in the best of humours and prone at such times to speak his mind in terms more fitted for the quarter-deck than for the council-chamber, wrote again on receiving the King's peremptory instructions to prevent an outburst which would only prejudice him in William's eyes.

"Though...I find you are not in a very good humour", he said, "I doubt the orders you have received since will put you in a worse. The doctrine you used to preach to me, that public good ought to be considered before private ease, will now come to your share to practise, in a more tedious and troublesome manner than you could foresee. Whether your stay this winter, at Cadiz, will be advantageous to the common cause may bear many arguments, for and against, which having been laid before his majesty, he is come to so positive a resolution for your continuing, that...I find he is in pain, lest the liberty the queen gave in her instructions, that, upon great necessity, you might return, should too much encourage you to do it. He has therefore renewed his commands to me to signify to you the importance of your stay; and I am sure you will so well understand his intentions, by this, as not to disagree, if there be a possibility of obliging, without the ruin of the fleet. I have but this more to beg, that if the orders his majesty has sent, be contrary to your opinion or inclinations, that may not so put you out of humour, as not to prosecute them in the most

[1] Same to same, Aug. 14/24, in *ibid.* p. 69.
[2] William to Shrewsbury, Aug. 30 n.s., in *ibid.* pp. 70–1.

admirable and best manner....Dear Mr. Russell, let a man that truly loves and values you, prevail upon you to practise patience and submission; and if his majesty is in the wrong in his commands, do you represent what you please; but then obey them with a prudence you can be master of, if you please. Advice is a thing, you know, against my temper to trouble people with; part of this is by command, but much the greatest, out of a real concern I have for you and your credit...."[1]

Russell still continued to complain to Shrewsbury of his health and of the conduct of the Spanish Government, but he was constrained to admit that the expectations of the King were not altogether unfounded,[2] and the signal success of the scheme, and the general approval with which it met,[3] to some extent compensated for the disaster in Camaret Bay. The salutary effect upon the allies' fortunes in Spain exerted by the maintenance of an English fleet in the Mediterranean is perhaps the most remarkable instance of William III's military prescience.

Shrewsbury's attention had, meanwhile, been diverted to home politics. One of the chief events of the summer was the establishment of the Bank. Within a fortnight of the day on which the subscription list was opened the whole amount had been subscribed, Shrewsbury, as a loyal Whig, advancing £10,000.[4] Nevertheless, these were troubled and anxious days for him. The department of secret service belonged peculiarly to the Duke's office, and it involved a considerable addition to the duties and responsibilities of the post of

[1] Shrewsbury to Russell, Aug. 26/Sept. 5, in Coxe, pp. 201–2.
[2] Russell to Shrewsbury, Nov. 2/12, in *ibid.* pp. 210–13.
[3] Shrewsbury to Russell, Mar. 12/22, 1694/5, in *ibid.* p. 225.
[4] L'Hermitage, June 22/July 2, 1694, in Add. MSS. 17,677, vol. O.O. f. 279. "It is generally believed that the money will come in apace" [Shrewsbury had written on the eve of the opening of the subscription list] "but many question what the consequence may be if they grow to such a greatness as they seem to promise themselves" (Letter to Blathwayt, June 8, in *Buccleuch MSS.* vol. II, pt i, p. 79).

Secretary of State. The reign of William III was marked by a constant succession of plots, some real, others invented by unscrupulous disciples of Titus Oates, sometimes with a real foundation of facts elaborated with additions of their own, sometimes with no foundation whatever. The office of the Secretaries of State was besieged by informers all anxious for rewards; much of the time of the Secretaries themselves as well as of their subordinates was spent in endeavouring to unravel the complicated narratives with which they were regaled, and it was often a problem of no small difficulty to distinguish between the real and the sham conspiracies.[1] Among the Government's spies was an Irish priest named Taaff, who had changed his religion and who received a small pension. He succeeded in persuading Lunt, a Jacobite agent—"an Irishman who was bold and poor and of a mean understanding"—to go with him to the Secretary's office and give information as to concealed arms in Lancashire and Cheshire.[2] The messengers sent to investigate the charges did in fact discover some secret stores of arms and various arrests followed on warrants signed by Shrewsbury upon whom the supervision of this affair mainly fell, his colleague Trenchard being incapacitated by illness. The prisoners were brought to London, examined, and committed to the Tower or Newgate, to await their trial. A month later they were sent down to Manchester and Chester to be tried, the Government confidently expecting that they would be convicted. But to their surprise and dismay, the result proved very different. Taaff was dissatisfied with his reward and had been

[1] During the year ending Sept. 28, 1695, Shrewsbury drew £3000 from the Exchequer for secret service, and on May 18, 1696, a warrant for £10,000 was drawn in his favour for the same purpose. *H.L. MSS.* 1695–7 (n.s.), vol. II, p. 165; *Cal. of Treasury Papers*, 1557–1696, p. 511.

[2] Burnet, vol. II, p. 141. The information is printed in the *MSS. of Lord Kenyon* (H.M.C. Rept. XIV, app. pt iv), pp. 292–301. For an account of Lunt, see *ibid.* pp. 310–20.

heavily bribed by the friends of the accused. When placed in the witness box, he unblushingly contradicted all his previous evidence, and denounced Lunt, whose credibility as a witness was easily shaken. The case for the prosecution naturally collapsed at once.[1] "There appears to have been great villainy among the King's evidence", Shrewsbury wrote to Blathwayt, "and some who put them upon swearing this Plot in order afterwards to discover their perjury....I hope all the actors in this villainy will be prosecuted and punished to the utmost."[2]

The loss of prestige resulting from the failure of the Lancashire prosecutions did not augur well for either a peaceful or satisfactory session. On the whole, however, the Government had no reason to complain of the results of the debates when the House assembled on November 12. Harley, it is true, asserted that the session began angrily "with some touches of the Northerne plot", which he characterised as "a mystery of villanous perjury scarce to be imagined".[3] Burnet, on the contrary, considered that it opened with a calmer face than had appeared in any session since the Revolution.[4] The success of the Bank had done much to relieve the King and his advisers in the important department of finance. The Continental campaign too had been a great improvement on those which had preceded it; if there had been no striking victory there had at least been no serious disaster, and to that extent the result satisfied the cautious who, like Shrewsbury, had been "so accustomed to hear ill news" that they began "to be very willing to compound to hear no news at all".[5] The most important feature of the session from Shrewsbury's point of view was a new Bill for Triennial

[1] Burnet, vol. II, pp. 142, 143.
[2] Shrewsbury to Blathwayt, Oct. 26, in *Buccleuch MSS.* vol. II, pt i, p. 152.
[3] R. Harley to Sir E. Harley, Nov. 13, in *Portland MSS.* vol. III, p. 559.
[4] Burnet, vol. II, p. 132. [5] Coxe, p. 52.

Parliaments which was introduced on the first day of the session and passed both Houses with little or no opposition, November 1696 being fixed as the time-limit for the duration of the existing Parliament. It remained to be seen what its fate would be when it was again tendered for the royal assent. Whether or not the bargain made between the King and Shrewsbury on the latter's return to office in the spring had expressly included the acceptance of this Bill by the Crown— and there is good ground for believing that it did—the King had certainly given Shrewsbury an assurance that "they should not disagree in anything material". The time had now come for testing whether William and his Secretary of State placed the same construction upon that assurance. On December 22, the Bill was again presented to the King and the answer of the Clerk of the Parliaments was "Le Roy et la Reyne le veulent", which elicited "a great humm" of approval and clapping of hands from the Commons assembled to hear its fate.[1]

The struggle which had been carried on for the past two years over this Bill was thus terminated in the victory of the cause for which Shrewsbury and his Whig followers had striven so long. But other events of the closing months of the year did much to counteract the legitimate pride which he felt at this success. A month before the Bill was passed, Tillotson, who had been mainly responsible for his conversion to the Church of England, was suddenly taken ill, and died on November 23, after lingering for five days.[2] The Primate had been his firm friend for the last fifteen years,

[1] Luttrell, Dec. 22, vol. III, p. 416; L'Hermitage, dispatch of Dec. 25/Jan. 4, 1694/5, in Add. MSS. 17,677, vol. P.P. f. 106; Burnet, vol. II, p. 133; Bonet's report, Dec. 25/Jan. 4, 1694/5, in Ranke, vol. VI, p. 262. Two days earlier the King had visited Shrewsbury at the latter's house and been closeted with him for half an hour, but whether the Bill was the subject of the interview there is nothing to shew. Vernon to Lexington, Dec. 21, 1694, in *Lexington Papers*, p. 26.   [2] Burnet, vol. II, p. 134.

and his death was felt by none more deeply than by his former convert. "We have had a great loss in the Archbishop", he wrote to Russell, "but I hope it will be better filled than is generally expected."[1] Many were in favour of the appointment of Stillingfleet, then Bishop of Worcester, as Tillotson's successor, and his adherents were supported by the Queen, who, in addition to pressing her husband to support him, several times urged Shrewsbury to use his influence on the same side. The Whigs, however, "apprehended that both his notions and his temper were too high", and favoured the claims of Tenison, who then held the see of Lincoln. The partisans of the latter won the day.[2]

The loss of Tillotson was soon followed by another which was much more serious, and which added materially to the anxieties of Shrewsbury's position. The Queen had been ill for some days, and the illness soon proved to be small-pox, and terminated fatally on December 28. From Shrewsbury's point of view as a member of the Government, as well as from that of the King himself, this was a serious blow. Mary had been deservedly popular with all with whom she had come in contact, and her death added considerably to the difficulties and responsibilities of the King's Ministers by removing one of the chief sources of strength of the Revolution settlement. "Certainly there never was anyone more really and universally lamented", Shrewsbury wrote in informing Russell of the "melancholy news;"

but the king, particularly, has been dejected by it, beyond what could be imagined; but I hope he begins to recover out of his great disorder, and that a little time will restore him to his former application to business. The lords and commons have behaved themselves upon this occasion with great duty and affection to his majesty, in their seasonable resolutions to stand by him in the defence and support of his person and government.[3]

[1] Shrewsbury to Russell, Dec. 4/14, in Coxe, p. 213.
[2] Burnet, vol. II, p. 136.
[3] Shrewsbury to Russell, Jan. 1/10, 1694/5, in Coxe, p. 218;

At the same time signs were not wanting that Shrewsbury's own health was beginning to give way under the strain imposed upon it by constant attention to the duties of his office and the added anxieties caused by the death of the Queen. To make matters worse, Trenchard, his colleague in the Secretary's office, was suffering from consumption, and was often unable to attend to business. The Duke had already had an attack of fever in November, and lameness in the knee.[1] This was followed in December by symptoms of gout, which confined him to the house for nearly a fortnight "for want of legs", as he told the King, and prevented him from attending either the debates in the Upper House on the Triennial Bill, or the adjournment on December 22 when the Bill at length received the royal assent.[2] Although he did not complain to the King, he gave vent to his feelings with more force than usual in writing to Russell. To the latter he could unburden his mind with more freedom, for the Admiral was much given to grumbling himself. "I am very much out of humour", Shrewsbury wrote, "with the apprehensions of the gout, which will certainly increase whilst I am tied to this hateful, unnatural, sedentary life."[3] While there was no hint of resignation—for there was now no disagreement with

same to Lexington, Dec. 28, 1694, in *Lexington Papers*, pp. 32–3. The malevolence of Howe, who had been the Queen's Vice-Chamberlain, did not spare her even after her death. He told Dartmouth a story of her supposed feelings towards Shrewsbury which would not have suggested itself to anyone except Howe or a Jacobite of the worst type; and Dartmouth thought fit to repeat it when commenting on Burnet's *History*. See note to Burnet, vol. II, p. 546. Shrewsbury was one of the commissioners appointed for endowing the Hospital at Greenwich in her memory and subscribed £500 to the fund raised for the purpose. *Evelyn's Diary*, May 5, 1695, pp. 437, 442.

[1] Luttrell, Nov. 17, 1694, vol. III, p. 401. Shrewsbury to Russell, Dec. 18, in *Buccleuch MSS.* vol. II, pt i, p. 166.

[2] Same to William, Dec. 15/25, in Coxe, p. 77; same to Capel, Dec. 22, in *Buccleuch MSS.* vol. II, pt i, p. 167.

[3] Shrewsbury to Russell, Dec. 18/28, in Coxe, p. 214.

the King, or with other members of the Ministry, on matters
of policy as there had been in 1690—it soon became clear
that his health demanded some respite from the duties of his
office. In January he was ordered by his physicians to "for-
bear all studious business", as it might endanger the sight
of his eye, which had been affected by the gout, and he went
to Windsor, "to try if rest and air would give him any relief".[1]
The experiment was only partially successful. He returned
to London on the 24th, but was unable to attend at the
Secretary's office for nearly a week, and then only appeared
there on his way to the House of Lords where the Peers were
engaged in investigating the Lancashire Plot.[2] Almost immediately he was again attacked in a more acute form by his
illness, and was unable to attend to any business whatever,
and Normanby had to act as his deputy in Parliament. His
only course was to leave London again for some more
distant spot in the hope that a longer period of rest might
effect the cure which the air of Windsor had failed to do.
Early in February, having requested and obtained the King's
leave, he retired to his seat at Eyford, in Gloucestershire, as
far as possible from the cares and anxieties of office, and a
rumour was current that he was about to relinquish his post
and take the sinecure of Master of the Horse.[3]

[1] Shrewsbury to Russell, Jan. 15/25, 1694/5, in Coxe, p. 219;
Luttrell, Jan. 17, vol. III, p. 428. "Poor Duke Shrewsbury will be
quite blind and Sir J. Trenchard stone dead very shortly", Stepney
to Lexington, Feb. 13/23, 1694/5, in *Lexington Papers*, p. 61.

[2] "My Lord Duke of Shrewsbury has forced himself to come
abroad these two days, as thinking it fit for him to hear what passed
in the examination of the Lancashire business, though my Lord
Nottingham had before declared that no reflection could be in this
matter, upon him, since he had done no more than the duty of his
place required" (Vernon to Lexington, Jan. 29, 1694/5, in *Lexington
Papers*, p. 53).

[3] Luttrell, Feb. 5, 1694/5, vol. III, p. 436; Countess of Nottingham to Viscount Hatton, Feb. 9, in *Hatton Corr.* vol. II, p. 213, and
see Shrewsbury to Russell, same date, in *Buccleuch MSS.* vol. II,
pt i, p. 174.

After a month spent in the solitude of his country retreat, Shrewsbury was so far recovered as to be able to return to London. His presence in the Secretary's office was urgently needed, for Trenchard was now in the last stages of disease, and there were other reasons demanding his reappearance at Whitehall. One of the chief of these concerned Marlborough. One result of Mary's death in December had been to assure her sister's position as the next in succession to the Crown on the death of William under the terms of the Bill of Rights, and the Princess of Denmark had now composed her differences with her brother-in-law. The inevitable corollary of this reconciliation was the readmission to the royal favour of Anne's confidante and her husband. The latter at once began to work to this end, but for some time without much result. For it was not easy to overcome William's aversion, and when Shrewsbury returned to London at the beginning of March the King was still undecided, and it required all the Duke's influence with him, added to the other causes which were working in Marlborough's favour, to persuade the King to admit him to an audience. At length, however, the Earl's advocates won the day, and on March 29, Marlborough kissed the King's hand, and the two were outwardly, at least, reconciled. According to the general opinion he owed this very largely to the efforts made on his behalf by his friend Shrewsbury.[1]

Whilst the latter's credit was enhanced by the success which attended his efforts in this matter, the course of events during the following month contributed still further to strengthen his position as the King's most trusted minister. Trenchard died on April 27, and Shrewsbury thus recovered

[1] "Le Comte Marlborough qui, depuis deux ou trois ans étoit en disgrace, a ce matin baisé la main du roi et ira, à ce qu'on dit, en Flandre commander les troupes angloises. Le duc de Sheersbury, Secretaire d'état, est de ses intimes amis, et n'a pas peu contribué à ce qu'on croit à ce favorable retour" (L'Hermitage, Mar. 29/April 8, 1695, in Add. MSS. 17,677, vol. P.P. f. 209).

the post of first Secretary of State, of which his tardiness in accepting the seals had deprived him twelve months earlier. His new colleague in the Secretary's office was Sir William Trumbull. This appointment involved a change of methods as well as of men. Both were Whigs; but whilst Trenchard had been a Whig of the most stern and uncompromising type with a strong character, Trumbull was one of moderate opinions, and, according to Ailesbury, was not a friend to any "but your obedient humble servant to all, like my Lord Plausible in the 'Plain Dealer'".[1] The change was one which made Shrewsbury unquestionably the first Secretary of State in fact as well as in name.[2]

Nor was it on the Whig side only that changes took place. For some time past the Commons had been engaged in investigating charges of corruption which had resulted in the exposure of more than one prominent Tory politician, to the great glee of the Whigs, and which culminated in the disgrace of the foremost member of the party. "One discovery [as Burnet said] made way for another".[3] Suspicion

[1] *Ailesbury's Memoirs*, vol. II, p. 373.

[2] An illustration of the light in which he was at this time regarded by foreign observers and of the importance attached to his opinion is afforded by the correspondence of the Count Auersperg, Imperial Minister in England, with his Government. The latter wished the English Parliament to join the Alliance in its own name, and to this end Auersperg was recommended to sound Shrewsbury rather than Portland on the subject and act according as he approved the idea or not. Auersperg, however, replied that he would approach Portland first rather than Shrewsbury. He did not know whether the King would wish the matter to be discussed with the Duke, seeing that the only sphere left to the royal authority without consulting Parliament consisted in the power to make peace and war, and as Shrewsbury was—or at least pretended to be—a good Presbyterian (*i.e.* a Whig) he would willingly give his assistance to a proposal which would have the effect of limiting it still further. See instruction of Count Kinsky for Count Auersperg, April 6, and Auersperg's reply dated April 26, 1695. Onno Klopp, *Der Fall des Hauses Stuart*, (14 vols. Vienna, 1875–88), vol. VII, pp. 504–5.

[3] Burnet, vol. II, p. 145.

was aroused as to the transactions of the East India Company. Under threat of a Bill of Pains and Penalties, Cook, the Governor of the Company, was induced to offer "to make a full discovery if he might be indemnified for all that he had done or that he might say". A Bill of Indemnity was accordingly introduced and passed, and a joint committee of both Houses appointed to examine him. Shrewsbury was one of the twelve representatives of the Peers on the committee, having received more votes than any of his colleagues.[1] When the committee met, sufficient evidence was soon forthcoming to prove the secret dealings of the Duke of Leeds with the Company, and the Whigs began eagerly to prepare for his impeachment before the Lords. But they were suddenly deprived of the anticipated pleasure of having him tried and condemned by the Peers, as the chief witness against him absconded and escaped to the Continent. After a conference with the Commons, the Lords had a long debate about throwing out the impeachment, and precedents were sought, but without success. Shrewsbury then suggested that they should follow the practice of the ordinary courts in similar cases, and suspend the trial. The suggestion met with general approval, and was unanimously adopted by the House.[2] The impeachment was never revived, for within a few days Parliament was prorogued and did not meet again as a dissolution intervened before the time arrived for the commencement of the following session. Shrewsbury appears to have

[1] *H.L. MSS.* 1693–5, p. 551.
[2] *Ibid.* p. 581; Greenwich Hospital News-letter, May 4; *C.S.P.* (*Dom.*), 1695 (addenda), p. 328; Burnet, vol. II, pp. 144–7. These attacks provoked retaliation, and during the enquiries Normanby was attacked for accepting money to facilitate the passage of a Bill on the subject of convex lights and was defended both by Leeds and Shrewsbury. The latter's action was scarcely consistent with his attitude towards the attacks upon Leeds and other Tories, but Normanby was a Whig, and had ably supported him when in opposition. L'Hermitage, April 19/29, in Add. MSS. 17,677, vol. P.P. f. 237.

anticipated this when he moved the suspension of the trial, for he had written to Russell early in April saying that the enquiries had thrown so much dirt that he concluded the same Parliament could never sit again.[1] Whether the impeachment was ever revived or not was a matter of comparative unimportance, as the object of the Whigs in promoting it—the overthrow of Leeds—had already been accomplished quite as effectively as if the trial had actually taken place and resulted in a verdict of guilty. Leeds was irretrievably ruined, and, although he was allowed to retain the office of Lord President for a time, his influence was destroyed and his chances of rivalling the principal Secretary of State were at an end.

On May 12 the King left Kensington for Holland. Owing to the death of the Queen, a new arrangement was necessary for carrying on the Government in his absence. The most natural course to adopt, and the one which many, including Burnet,[2] considered should have been adopted, would have been to appoint the Princess of Denmark to be Regent. But, although William had been formally reconciled to her, he was not yet prepared to trust her with all the secrets of the Government. A board of Lords Justices was accordingly established, consisting of Tenison, Shrewsbury, Pembroke, Devonshire, Dorset, Somers and Godolphin, the name of Leeds being conspicuous by its absence.[3] The only Tory amongst the seven was Godolphin. The Whigs were masters of the situation, and amongst his Whig colleagues there was not one capable of challenging Shrewsbury's claim to the chief place on the board. Trumbull acted as Secretary to the Lords Justices and countersigned all their orders, thus relieving his colleague of some of the routine work of the

[1] Shrewsbury to Russell, April 9/19, 1695, in Coxe, p. 226.
[2] Burnet, vol. II, p. 149.
[3] Privy Council Minutes, May 4, in *Buccleuch MSS.* vol. II, pt i, p. 182; Luttrell, same date and May 18, vol. III, pp. 467, 474.

Secretary's office, as Shrewsbury only signed in his capacity of Lord Justice.[1]

In England the summer passed uneventfully. Nor had the Government any reason to be dissatisfied with the result of the year's campaign, which was the most successful since the outbreak of the war. The effect of the order to Russell to winter in the Mediterranean had fully justified the King's insistence upon carrying out the scheme, and William was anxious that the experiment should be repeated, but did not press Russell to retain the command. Shrewsbury had procured him the commission of Captain-General, in addition to that of Admiral-General which he already held, and had done what he could to lessen his detestation of the post. He was, however, well aware that his efforts had had little or no result, and, anticipating a refusal to comply with the King's wishes, had done his best to prepare the latter for it.[2] Russell did in fact decline to spend another winter in the Mediterranean,[3] and Rooke was accordingly appointed to succeed him. Russell was always prone to grumble without troubling himself overmuch either about the justice of the complaints he made, or as to the channels through which they passed. One of his letters to Shrewsbury containing information about the state of his squadron and also an attack upon the Dutch Admiralty was sent through France, and being under cover to Blathwayt was opened by the King, who was naturally indignant.[4] Shrewsbury did his best to whitewash Russell's indiscretion, but even with exaggerated assurances of his loyalty, he could not do much,[5] and moderate though the

[1] L'Hermitage, May 7/17, in Add. MSS. 17,677, vol. P.P. f. 259.
[2] Shrewsbury to Russell, Mar. 12/22, in Coxe, pp. 224-5.
[3] Russell to Shrewsbury, April 16/26, in *ibid.* pp. 226-7.
[4] Russell to Shrewsbury, July 21/31, William to same, Sept. 6 (n.s.), in Coxe, pp. 104, 234-6.
[5] "If Mr. Russell has writ anything to give your majesty offence, I am heartily sorry for it, and dare answer he will be so too. I am sure your majesty will not impute his sending whatever he has writ

tone of his reply to his friend was, it implied the strongest disapproval of his conduct.

"You must give me leave to think you even in the wrong" [he wrote], "to send any letter through France, that gave so exact an account of the condition of your fleet and how it was to be disposed of the rest of the summer; but if that was not very cautious, with respect to the public, the inclosing a letter to me in one to Mr. Blathwayt, of the nature of your's, was not more careful of yourself, since curiosity or suspicion might very well invite the king to do what has unluckily happened."[1]

Closely connected with the maintenance of the fleet in the Mediterranean was the alliance with the Duke of Savoy, and it was hoped that the latter's army would act in concert with the fleet. The affairs of Savoy had now come within Shrewsbury's province, and he took the opportunity of urging the advantages to the allies in general and to England in particular of an attack upon some of the French ports, and particularly upon Toulon, or Marseilles, in concert with Russell's fleet, although, with his usual diffidence, he begged Galway, our envoy at Turin, to "excuse his ignorant thoughts upon this

through France, to anything but inadvertence; and if there be expressions more warm, or free, than became him, you will charitably allow for his temper, and the time they were writ at, just upon receiving the first orders to stay, contrary to his own opinion, with regard to the safety of the fleet, as well as his own inclination of returning hither, he seeming to think it necessary for his health. Besides, Sir, they were writ to one, whose friendship he is persuaded he may so entirely depend upon, that if anything were expressed in his letter improper for him to say, it would be as secure from being made public, as if it still remained in his own breast; so that opening his mind to a friend, he reckoned no more than talking to himself, and I, who pretend to know Mr. Russell's heart as well as most men do, will venture to engage, that if your majesty saw it, and every secret thought in it, you would be sufficiently convinced of his zeal for your service and government, and of his respect and affection for your own person" (Shrewsbury to William, Sept. 6/16, in Coxe, p. 105).

[1] Shrewsbury to Russell, Aug. 27/Sept. 6, in Coxe, p. 237.

subject ".[1] The King, Galway, and Russell were all agreed as to the merits of this scheme, but when it was broached to the Duke of Savoy, he declined to fall in with it, and insisted upon undertaking the reduction of Casale, which surrendered unexpectedly and under somewhat suspicious circumstances after a short siege. Shrewsbury had his doubts of the Duke's fidelity to the alliance and communicated them to the King; but the latter did not share them, and Shrewsbury, "very glad to find that they were groundless, joyfully submitted to his majesty's better judgment and information ".[2] Galway also declined to believe that the Duke was playing them false,[3] but as events soon proved, Shrewsbury's suspicions had been well-founded, for secret negotiations with France were in fact pending, and it was not many months before Savoy openly abandoned the coalition.

William was in fact too deeply engrossed in his own campaign to be able to pay minute attention to those of his allies. His operations centred in the siege of Namur. Shrewsbury, when informed of his intention to undertake the task of reducing the fortress, with his habitual caution was chiefly concerned with the risks involved, and reiterated the fears which he had already expressed to the King for his personal safety.[4] But his forebodings were soon ended, for at the beginning of August news arrived of the capture of the town, and the citadel also fell less than a month later.

Shrewsbury availed himself of the opportunity thus afforded to revert to a matter upon which he had been pressing the King for some time past—the question of dissolving Parliament—and to point out the advisability of taking

[1] Galway to Shrewsbury, May 31/June 10, Shrewsbury to Galway, June 28/July 8, in Coxe, pp. 261, 263–4.

[2] Shrewsbury to William, July 16/26 and July 30/Aug. 9, William to Shrewsbury, Aug. 1, in *ibid.* pp. 94, 97, 99.

[3] Galway to Shrewsbury, Aug. 16/26, in *ibid.* p. 270.

[4] Shrewsbury to William, June 4/14, July 12/22, in *ibid.* pp. 85, 92.

advantage of the prestige which this success gave him for the purpose. Before William left England in May, Shrewsbury had discussed the subject with him together with Somers and Sunderland (the latter of whom was now becoming more and more prominent as an ally of the Whigs), and he had agreed to a dissolution in the autumn. While the siege of Namur was in progress, the Duke had written to him at the instance of Sunderland and the Lord Keeper, reminding him of this arrangement, and requesting that he would return as soon as possible.

"Though it is not to be questioned but the country will generally elect persons well affected to the government", he said, "yet your majesty's presence, a little time before the election, and a few things it will be necessary for you to say to some, who, by the employments you gave them, have gained interests it would be very unreasonable they should employ against you and the public good, will make that matter much more secure and easy, than otherwise it would be, the consequence of which is too obvious to enlarge upon."[1]

He wrote again three weeks later representing that the general uncertainty as to whether a dissolution was intended or not was producing most undesirable results. "It has been very industriously spread about", he said, "that a new parliament is not intended; by which your majesty's friends are discouraged from making their interests in the several places they have pretensions to be chose in; whilst others, worse affected, as warm as ever solicit their elections."[2] Shrewsbury's fears were groundless, for the King replied assuring the Duke that he had never entertained any other thought than to call a new Parliament on his return and authorised him "boldly to announce his resolution", so as to remove the

[1] Shrewsbury to William, July 26/Aug. 5, in Coxe, pp. 96–7.
[2] Shrewsbury to William, Aug. 16/26, in *ibid.* pp. 101–2; and see R. Harley to Sir E. Harley, Sept. 3, in *Portland MSS.* vol. III, p. 566, and Burnet, vol. II, p. 160.

"unfavorable impressions" which had been created.[1] Shrewsbury, much relieved, at once assured him that "the nation was disposed to elect persons well affected to his interest and government". On the whole the result of the election was satisfactory to the Government, for a Whig majority was returned, although, according to Burnet, there were "many of the sourer sort of whigs, who were much alienated from the king".[2] The main business of the new Parliament, apart from the granting of supplies for carrying on the war, related to the reform of the currency and the mode of trial in cases of high treason. The former was a problem which had for some time past been demanding attention. It was one that affected every department of the Government, and it had already been the cause of much anxiety to Shrewsbury as the head of the Administration during the King's absence.

"One of the main difficulties we lie at present under", Shrewsbury had written to Russell in July, "is the scarcity of good money and the quantity of bad. This will, I believe, necessitate parliament to an expense for the regulating the coin for the future, and for the present raises guineas to above thirty shillings....This being the case, makes me put you in mind, that bullion, whether of gold or silver, would never be so welcome to us as in this conjuncture if you have any opportunity of bringing a quantity, when you return, or sending it by a safe conveyance, that may come upon other occasions."[3]

The disorganisation of the currency had by this time reached such a pitch that the matter would brook no further delay. After much consideration a Recoinage Bill designed to rectify the existing state of affairs was drafted and brought into the Commons by Montagu and passed. It was then sent up to the Lords and passed by them with amendments to some of which the Commons were not inclined to agree on the ground

[1] William to Shrewsbury, Sept. 6 (n.s.), in Coxe, p. 104.
[2] Burnet, vol. II, p. 160.
[3] Shrewsbury to Russell, July 2/12, 1695, in Coxe, p. 231.

that they were an encroachment on their privileges. A compromise was, however, effected, Charles Montagu bringing in a new Bill framed so as to meet some of the objections of the Peers, and in this form the measure was passed.[1]

This arrangement was one part of a bargain between the two Houses. The other part related to the regulation of trials in cases of high treason. The Treason Bill made its appearance for the fourth, and, as it proved, the last time, for the Commons now at length agreed to accept the Lords' amendments with reference to the composition of the Court of the Lord High Steward in return for the concession in the matter of the Recoinage Bill. Shrewsbury again supported the Bill strongly. His conduct in the matter, whilst it caused Ailesbury no little amusement, was witnessed by Portland with the utmost astonishment. The former, compromising as his conduct had been since the Revolution, was naturally in favour of the Bill and was at no loss to explain Shrewsbury's conduct to his own satisfaction, as he "knew that he had been dipped in 1693". Portland was not surprised that Ailesbury supported the Bill; but he told him that he stood "amazed for to see persons so near the King in his Councils be so warm against his interest and that of the Crown".[2] Apparently it did not occur to him that a Whig might continue to hold the principles of the Whig creed and to act upon them when he was in office as well as when he was in opposition.

The Bill received the royal assent on January 12. It provided that the new regulations should come into force at the new year—on March 25. Before that date arrived, however, events occurred which were calculated to make the more timid amongst its Whig supporters regret that the measure had been placed upon the statute book. For some time past the Jacobites had been engaged in concocting a scheme for overthrowing the Revolution settlement, and they

[1] Burnet, vol. II, p. 161; *H.L. MSS.* 1695–7, pp. 128–31.
[2] *Ailesbury's Memoirs*, vol. II, p. 371.

had now evolved one which comprised the assassination of the King and a simultaneous invasion from France. For some time past vague rumours of a plot had been in circulation and hints had been dropped, but the Government had not forgotten the case of Taaff, and were not at first inclined to pay overmuch attention to them. At length, however, they received information which convinced them that a serious conspiracy really was in existence. Prendergast, one of the Jacobites to whom the scheme had been communicated, disapproved of assassination as a means of achieving a restoration, and on the eve of the day fixed for the murder, went to Portland and warned him of the King's danger. His information led to the discovery of the whole plot, and Shrewsbury was soon busily engaged in the task of hunting out and securing the plotters.[1] By the King's orders he wrote to Russell immediately to collect his fleet and threaten the French coast, so as to guard against any attempt on the part

[1] Examinations touching Jacobite plots, March to June 1696, in *Buccleuch MSS.* vol. II, pt i, pp. 319–22; Luttrell, Mar. 5, April 18, 23, vol. IV, pp. 26, 46, 49. On May 18 a warrant was signed for Shrewsbury for £10,000 for secret service, a large part of the sum being no doubt intended for use in connection with the investigations into the plot (*Cal. Treasury Papers*, 1557–1696, p. 511). Ailesbury was one of those who were immediately arrested on the discovery of the plot. He had been recommended by some of his friends to make his escape while there was time, but took the advice of Sir Philip Meadows that he should go to the Secretary of State. "I repaired forthwith to the Duke of Shrewsbury [he says] in Duke Street, St. James's, as I take it. I told him that I came there to offer myself. He received me with the last coldness and reservedness, perhaps out of policy; he answered me with a grave countenance that he had heard nothing of me, and so I went to my old acquaintance, Sir William Trumbull...." The latter signed the warrant for his arrest, Shrewsbury, according to the Jacobite Earl's account, having declined to do so. Shrewsbury had certainly been a friend of Ailesbury in the past, and when the latter was in confinement did what he could to mitigate its rigours; but his friendship had cooled considerably during the last few months. *Ailesbury's Memoirs*, vol. I, pp. 287–8; vol. II, pp. 373, 374, 378–9, 383, 404–5.

of the Jacobites and their French allies to execute the second portion of their scheme.[1] The prompt and energetic action of the Ministry soon averted any danger of an invasion and the Whigs took advantage of the popular indignation aroused by the discovery of the plot to set on foot a voluntary Association for the defence of the King's person and Government. For this Association they soon succeeded in obtaining statutory sanction, for an Act was passed making adherence to it obligatory upon all members of Parliament and all holders of civil or military office.

"I have neglected writing so frequently as I would," Shrewsbury wrote to Galway at the beginning of April, "if the perpetual attendance I am forced to give to the enquiry into this horrid plot, besides that upon the Parliament, did not almost take up my whole time and thoughts. This villainous intention has not only miscarried, but I hope it has opened the eyes of many deluded though well affected persons in these kingdoms, for there appears everywhere upon this occasion a hearty affection and zeal for his Majesty's person and government, which I am confident may be improved to the securing of both."[2]

Towards the end of the month he was able to assure him that the state of affairs was most satisfactory. "The zeal that has been shewed throughout the whole kingdom upon the discovery of this horrid conspiracy is so general", he wrote, "and so hearty for the preservation of his majesty's person and government, that it is a great encouragement to the honest party; so no doubt it must leave the contrary effect upon the ill inclined."[3] The conspiracy had, in fact, been of

[1] Shrewsbury to Russell, Feb. 25, in Coxe, pp. 247–8.
[2] Shrewsbury to Galway, April 3, in *Buccleuch MSS.* vol. ii, pt i, p. 322.
[3] Shrewsbury to Galway, April 21/May 1, in Coxe, p. 286. See *A true and Impartial History of the Conspiracy against the Person and Government of King William III*, by Sir R. Blackmore (London 1723), compiled under the supervision of Shrewsbury and Somers. The former "thought fit to delay the publication of it so long that

the utmost utility to the Whigs, for it had enabled them to form the Association, and, having had it confirmed and made binding by Act of Parliament, to discriminate further between the adherents of William and the adherents of James, and to brand those who declined to sign it as traitors to the Revolution Settlement.

At the beginning of May, Shrewsbury attended the King as far as Margate on his way to the Continent. The Government in William's absence was again delegated to a body of Lords Justices, the board being constituted of the same members as in the previous year.[1] Shrewsbury, as the most important member, was therefore once more the virtual head of the Administration, and was more trusted than ever by the King, who regarded him as indispensable. But his distaste for the cares and responsibilities of office was as great as ever. To James Johnston, the Scottish Secretary, who was of the same mind with him on this subject,[2] he wrote:

I never yet was a month in business without wishing thirty times to be out of it. Even when things go the best, it has its disgusts; but to be in a post where much good is expected, and see how little one is able to do is hardly to be borne; and yet, whilst one is able to do any good, or prevent much mischief, when it is plain one's retirement would make room for knavery and treachery, I doubt one is obliged to consider the public so much more than one's self, that it is hardly honest to retreat. This doctrine is much easier, I confess, to preach than to practise.[3]

The Venetian envoys, Soranzo and Venier, who reached England in April and were "nobly entertained" by him on

the negotiations for a treaty of peace with France intervening, it was then judged improper to let it go abroad", and it was not actually published until 1723.

[1] L'Hermitage, May 5/15, 1696, in Add. MSS. 17,677, vol. Q.Q. f. 415; Luttrell, May 7, vol. IV, p. 55.

[2] Cf. Johnston to Shrewsbury, July 19, 1695, in *Buccleuch MSS.* vol. II, pt i, p. 202.

[3] Shrewsbury to Johnston, Aug. 1, 1695, in *Buccleuch MSS.* vol. II, pt i, p. 210.

their arrival,[1] soon discovered that Shrewsbury was more inclined to pleasure than to business and that he held the office of Secretary of State most unwillingly. This they attributed, not unnaturally, to the loss of one of his eyes and the weakness of the other. They observed that he relied to a great extent upon his subordinates, an opinion which is to some extent confirmed by Ailesbury's estimate of his character. But whatever they may have thought of his fitness for the office which he held, and whilst they found his manner somewhat reserved and cold, they were struck with his dignity and courtesy.[2]

In the summer of 1696, more than ever, Shrewsbury found that the chief weight of responsibility in the King's absence rested upon him. The first letter which the King wrote to Shrewsbury after leaving England contained an urgent request for immediate supplies and that request was only the first of a series which became more and more urgent as the summer advanced, and which became more and more difficult to satisfy. The financial problem had indeed been aggravated for the time as a result of the very means which had been adopted to cope with it. The Recoinage Act had provided that after May 4 clipped money should no longer be accepted in payment of taxes. May 4 was followed by a financial crisis, the most serious through which the country had ever passed, and throughout the summer the chief care of the Government was to find means for averting the complete paralysis with which it was threatened by the lack of funds.

"We discoursed this morning with several of the most eminent

[1] Luttrell, April 25, 1696, vol. IV, p. 50. The Republic had acknowledged William as King of England at the end of 1694, when the fleet had been ordered to winter at Cadiz for the first time.

[2] "Relazione d' Inghilterra di Lorenzo Soranzo e Girolamo Venier, ambasciatori straordinarii a Guglielmo III nell' anno 1696" (Barozzi e Berchet, *Le Relazioni degli Stati Europei...nel secolo decimosettimo*, Serie IV, Inghilterra (Venice, 1863), pp. 505–6.

CHARLES TALBOT, DUKE OF SHREWSBURY

From the portrait by Sir Peter Lely in the Charterhouse

goldsmiths, and with some of the bank ", Shrewsbury wrote to the King on May 15 in answer to his request for supplies, "and had the dismallest accounts from them of the state of credit in this town, and of the effects it would soon have upon all the traders in money: none of them being able to propose a remedy, except letting the parliament sit in June, and enacting the clipt money to go again, the very hopes of which locks up all the gold and good money, and would be to undo all that has been done."[1]

Scheme after scheme was suggested and considered, whilst the King wrote letter after letter to Shrewsbury begging him to do his utmost to procure money from any source, by any means, and at almost any cost. But each method that was suggested was in turn found impracticable and was abandoned, and at last, in desperation, William hastily sent over Portland to assist Shrewsbury in his task, in the hope that together they might be able to devise some means of averting a catastrophe.[2] For some time, however, even with Portland's assistance, no solution was discovered. Every possible scheme was considered in conjunction with him, with a view to raising sufficient funds to satisfy some portion at least of the King's demands, but without avail. One source from which it was hoped that some assistance might be forthcoming was the new National Land Bank, which Harley had succeeded in inducing Parliament to establish at the end of the last Session, and which the Tories hoped would prove a formidable rival of Montagu's foundation.[3] The Land Bank, however, proved to be a dismal failure, and at the end of July, after negotiating for two months, Shrewsbury had to report that all that had so far been subscribed was £40,000, and that at the last interview with the directors, the latter

[1] Shrewsbury to William, May 15/25, in Coxe, p. 116. Cf. C.S.P. (Dom.), 1696, p. 203.
[2] Bonet's report, July 28/Aug. 7, in Add. MSS. 30,000, vol. A. f. 192.
[3] Cf. Portland to the King, July 28, in C.S.P. (Dom.), 1696, pp. 297–9.

had appeared "so willing to quarrel" that he had serious
doubts as to their performing what had been so often and so
positively promised.[1] As a final resort they applied to the
Bank of England for an advance of £200,000 to enable them
to carry on the several services till the meeting of Parliament.
"If this should not succeed", Shrewsbury wrote to the King
on August 7, "God knows what can be done." Fortunately,
the Proprietors of the Bank of England, realising that their
interests were bound up with the continued existence of the
Revolution Government agreed to advance the money, and
Portland was able to return to Holland after their meeting,
with the welcome news that, for the time at least, the situation
was safe. He was loud in his praises of the manner in which
he had been assisted in his task by the chief Secretary of
State. "He cannot say enough in favour of your civilities
and frankness", the King wrote to Shrewsbury after Portland's return, "and has acquainted me with your zeal and
endeavors for my service, for which I am obliged to you, being
greatly concerned that you are not seconded as we could wish,
which would produce more activity in our business than we
find."[2]

Still the King's full requirements for the prosecution of
the war were not being met. Force of circumstances, indeed,
at length compelled him to listen to the suggestions which
Shrewsbury had been making for some time past as to the
advisability of entering into negotiations for peace. "It is
certain", the Duke had written towards the end of June,
"that a peace is much discoursed of; a good one everybody
would desire, and many are so weary as to be content with
a bad one."[3] The news that the Duke of Savoy had deserted
the alliance, and an intimation from the King that "he could
give no hopes of undertaking anything considerable this

---

[1] Shrewsbury to William, July 31/Aug. 10, in Coxe, p. 133.
[2] William to Shrewsbury, Aug. 24/Sept. 3, in *ibid.* p. 137.
[3] Shrewsbury to William, June 23/July 3, in *ibid.* p. 126.

campaign"[1] afforded him a good opportunity for pressing the point, and he at once availed himself of it.

"I imagine he [the Duke of Savoy] has not made this step", Shrewsbury wrote, "but at the same time, he has agreed with France to join his forces, for the quieting of Italy, if there shall be occasion, in which case, how successfully the war can be carried on in those parts, nobody can judge so well as yourself.

The posture of affairs in Flanders being such, that I perceive your majesty has no great hopes of doing anything considerable there, I cannot see there is a prospect in any other part of the world of more than acting defensively; so that, in all appearance, this campaign will end in a very discouraging manner for the allies. And how far such circumstances, improved by French money and artifice, may prevail upon other princes to follow the duke of Savoy's example, is to me a very melancholy reflection, and much more so when I consider our own condition at home, encompassed with so many difficulties, from the ruin of all credit, the scarcity of money, the deficiency in the supply for restoring the coin, and other anticipations, that I dare confidently affirm, no remedy so speedy and effectual can be found as will put the nation in a capacity, the next year, to furnish such sums as have been given in former sessions. A willing parliament may pass acts, but I fear the money can neither be raised nor borrowed. I think it my duty to lay this before your majesty, and because I think it of the last importance in this conjuncture, that you should be exactly informed of affairs at home, which might otherwise misguide you in your consideration of those abroad.... I cannot see that a town more or less is very material to your majesty's interest, provided the princes more nearly concerned are contented with it.

Above all things, it is necessary the allies should be satisfied with the conclusion of the war; that, continuing their just opinion of your majesty's unshaken constancy and virtue, they may be ready to engage with you upon any other occasion; but if they are pleased, though they should be a little more exposed, and not have such a barrier to protect them, as were to be wished, yet, by that weakness, they seem the more necessarily obliged to seek their safety, only from strength and firmness of the alliance. If the condition of affairs in Europe could give a reasonable prospect, that in a short time the power of France, by sea and land, would be

[1] William to Shrewsbury, July 23, 1696, in Coxe, p. 127.

reduced to what it was but forty years since, a great deal ought to be ventured to attain such a state of quiet and security; but, under the circumstances before mentioned, whether that can be hoped, and whether any less design be worth the hazarding all, is humbly submitted to your Majesty."[1]

The King, as Shrewsbury found from his reply, was by no means disposed as yet to admit the necessity of opening negotiations for peace.[2] Whilst the Duke was writing to him, he himself was writing to the Duke, informing him of Portland's mission to assist him in finding means for continuing the struggle.[3] He was greatly mortified by Shrewsbury's letter, and could not bring himself to believe that the position was really as bad as the Secretary represented it to be. In his unwillingness to acquiesce in the Duke's view, he wrote to Portland requesting him to ascertain whether Shrewsbury's letter represented his real opinion or not, as the latter was "very reserved".[4] But from his own experience Portland could not but confirm what Shrewsbury had already told the King, and, when the Land Bank had proved a failure, and the Government was driven to making a last appeal to the Bank of England, the Duke once more pressed his views upon the King in firmer language than he usually employed in writing to him, though still with the same deference to his opinion.

"I desire no more than that your majesty should know the truth," he wrote, "and then nobody can judge so well as yourself. Only...

[1] Shrewsbury to William, July 21/31, in Coxe, pp. 128–9.
[2] William to Shrewsbury, Aug. 6, in *ibid.* p. 132.
[3] Same to same, July 21/31, in *ibid.* p. 130.
[4] "J'ay receu par le dernier courier d'Angleterre une lettre du Duc de Shrewsbury par laquelle il s'explique nettement qu'il ne voit point d'aparance que l'affaire de la monnoye et le credit se retablissent et qu'ainsi le seul party que j'ay à prendre c'est de faire la paix, peut estre qu'il vous dira la mesme chose mais comme il est fort reservé j'ay voulu vous l'escrire à tout hasard affin que vous fussiez informe de ses sentimens." William to Portland, Aug. 6, in Add. MSS. 34,514. (Mackintosh Collection, vol. xxxiii, f. 87.)

I shall presume to offer, that if a peace must not be concluded, till so many humours and interests are contented, as compose this alliance, I shall despair that such a conjuncture will ever be found. All people agree, that the states are satisfied by these offers in the most material things they desire. The letters from Vienna say, the emperor and his minister are fond of the peace on the same conditions. These I take to be the most, if not the only important members of your majesty's alliance. It is said the circles of Suabia and Franconia, will be uneasy at the demolishing the new fortifications of Strasburgh; but is it reasonable your majesty should hazard your crown, and Europe its liberty, to please those gentlemen who judge upon expectations from hence, and perhaps from Holland, which possibly neither the one nor the other is able to make good?

It would not be advisable to lay open the state of this country, I own, equal to what I fear is the truth, but yet enough might be said to shew them, that a tolerable peace is very desirable; and although we are not in a condition to prosecute the war with that vigour it has hitherto been carried on, yet a trading and a free people, like England and Holland, will, in one year of quiet, recover more strength, than France can in five. The circumstances here are different from those of any country: suffering makes men dissatisfied; and how far that, by degrees, may be improved to the ruin of the whole, nobody can tell. But I hope I shall be pardoned for the ignorant freedom with which I write."[1]

Whether Shrewsbury's argument had any influence with him or not, William was gradually being driven, though sorely against his will, to see the impossibility of continuing the struggle in face of the difficulties with which he was confronted. It was some time, however, before he could bring himself to admit this to Shrewsbury, and the latter received his first intimation of the King's conversion from Villiers, who was then at The Hague as envoy from England. Villiers wrote to him privately that "want of money had made his Majesty resolve to accept of the peace".[2]

[1] Shrewsbury to William, Aug. 7/17, in Coxe, pp. 135-6.
[2] Villiers to Shrewsbury, Aug. 25 (n.s.), in *ibid.* pp. 320-1.

CHAPTER V

The Fenwick Case

Meanwhile events had been taking place, which, though unknown to Shrewsbury at the time, proved to be of the first importance to him in their results, and which, when they came to his knowledge, left little room in his mind for other things. In the months following the discovery of the Jacobite conspiracy of the previous winter, the Government had been actively engaged in tracking down and securing those who were known or suspected to have been privy to it. Amongst those of whom they had been in search was Sir John Fenwick. The latter was a descendant of an old Northumberland family, and had sat in the House of Commons in the time of Charles II, and also in the short-lived Parliament of James. He was well-known as an adherent of the exiled Stuarts and had already been arrested once, soon after the Revolution, and imprisoned in the Tower for fomenting disturbances in the North but had been released a few months later. In the commission sent by James from France at the time of the assassination plot he had been nominated as Major-General of the troops to be raised to aid the projected invasion, and he was probably cognisant of the other object of the conspiracy—the murder of William. When the plot failed, he remained in hiding until after the trials of the captured conspirators and he learned from the reports of the proceedings that there were only two of the prisoners who could give evidence sufficient to convict him. Fenwick, not unnaturally, attempted bribery as a means of getting rid of the evidence against him. The attempt proved in the end to be his undoing, for Porter, the conspirator whom he attempted to bribe, played a double game, and whilst affecting to listen, gave information to the Government, with the result that the agent employed to bribe him was arrested.[1] This was followed by a Bill of Indictment at the next Sessions at London, and Fenwick, realising that he was no longer safe in England, attempted to cross over to France. His disguise was detected, however, before he reached the coast, and he was arrested on June 13. He was brought before the Lords Justices and examined without their being able to get any information out of him. But they had ample evidence against him, as well as a virtual confession of his complicity in the plot in a letter which he had written to his wife, and which had been intercepted before it reached its destination. He was accordingly sent to the Tower to await his trial for high treason.[2] The Government were not without hope that when he was left in solitary confinement to consider his position, he might be induced to give valuable information about the conspiracy and the conspirators.

The prisoner found himself in a most painful dilemma. If he was to avoid the block it could only be done at the price of betraying his friends. For days Fenwick racked his brains to find some way of escape from the toils, whilst the Government waited and made preparations for his trial. At length after nearly a month in confinement he had an inspiration. He had learned something of the dealings of the agents of St Germain in the past with several peers who now held high office under the usurper, and it occurred to him that he might be able to serve the cause of James II as well as to save his own life by repeating the tales which he had heard. The

[1] Part of the bribe consisted of a sham letter of recommendation to James. On receiving the letter Porter took it at once to the Secretary's office where it was opened and proved to contain nothing but a blank sheet of paper. Bonet, May 12/22, 1696, in Add. MSS. 30,000, vol. A. f. 137.

[2] Burnet, vol. II, p. 182; W. Patten to R. Kenyon, June 20, in *Kenyon MSS.* p. 409.

Jacobites had relied upon Shrewsbury, Marlborough, Godolphin and Russell for assistance, but they had relied in vain. The destruction of those broken reeds was a most desirable object, and one which it was worth a good deal to attain.[1] Accordingly Fenwick sent a message to Devonshire offering to give valuable information to the Government. The prisoner's trial was hastily postponed and an authority obtained from the King for the Lord Steward to take his confession. This Devonshire proceeded to do, and he transmitted Fenwick's written statement to William at Loo without communicating its contents or character to any of his colleagues.

"I am not acquainted with the particulars my lord steward has sent your majesty from sir John Fenwick", Shrewsbury wrote to William shortly afterwards. "He is generally reputed a fearful man, and though now he may not offer to say all, yet beginning to treat is no contradiction to that character. I am confident he knows what, if he will discover, may be much more valuable than his life. If he were well managed, possibly he might lay open a scene that would facilitate the business the next winter, which, without some such miracle will be difficult enough."[2]

But Fenwick, as Shrewsbury was soon to discover to his cost, had no intention, if it could possibly be avoided, of performing the miracle of "laying open a scene that would facilitate the business the next winter", in the sense in which the Duke understood that phrase, and this became plain as soon as the document was opened and read. Of the information which the Government had hoped and expected to find in it, there was not a trace. Instead of the real adherents of the Jacobite cause the names which figured most prominently

[1] It was afterwards suspected that the scheme was partly of French origin. "I believe Sir John Fenwick's plot, like all the rest we have had, is part French and part English", Shrewsbury wrote to Villiers a few weeks later; "let it begin where it will, there is a good share of impudence, as well as villainy in the contrivance", Nov. 21/Dec. 1, 1696, in Coxe, p. 329.

[2] Shrewsbury to William, July 28/Aug. 7, in *ibid.* pp. 131–2.

in the "information" were those of four of the men who had rendered the most conspicuous services to William III— Russell and Marlborough, Godolphin and Shrewsbury. The two former were accused of endeavouring to make their peace with St Germain by undertaking to seduce the fleet and the army from their allegiance, and Marlborough was stated to have done "a considerable piece of service", which was probably a veiled allusion to the information sent by him to France with regard to the Brest expedition of 1694. Godolphin was charged with having corresponded with James after the latter's return to France from Ireland, and with having negotiated with James's principal adviser, the Earl of Middleton, before he left England. As for Shrewsbury, Fenwick asserted that he had also treated with Middleton during the time between his resignation in 1690 and Middleton's departure, and that he had arranged to keep up a correspondence with him afterwards. He also told how James had reassured his followers at St Germain when Shrewsbury resumed office in 1694, by telling them "not to be dissatisfied, for it was with his consent he came in; that he was more capable of doing him service and took off all suspicion of the correspondence he held".[1]

---

[1] C.S.P. (Dom.), 1696, pp. 492–5; *Buccleuch MSS.* vol. II, pt i, pp. 393–6. The reference to Shrewsbury's resumption of office in 1694 is probably correct, as it agrees with the story told in the *Life of James II*. As regards the correspondence with Middleton, Ailesbury afterwards asserted that Shrewsbury and the rest were engaged in it with the King's full knowledge and consent as a means of deceiving Middleton and discovering the secrets of the Jacobite Court, but this assertion is not corroborated by other evidence, and Shrewsbury does not refer to it in his letters to the King at the time (*Ailesbury's Memoirs*, vol. II, pp. 391–2). Cf. Godfrey Davies, "Macpherson and the Nairne Papers", *E.H.R.* vol. XXXV, p. 373, where it is argued that Ailesbury was in any case not in a position to know and was writing after thirty years of exile. Had Shrewsbury obtained permission to correspond with St Germain from William himself, he would not have been at such pains to exculpate himself.

But in spite of the unsatisfactory character of the information, the paper was not without a certain cunning in its composition, and had William been other than he was, it might have entailed serious consequences for those who were named in it. There was an air of verisimilitude about the story, imparted by the substratum of truth which undoubtedly underlay some of the assertions. But the King was clear-sighted enough to perceive at once with what object it had been written. Whatever the substance underlying Fenwick's charges might be, even in the case of Marlborough, he decided to ignore them, and to judge the accused by the actual services which they had rendered to him, rather than by the promises of support and assistance which they were alleged to have given to his rival. Having made up his mind on this point, he at once sent Fenwick's paper to Shrewsbury, the chief of those who were accused in it.

"You may judge of my astonishment at his effrontery, in accusing you," he wrote. "You are, I trust, too fully convinced of the entire confidence which I place in you, to imagine that such an accusation has made any impression on me, or that if it had, I should have sent you this paper. You will observe *the sincerity of this honest man*, who only accuses those in my service, and not one of his own party."

Portland echoed the King's words, saying that Shrewsbury was "above suspicion", and Devonshire was ordered to inform Fenwick that unless he proved what he had written, and moreover confessed all he knew, without reserve, the King would not permit his trial to be deferred, which he perceived was his only aim.[1]

Some rumours as to the nature of Fenwick's paper appear to have already reached Shrewsbury; but he was unprepared for what he found it actually to contain, and he protested with an indignation which does not altogether ring true. "Sir

[1] William to Shrewsbury, Sept. 10, Portland to same, same date, in Coxe, pp. 145, 146. Cf. *C.S.P. (Dom.)*, 1696, pp. 389–91.

Jo[hn] Fen[wick's] story is as wonderful to me as if he had accused me of coining", he wrote to Portland.[1]

"I want words to express my surprise at the impudent and unaccountable accusation of sir John Fenwick", he wrote in answer to William's letter. "I will, with all the sincerity imaginable, give your majesty an account of the only thing I can recollect, that should give the least pretence to such an invention; and I am confident you will judge there are few men in the kingdom that have not so far transgressed the law. After your majesty was pleased to allow me to lay down my employment, it was more than a year before I once saw my lord Middleton; then he came, and staid in town awhile, and returned to the country; but a little before the La Hogue business, he came up again, and upon that alarm, being put in the Tower, when people were permitted to see him, I visited him as often as I thought decent, for the nearness of our alliance.[2] Upon his enlargement, one night at supper, when he was pretty well in drink, he told me he intended to go beyond seas, and asked if I would command him no service. I then told him, by the course he was taking, it would never be in his power to do himself or his friends service; and if the time should come that he expected, I looked upon myself as an offender not to be forgiven, and therefore he should never find me asking it. In the condition he was then, he seemed shocked at my answer; and it being some months after before he went, he never mentioned his own going, or any thing else, to me, but left a message with my aunt, that he thought it better to say nothing to me, but that I might depend upon his good offices upon any occasion, and in the same manner he relied upon mine here; and had left me trustee for the small concerns he had in England. I only bowed, and told her I should always be ready to serve her, or him, or their children. Your majesty now knows the extent of my crime, and if I do not flatter myself, it is no more than a king may forgive. I am sure when I consider with what reason, justice, and generosity your majesty has weighed this man's information, I have little cause to apprehend your ill opinion upon his malice. I wish it were as easy to answer for the reasonableness of the generosity of the world. When such a base invention shall be made public,

[1] Shrewsbury to Portland, Sept. 8, in *Buccleuch MSS.* vol. II, pt i, p. 400.
[2] Middleton's wife was Shrewsbury's aunt on his mother's side.

they may perhaps make me incapable of serving you; but if till now I had had neither interest nor inclination, the noble and frank manner with which your majesty has used me upon this occasion, shall ever be owned with all the gratitude in my power."[1]

Shrewsbury's own statements, uncorroborated by extrinsic independent testimony, cannot of course be accepted as satisfactory evidence as to the character of his relations with the Jacobite faction. A vindication of his conduct with regard to Middleton in recent months does not exonerate him from suspicion of having been engaged in treasonable correspondence prior to that. Direct evidence against him is, however, almost entirely lacking for the simple reason that while Shrewsbury's demeanour towards the adherents of James appears to have been uniformly courteous, it seems to have been very non-committal. He thereby encouraged hopes which the plotters in their enthusiasm were too eager to cherish, but which probably he had no intention whatever of fulfilling. On the other hand, there is no real evidence to disprove his statements. Nor is there any good ground for doubting that he spoke the truth when he said he had told Middleton that he "looked upon himself as an offender not to be forgiven". Whatever private opinion he may have had on the subject, William accepted the Duke's explanation without question, and in terms of great generosity.

"In sending you sir John Fenwick's paper, I assured you", he wrote, "that I was persuaded his accusation was false, of which I am now fully convinced, by your answer, and perfectly satisfied with the ingenious confession of what passed between you and lord Middleton, which can by no means be imputed to you as a crime. And indeed you may be assured, that this business, so far from making on me any unfavourable impression, will, on the contrary, if possible, in future, strengthen my confidence in you, and my friendship can admit of no increase."[2]

[1] Shrewsbury to William, Sept. 8/18, in Coxe, pp. 147-8.
[2] William to Shrewsbury, Sept. 25, in Coxe, p. 151.

By the King's order Shrewsbury at once informed his colleagues of the contents of Fenwick's paper. They began immediately to make arrangements for the prisoner's trial, whilst those of them who were named with Shrewsbury in the document vented their wrath upon the Lord Steward for not informing them of its contents before sending it to Holland. Lady Mary Fenwick did her utmost to induce them to delay the trial by holding out hopes that her husband would give further information, whilst Sir John, for his part, through the Duke of Norfolk, declared himself "willing to give all proofs of his sincerity". He succeeded in postponing his arraignment, but only for a few days. It took place on September 17, much to the satisfaction of Portland, who sincerely hoped that the trial would be over before the King returned to England, and complained strongly to Shrewsbury of the way in which the matter had been managed.[1] His hopes, however, were soon dashed. Just before the date fixed for his trial, in answer to an intimation from the Lords Justices that it could be deferred no longer unless he chose to "recollect himself by tomorrow at nine in the morning",[2] Fenwick gave Vernon, who was sent to interview him, some more written information, which secured him a further indefinite delay. This document was of a very different stamp from the one which had preceded it. No attempt whatever was made to substantiate the previous charges against Shrewsbury and his friends—a tacit admission on the part of the prisoner that his scheme of ruining them with William by arousing suspicions of their fidelity had miscarried, and that he could not produce enough evidence against them to redeem his failure. Instead of this, almost the whole of the second paper was taken up with the doings of Ailesbury, and

[1] Shrewsbury to Portland, Sept. 11/21, 15/25, 18/28, Portland to Shrewsbury, Sept. 27 (n.s.), Sept. 24/Oct. 4, in Coxe, pp. 149–53.
[2] *Buccleuch MSS.* vol. II, pt ii, pp. 409–10; Vernon to Shrewsbury, Sept. 24, in *Vernon Corr.* vol. I, p. 1.

the men who had figured so prominently in the former document were not even mentioned. It was obvious that Fenwick had not so far revealed by any means all that he knew, but the character of the later paper was an indication that his resolution was not altogether proof against the fate which awaited him if he remained obdurate, and that under further pressure some valuable information might even yet be extorted from him.[1]

Whilst Fenwick was thus beginning to shew signs of wavering, Shrewsbury left London for Eyford, as he had done the previous autumn for a short rest before the return of the King and the opening of the session. Vernon, his Under-Secretary, was left in charge of the office, and ordered to keep Portland informed of the progress of the case against Fenwick. It was not long, however, before he heard from Portland that the King was on the point of starting for England,[2] and this intimation was soon followed by the news that William had reached Kensington late in the evening of October 6. On the next day the Palace was crowded by a throng of courtiers who came to kiss the King's hand. William looked long and anxiously amongst them for a sight of his principal Secretary of State, who had been summoned to return to London as soon as his arrival had been notified. But he looked in vain; Shrewsbury was nowhere to be seen. He inquired of Vernon when the Duke would arrive, and whether he had given him notice of his arrival, but the Under-Secretary could give no explanation of his principal's absence. At length a messenger arrived from Eyford with the news that Shrewsbury was detained there owing to a fall from his horse whilst hunting. At first it was hoped that this

[1] See the information dated Sept. 23 in *Buccleuch MSS.* vol. II, pt ii, pp. 410–13; L'Hermitage, Sept. 25/Oct. 5, in Add. MSS. 17,677, vol. Q.Q. f. 549.
[2] Portland to Shrewsbury, Oct. 2/12, in *Buccleuch MSS.* vol. II, pt ii, p. 414.

would not prevent his immediate return to Whitehall, and the meeting of the Council was postponed pending his arrival.[1] Both the King and Portland, in writing to condole with him on the accident, insisted upon the necessity of his presence in London at the earliest possible moment,[2] and their letters were almost immediately followed by others from Somers and Sunderland urging his return as soon as ever he was able to travel. "I beg of your grace", Somers wrote, "that you would come to town as soon as your health will possibly allow. Give me leave to say, I hope you will not unnecessarily delay one hour. I am confident, were you here, it would be easy to give the right turn to this business, which I fear will not otherwise be possible."[3]

Time went on, however, and still the Duke did not return to town, and at length people began to realise that his accident had been more serious than they had been led to understand. In his fall he had injured his lungs, and rest and quiet were essential, as the immediate result of any exertion was to cause an attack of blood-spitting.

"I am so sensible that this is a most improper time for me to be absent", he wrote to the King, "both in regard to my duty to your majesty and my own private concern, that nothing less than necessity could have obliged me to it; but the weakness and soreness of my breast, as well as my spitting of blood, though not violent, whilst I remain quiet, do so immediately increase, upon the least sudden motion that I have made unawares in my own chamber, and these are followed by such a sickness and faintness

[1] Vernon to Shrewsbury, Oct. 8, in *Vernon Corr.* vol. I, pp. 14–15; L'Hermitage, Oct. 13/23, in Add. MSS. 17,677, vol. Q.Q. ff. 563–4.

[2] Portland to Shrewsbury, Oct. 9, in *Buccleuch MSS.* vol. II, pt ii, p. 414. "I am much concerned to hear that you have been hurt by a fall from your horse in hunting (William wrote the same day); I hope you will soon be able to bear the motion of a carriage, and that I shall have the pleasure of seeing you here, where your presence is much wanted. I am very impatient to embrace you and to assure you of the continuance of my esteem" (Coxe, p. 154).

[3] Somers to same, Oct. 15/25, in *ibid.* p. 410.

upon my spirits, that I am next to certain I cannot yet be able to endure the coach; but I will try as soon as possible, for I am sure there is nothing in the world I more earnestly desire, than to kiss your majesty's hands, and to give you thanks, Sir, for the generosity and confidence you have used towards me.

I understand there are some people fully determined to put all in heat and confusion this sessions, and considering the materials they will have, and the usual disposition of a parliament, they can hardly miss their aim; but when such a thing is once begun, and a maxim settled, that hear-say is ground sufficient to defame any one, how far it may go, or where it may end they nor nobody but God knows. I am told the animosity of some persons to me is the great occasion of this. I presume, Sir, you may know who they are, and how little I have deserved it from them. It falls out by my misfortune, and not by my fault, that possibly they have it in their power to cast a reflection on me, that I should be extremely uneasy under, not because I shall be obliged to part with a considerable employment; your majesty may be much better served, and you are too well acquainted with my thoughts and inclinations on this subject, to believe that the cause; but that having all my life acted like an honest man, it will be a severe mortification to be suspected for the contrary, though by a few and for a little time. I am certain, however, at the end truth will appear, and I hope I shall shew your majesty, and the world, that you were not mistaken in my fidelity, nor I ungrateful for your good opinion, and the many favours I have received."[1]

So anxious were the King and the Whig leaders to secure Shrewsbury's presence at Whitehall that they did not even yet abandon their efforts as useless. Sir Thomas Millington, one of the most eminent physicians of the time, was called into consultation and, on his advice, a horse-litter was despatched to Eyford in the hope that the Duke would be

[1] Shrewsbury to William, Oct. 11/21, in Coxe, pp. 154–5; C.S.P. (Dom.), 1696, p. 413. On the same day he wrote to Portland, "You may be sure my own circumstances, as well as my duty to his majesty, will oblige me to make all possible haste to London; but at present any motion, more violent than gently walking in my chamber, immediately occasions my more than ordinary spitting of blood, and brings such a faintness on my spirits that I am ready to swoon away" (Coxe, p. 156).

able to travel in it if he could not endure the motion of a coach.[1] When the litter arrived, in his anxiety to return to London Shrewsbury endeavoured to make the journey by that means, against the advice of his physician, but found that it was impracticable as he could endure the litter no better than a coach, and he was obliged to abandon the attempt. Being convinced by this result that he must remain at Eyford for a considerable time if he was to entertain any hope of ultimate recovery, he determined to resign the seals, and wrote at once to William for permission to do so, in language which certainly suggested a troubled conscience as well as a suffering body.

" I have endeavoured to come to London to receive your majesty's commands and directions", he said, "but by what happened yesterday, I find it is impossible for me, and in all appearance will be so for a long time. I am very sensible your majesty's affairs must necessarily receive great prejudice, by the absence of one in my post; and since it is very doubtful whether I shall ever so well recover this accident, as to be capable of serving in the station I have the honour to be in at present, and most certain it cannot be of a long time, I humbly and earnestly entreat your majesty will allow me to return the seals into your hands. Besides my incapacity upon this illness, I am sure, Sir, you must think it impossible for any man to serve in so nice an employment as your secretary, that has the misfortune to be under the suspicion, though but of a few. I do not doubt but in my private capacity, I shall have occasions to demonstrate my fidelity and loyalty to your majesty. In the mean time I repeat my request, and beg leave to put you in mind of your promise at my receiving the seals, that I should be at liberty to return them, without your majesty's displeasure, whenever I found the place uneasy."[2]

But the King declined altogether to allow Shrewsbury to

<hr>

[1] Vernon to Shrewsbury, Oct. 13, 15, 20, in *Vernon Corr.* vol. 1, pp. 18–25.
[2] Shrewsbury to William, Oct. 18/28, in Coxe, pp. 156–7; *C.S.P. (Dom.)*, 1696, p. 418; L'Hermitage, Oct. 20/30, in Add. MSS. 17,677, vol. Q.Q. f. 571.

compromise himself in the eyes of the public, as he must inevitably do if he insisted on resigning then.

"You could not have chosen a more improper time to execute such a design", William wrote, "as well on your own account as on mine. I have, indeed, so great a regard for you, that were it in my power, I would never permit you to do what will draw on you so much blame. I am fully sensible that your resignation would be injurious to my service, but I protest to you that on this occasion, I consider your interest more than my own; I hope, therefore, that on due consideration, you will think no more of it. Doubtless it is much to be wished that you could have been here before the opening of parliament, but I do not see that my service will suffer much by your temporary absence, which will enable you to attend to the re-establishment of your health. May God speedily restore it, that I may have the satisfaction of embracing, and assuring you in person of my sincere friendship, which is greater than you can imagine."[1]

This remonstrance was accompanied by others from Portland, Somers and Sunderland, and Vernon was despatched to Eyford to press their views upon the Duke.[2] But Shrewsbury still insisted that before long it would become necessary for him to retire, and he considered that "it would look very odd to keep the seals, whilst his health prevented his executing the office, and then quit them when perhaps he might grow better". Nevertheless he "entirely submitted himself to be disposed of as his Majesty should think best", and agreed to retain the seals if the King did not judge his reasons for wishing to resign them a sufficient ground for allowing him to do so.[3]

Having thus consented to retain office under conditions which rendered it less endurable than ever, Shrewsbury had

[1] William to Shrewsbury, Oct. 20 (o.s.), in Coxe, pp. 157–8.
[2] Portland to Shrewsbury, Oct. 20/30, Somers and Sunderland to same, Oct. 19/29, in Coxe, pp. 158–9, 411–13; Bonet, Oct. 16/26, in Add. MSS. 30,000, vol. A. ff. 227, 231.
[3] Shrewsbury to William, Oct. 22/Nov. 1, in Coxe, p. 159; C.S.P. (Dom.), 1696, p. 421.

perforce to resign himself to remain in seclusion at Eyford and watch events from there, without being able to take any active part in vindicating himself from the charges brought against him by Fenwick. His anxieties were not lessened when the Houses reassembled on October 20. "You may believe", he wrote four days later, "I am very uneasy to be here at a time that 'tis so much my duty to wait upon the King, and attend the Parliament, but how long the same mortification will continue I am not yet able to judge."[1] It was more than a fortnight before the Fenwick question was brought forward, the Commons being occupied at first with the pressing business of supply. The Whig leaders, meanwhile, were holding frequent meetings to decide what was the best course to adopt, and, in addition, were doing their best to pacify the restless Monmouth. The latter was indefatigable in the search for opportunities to create a disturbance, and, in the very legitimate belief that the Fenwick case afforded a most admirable opening for doing this, had for some time past "been very busy in blowing these coals", though it was hoped that he might be kept quiet by the fear that he had himself been named by the prisoner, as was generally reported, to his great indignation.[2] After much discussion it was decided that the most satisfactory plan would be to request the King to examine Fenwick himself, and then for Russell to ask permission to bring the matter

[1] Shrewsbury to Hill, Oct. 24, in *Buccleuch MSS.* vol. II, pt ii, p. 418.
[2] Shrewsbury had been informed by Somers, just at the time when he retired to Eyford, that Monmouth was engaged in a scheme for making trouble, but it was hoped that he had been persuaded not to take any steps until he had seen the Duke. Of the latter, according to Vernon, he spoke with esteem but regarded him as "mené par le nez by the Lord he threw out all his suspicions upon"—an allusion probably to Sunderland. Somers to Shrewsbury, Sept. 24/ Oct. 4, Oct. 19/29, Sunderland to same, Oct. 15/25, in Coxe, pp. 408, 411–13; Vernon to same, Oct. 1, in *Vernon Corr.* vol. I, p. 13.

before the Commons. It was hoped that if Fenwick was sent for suddenly by the King and questioned by him, his courage would give way, and that he would then "tell things of his own knowledge", instead of repeating mere reports which were not, and were not intended to be, of any service to the Government.[1] Shrewsbury had recommended this arrangement some weeks before, but William had not then been inclined to act upon the suggestion.[2] At the instigation of Sunderland he was now committing himself more and more to the side of the Whigs, and after some manœuvring on the part of the Earl, Godolphin, who as the only Tory still remaining in the Ministry was obnoxious to them, was induced to offer his resignation. To his surprise and annoyance it was immediately accepted by the King, and the Whigs were left in undisputed possession in the Cabinet Council.[3]

The examination of Fenwick by the King took place on November 2. It failed entirely to answer the expectations of the Whigs. Since his arrest, Fenwick's wife and friends had been doing their best to corrupt the witnesses against him, and, just before his interview with William, he had heard that they had succeeded in bribing "Scum" Goodman to leave England.[4] Without the evidence of this witness a conviction could not (in accordance with the new Trial of Treasons Act passed in the previous January) be secured in a court of law, and, secure in this knowledge, Fenwick refused to give any information whatever.[5] The flight of

[1] Somers to Shrewsbury, Oct. 31/Nov. 10, in Coxe, p. 419.
[2] Shrewsbury to Portland, Oct. 11/21, in Coxe, p. 156.
[3] Somers to Shrewsbury, Oct. 31/Nov. 10, in Coxe, p. 420.
[4] See same to same, Nov. 3/13, in *ibid.* pp. 420–2.
[5] There was a possible second witness to corroborate Porter in Cooke, one of the conspirators who had been condemned but reprieved from time to time in the hope of obtaining evidence from him, but he was "so shatter-brained a fellow" that it was considered doubtful whether he could be relied upon even if he could be induced to give evidence. See Vernon to Shrewsbury, Nov. 3, in *Vernon Corr.* vol. I, p. 41.

Goodman rendered the Government's task of bringing Fenwick and his associates to book much more difficult, but it was essential that some steps should be taken, and taken soon. It was already currently reported that the prisoner's confession concerned persons of every rank, and included some who would never have been suspected,[1] and for some time past there had been "a good deal of impatience in a great many honest gentlemen of the House to be getting at this matter of the plot". The more zealous among the Whigs were not without hopes of finding a weapon with which to attack Godolphin. This would not have displeased some of their leaders, especially Wharton, but it was generally admitted that it was impossible to draw distinctions between different parts of Fenwick's paper, much as many would have liked to do so.[2] After much anxious consideration it was decided that the King should be asked to allow the matter to be brought before the Commons, and that Fenwick and his paper should be formally condemned by a vote of the members.[3]

The question was accordingly considered by the Council, and, the King's permission having been obtained, Fenwick's confession was presented to the House on November 6. The task of introducing the subject was entrusted to Russell. He had only just learned the contents of the paper at the Council meeting, and, as was to be expected, was furious both with its author and with Devonshire.[4] Vernon, in reporting the result of the debate which followed the presentation of the paper, informed Shrewsbury that Russell "spoke handsomely and modestly for himself and his Grace and put himself upon

[1] F. L. Bonet, Nov. 3/13, in Add. MSS. 30,000, vol. A. f. 242.
[2] Wharton to Shrewsbury, Oct. 27/Nov. 6, in Coxe, pp. 415–16.
[3] See Somers to same, Oct. 31/Nov. 10, Nov. 3/13, in *ibid.* pp. 419–21.
[4] "Lord steward, out of countenance, made like himself a foolish speech, asking your's and my pardon, he had not acquainted us with the matter" (Russell to Shrewsbury, Nov. 5, in *ibid.* pp. 423–4).

the justice of the House, to stand or fall by their opinions".[1]
The debate went on the whole day, and from the point of
view of the Whig leaders its results were all that could be
desired. Their followers were not only perfectly willing but
eager to absolve Shrewsbury and Russell, the former of
whom, at least, commanded general respect, and to wipe
away the stain which it was felt that Fenwick's charges had
left upon their party. The intimation that these two were
accused caused general surprise, for they had never been
suspected, and were regarded as being the most irreconcilable
of James's enemies, and there was no disposition for a moment
to give any credit to the charges brought against them. Nor
was any obstacle raised by the Whigs to the acquittal of
Marlborough who had long been out of office. Godolphin,
however, had only just resigned, and it was with some difficulty
that his friends succeeded in securing his absolution also.
Fenwick by his conduct once more assisted those whom he
had accused, for when he was brought from Newgate by
order of the House and put to the bar and recommended to
make a full confession, no information could be elicited from
him, but only excuses and requests for further time. After
his removal, the House resolved that his paper was false and
scandalous and a contrivance to undermine the Government
and to create jealousies between the King and his subjects,
in order to stifle the real conspiracy. By that time, "the
House was grown considerably thinner", many of the Tories
having left, and the Whigs seized the opportunity to follow
up their advantage. Another resolution was at once proposed,
and carried by 179 to 61 votes, that a Bill should be brought in
to attaint the prisoner.[2]

[1] Vernon to Shrewsbury, Nov. 6, in *Vernon Corr.* vol. I, p. 47.
[2] Vernon to Shrewsbury, Nov. 6, in *Vernon Corr.* vol. I, pp. 45–51;
Luttrell, Nov. 7, vol. IV, p. 136; Boyer, *Histoire de Guillaume III*
(Amsterdam 1703), vol. II, pp. 254–5; L'Hermitage, Nov. 6/16, in
Add. MSS. 17,677, vol. Q.Q. ff. 590–1.

Shrewsbury, meanwhile, had been waiting at Eyford in his "sick solitary chamber" (as he described it in writing to Portland)[1] to hear what effect Fenwick's paper had produced upon the Commons. Vernon wrote the same night to send "the joyful account of that day's success that had been carried as well according to his expectations as wishes"; and his letter was soon followed by others congratulating the Duke upon his vindication from the charges made against him by Fenwick. But their congratulations were accompanied by renewed exhortations that Shrewsbury should allow nothing to prevent him from returning to London at the earliest possible moment.[2] Shrewsbury was much relieved at the result of the proceedings, and expressed his gratitude to the friends who had helped to secure the condemnation of Fenwick's paper. He acquiesced in the decision to proceed against Sir John by Bill of Attainder, as it appeared to be the only means of bringing him to justice, but it was not without hesitation that he did so, as he was well aware that that method was likely to arouse considerable opposition, especially amongst the Peers. But urgent as he realised the need of his presence at Whitehall to be, he was as yet quite unable to undertake the journey. "I will not fail to make all the haste I can to town", he wrote to Sunderland, "but I have small hopes it will be very soon; for on Sunday I tried to take the air in my coach, and found I could not endure it yet."[3] "My Lord Duke", said Vernon, "is still confined to his country habitation, and is spitting blood while Sir John Fenwick is spitting venom. I don't care how soon the last is choked; I wish the other may recover as soon from his

[1] Shrewsbury to Portland, Oct. 24/Nov. 3, in Coxe, p. 161.
[2] Vernon to Shrewsbury, Nov. 6, in *Vernon Corr.* vol. I, pp. 45–51 (part of the letter is printed by Coxe also, see pp. 424–7); Somers and Sunderland to same, Nov. 7/17, Wharton to same, Nov. 10/20, in Coxe, pp. 427–9.
[3] Shrewsbury to Sunderland, Nov. 10/20, in Coxe, pp. 429–30.

distemper as he will from the rage and malice of Sir John and his party."[1]

The promoters of the Bill had therefore to resign themselves to proceed with it without Shrewsbury's assistance. In the Commons, as they anticipated, they met with strong opposition which increased as the Bill progressed; but they succeeded in carrying the motion that it should pass by a majority of thirty-three votes. They were well aware, however, that their chief difficulties had still to be surmounted in the Upper House, and it was with some misgivings that the supporters of the Bill looked forward to the contest. Consequently, whilst it was before the Commons, Shrewsbury's friends continued to write letter after letter urging him to return at once for his own sake, no matter what the cost might be to him.[2] These exhortations were, indeed, quite superfluous, for Shrewsbury himself was no less anxious to return to London at once than his friends were to see him there, and it was only his complete inability to bear the journey that prevented him from undertaking it. He made more than one attempt to do so, but always with the same result. "I have made some trials to get to London", he wrote to Galway at the beginning of December, "but instead of being able to perform the journey, I have fallen into relapses that have deferred it, and at this time have no near prospect of being in a condition to remove."[3]

The proceedings on the Bill in the Lords opened on December 1. Besides the opposition of the avowed antagonists of the Bill, the supporters of the measure had to deal with the

[1] Vernon to Prior, Nov. 13/23, in *Bath MSS.* (H.M.C.), vol. III (*Prior Papers*), p. 93.
[2] Wharton to Shrewsbury, Nov. 10/20. Somers to same, Nov. 19/29, in *ibid.* pp. 429, 431–2; L'Hermitage, Nov. 10/20, in Add. MSS. 17,677, vol. Q.Q. f. 596; Bonet, Nov. 27/Dec. 7, in *ibid.* 30,000, vol. A. f. 254; Portland to Shrewsbury, Nov. 18/28, in *Buccleuch MSS.* vol. II, pt ii, p. 424.
[3] Shrewsbury to Galway, Dec. 3, in *Buccleuch MSS.* vol. II, pt ii, pp. 427–8.

incessant intrigues of the restless Monmouth. Somers and others had done their best to prevent him from making mischief, but their efforts had proved of no avail.[1] Through the agency of the Duchess of Norfolk, he had transmitted to the prisoner by Lady Mary Fenwick a paper advising him to earn the King's pardon and favour by substantiating the charges against Shrewsbury and the other ministers contained in the first paper. Fenwick, however, ignored the advice, not being, in fact, in a position to comply with it, and Monmouth, on discovering this, promptly turned against him, and did his best to aid in securing the passing of the Bill.[2] With the removal of this factious source of opposition, there still remained the repugnance of a considerable body of Peers, who, whilst condemning Fenwick, strongly disapproved of the method of proceeding against him adopted by the Government. The majorities for the Bill steadily dwindled and the third reading was only carried by the narrow margin of seven votes. "One would wonder it passed at all when one considers who they were that voted against it", Vernon wrote to Shrewsbury.[3] The Bill having been passed by the

---

[1] Somers to Shrewsbury, Nov. 19/29, in Coxe, pp. 432–3.

[2] A copy of the advice is printed in *Buccleuch MSS.* vol. II, pt ii, pp. 426–7. See Luttrell, Jan. 12/22, vol. IV, p. 167; L'Hermitage, same date, in Add. MSS. 17,677, vol. R.R. ff. 178–9; *H.L. MSS.* 1695–7, pp. 294, 301; Wharton to Shrewsbury, Dec. 24/Jan. 3, Somers to same, same date, in Coxe, pp. 443–51. Ailesbury has a story that, hearing there was a design to impeach him, he sent word that in that event Shrewsbury would find himself impeached too, and that this threat sufficed to prevent his own impeachment (see *Ailesbury Memoirs*, vol. II, pp. 392–3, 413, 437).

[3] Bonet, Dec. 1/11, in Add. MSS. 30,000, vol. A. f. 256; L'Hermitage, Dec. 4/14, in *ibid.* 17,677, vol. Q.Q. f. 626; Wharton to Shrewsbury, Dec. 1/11, Dec. 24/Jan. 3, Somers to same, Dec. 10/20, in Coxe, pp. 437–40, 443–4; Marlborough to same (Dec. 2), in *Buccleuch MSS.* vol. II, pt ii, p. 427; *Vernon Corr.* vol. I, pp. 90–136; Burnet, vol. II, pp. 183–93; *H.L. MSS.* (n.s.), vol. II, pp. 274–302; *L.J.* Dec. 23, vol. XVI, p. 48. For proceedings on the Bill see Howell's *State Trials*, vol. XIII, pp. 538–758.

Lords, Fenwick's fate was sealed. In spite of further attempts on his behalf, the Bill received the royal assent, and Fenwick was executed on Tower Hill on January 28.

He had the satisfaction before he died of knowing that retribution had overtaken the man who had at first feigned to help and had then deserted him. His wife, furious at the abandonment by Monmouth of her husband's cause, determined to be revenged for the part he had played, and revealed his discreditable intrigues to the Peers. Monmouth was sent to the Tower, and on the presentation of an address from the Lords, was turned out of his place in the bed-chamber, and his name was removed from the list of Privy Councillors. He only obtained his release after ten weeks' confinement on making an abject submission and apology to the House.

With the passing of the Bill of Attainder and the disgrace of Monmouth, Shrewsbury might well have believed that his troubles arising out of the plot were ended. But no sooner had the intriguing Earl been removed from the scene than the Peers had to deal with one of his tools. Amongst the crowd of disreputable characters that were always to be found in the neighbourhood of Westminster Hall, Monmouth had fallen in with a discarded informer named Matthew Smith,[1] a nephew of one of the conspirators recently arrested and executed for complicity in the Assassination Plot. Smith had had some small knowledge of the plot and had written vaguely to Shrewsbury on the subject in the hope of obtaining a handsome reward. He had received small sums at different times from Shrewsbury, and also from Portland, but as these subsidies had never produced anything except pressing appeals for more and vague hints of little or no real value,

[1] For particulars as to Smith see *D.N.B.* vol. XVIII, p. 505. The account is based upon the assumption that in his dealings with Smith, Shrewsbury's "vigilance was benumbed by a guilty consciousness of his own intrigues with the exiles"—an assumption which is not warranted by the evidence.

they were at last discontinued. Since then, Smith had been
on the watch for some means of venting his spite against
Shrewsbury, and he was quite ready to fall in with any scheme
that seemed likely to injure his former employer. Having
ascertained Smith's past dealings with Shrewsbury, Monmouth had done his best to induce Fenwick to send for him
in the hope that this might lead to the production of Smith's
correspondence which had been left sealed up in the Secretary's office, and that it might be made to appear as though
the Duke had received early information of the conspiracy
against William's life, and had purposely suppressed it.
Moreover, the fact of Shrewsbury's retirement into the
country just before the date fixed for the execution of the
plot served to give an air of verisimilitude to the charge.

The scheme, however, had failed to answer the expectations
of its contrivers. In the first place, Fenwick would have
nothing to do with Monmouth's suggestions; then, the
latter's intrigues were discovered and he had to defend
himself as best he could. Smith's name was introduced into
the case in the hope that something might result from it, and
Smith himself was, with some difficulty, hunted out and
examined. He put on the air of one who had been very badly
treated, indulged (as Vernon expressed it) in "a large commendation of his own merits", and accused Shrewsbury of
"ingratitude". But his pose did not produce the effect he
had anticipated. Nor was the informer's case helped by the
fact of his association with Monmouth, which was well
known, though the latter had the effrontery to deny it. The
Lords appointed a committee to consider his correspondence,
and Somers was ordered to write to Shrewsbury requesting him
to send any of Smith's letters that were in his possession, or
to inform the House of their contents, so far as he could
remember them, if they had been destroyed. Shrewsbury
replied that almost all the letters had been destroyed, and
that most of those which were left were of an old date—when

he set more value on Smith's intelligence than he had afterwards. As to the recent plot, Smith had given some information; but his accounts varied, and it was suspected that
there was no truth in the story, as he was "never able to
bring any thing in confirmation of what he asserted, from
whom he had it, how he came by it, or at what time it was
to be executed". When the plot was discovered it appeared
that he was not enough in the secret to have prevented it, but
Shrewsbury said he had intended to do something for him
until he found that Smith "in very public places began to
threaten he would complain of him to the Parliament, whereupon he thought it neither safe nor decent to have more to
do with him". Such information as Smith had given with
regard to the assassination plot the Duke said he had always
communicated to the King.[1] Any doubt as to the truth of
this assertion was removed by the King, who personally confirmed Shrewsbury's statement. The committee appointed by
the House to consider Smith's correspondence, made its report
on January 20, and it was thereupon resolved with general
assent that he had no ground of complaint and did not deserve
any further reward. An order was then made that he should
be discharged by the Sergeant-at-Arms (in whose custody he
had been kept for more than a week during the examination
by the Lords), and he once more relapsed into obscurity.[2]

[1] Shrewsbury to Lord Keeper Somers, Jan. 13/23, 1696/7, in
Coxe, pp. 460-2.
[2] Burnet, vol. II, pp. 190-3; L'Hermitage, Jan. 12/22, 15/25,
19/29, Jan. 22/Feb. 1, in Add. MSS. 17,677, vol. R.R. ff. 179-80,
184-5, 191-2; Luttrell, Jan. 12, 19, 21, vol. IV, pp. 167, 170-2;
H.L. MSS. 1695-7, pp. 290-5, 299-300; Somers to Shrewsbury,
Dec. 24/Jan. 3, Jan. 5/15, 12/22, 16/26, 20/30, in Coxe, pp. 449,
455-65; Vernon to same, Jan. 9, 12; in Vernon Corr. vol. I, pp. 163-
171. The second resolution (that Smith did not deserve any further
reward) was moved by Rochester, whose conduct elicited a grateful
acknowledgment from Shrewsbury. See Shrewsbury's letter to
Rochester of Jan. 23, which is printed in Corr. of Clarendon and
Rochester, vol. II, p. 342, and Rochester's reply dated Jan. 26, in
Buccleuch MSS. vol. II, pt ii, p. 443.

CHAPTER VI

The Aftermath of the Fenwick Case

"All is now finished, entirely to your advantage", Portland wrote to Shrewsbury when Smith had been discharged by the Lords. "Nothing is now wanting but your presence, and I hope your health will permit you to return. If contentment of mind contribute to bodily health, yours ought to allow you soon to undertake the journey."[1] "For God's sake, come to us as soon as you are able", wrote Sunderland.[2] But Shrewsbury did not as yet possess either health or contentment of mind; and as his physicians told him that his full recovery would take some time longer, he remained at Eyford. It was not until the beginning of March, after another letter from the King, when the weather had become much warmer, that he felt able to move to London, and even then those who saw him at Court the day after his arrival were so much struck by the change in his appearance that they began to doubt whether he would ever fully recover.[3] He took lodgings close to Hyde Park instead of at the Secretary's official residence in Whitehall, in the hope that the air would better suit his health, but a fortnight later he had another attack of hæmorrhage.[4]

This relapse decided him to renew the request which he had made in the previous autumn for permission to resign

[1] Jan. 20, 1696/7, in Coxe, p. 163.

[2] Jan. 21, in *Buccleuch MSS.* vol. II, pt ii, p. 441.

[3] "Le duc de Shrewsbury est de retour, et il a ce matin fait la reverence au roy; il continue à cracher du sang, et il est si changé de visage, qu'on croy que sa santé aura peine à se retablir" (L'Hermitage, Mar. 5/15, in Add. MSS. 17,677, vol. R.R. f. 251).

[4] *Ibid.* pp. 254, 289, 303; Luttrell, April 10, vol. IV, p. 209; *Bath MSS.* vol. III, p. 112.

the seals. "After six months' experiment", he wrote to William, "I find myself in a condition as weak, and more desperate than I have yet been." He was sure that business would suffer from his inability to attend to it, and that "nothing but a considerable time of perfect quiet and leisure can give me the least hopes of overcoming such a kind of distemper". Retiring to the country while still retaining the seals of office was no remedy; the thought of work neglected caused him too much disquietude of mind, "so that remaining under this burthen can be of no use, but at the same time to neglect your majesty's affairs, and destroy my own health".[1] William remained adamant, promising, however, not to trouble the Secretary with business until he had recovered sufficiently to be able to reside in London and to undertake the duties of his post.[2] The Duke's name accordingly appeared once more in the list of Lords Justices commissioned to carry on the government in the King's absence. Sunderland, now Lord Chamberlain, was also included in the commission for the first time, and it was generally believed that "the secret and weight of the administration was wholly in them two".[3]

A few days later Shrewsbury was once more at Eyford. The other Lords Justices forebore to trouble him with business, except when it was absolutely necessary, and a few weeks of country air—first at Eyford, then at Grafton, together with almost entire freedom from the cares of office, produced their effect. By the end of June he had to all appearances completely recovered, and on July 6 he reappeared at Whitehall.[4] The King, in writing to express his pleasure at his return to

---

[1] Shrewsbury to William, April 19/29, 1697, in Coxe, p. 165.

[2] William to Shrewsbury, July 12/22, 1697, in *ibid*. p. 168.

[3] Luttrell, April 20, vol. IV, pp. 213, 215; Johnstone to Polwarth, Mar. 17, 1696–7, in *Marchmont MSS*. p. 132.

[4] L'Hermitage, dispatch of June 25/July 5, 1697, in Add. MSS. 17,677, vol. R.R. f. 372; July 6/16, in *ibid*. f. 382.

London, was able to give him at the same time the welcome news that the protracted negotiations for peace were at last nearing their conclusion.[1] Nearly a year had elapsed since Shrewsbury had first been consulted by the King as to the appointment of plenipotentiaries and the first tentative advances had been made. The King had conducted these negotiations, in accordance with his usual practice in dealing with diplomatic affairs, without reference to his Secretary of State, and the only point on which the latter was taken into his confidence related to the insertion in the treaty of a clause in which Louis XIV recognised William III as King of England.[2] After considering the French proposals on this head, and consulting Somers and Sunderland about them, Shrewsbury wrote to William urging the necessity of insisting upon an unequivocal recognition of his title as "William III, King of Great Britain, to avoid any cavilling interpretations hereafter", and of securing an undertaking that James should be removed farther from England and that he should not receive any assistance whatever from the French Government in future. On the first point he was soon reassured by Portland, who informed him that William's full titles would be recited at the head of the treaty. On the subject of James the situation was less satisfactory. Louis refused to give a definite undertaking to oust the royal refugee from St Germain, and William and Portland deemed it prudent "to take the thing as verbally granted" rather than risk a decided refusal. Though not without misgivings as to what might be thought of such an arrangement when it became known in England, Shrewsbury acquiesced in it as

[1] William to Shrewsbury, July 12/22, 1697, in Coxe, p. 168.
[2] When urged to give an opinion upon another of the questions in negotiation Shrewsbury excused himself on the ground of his "having never had anything communicated" to him except the matter of the acknowledgment of the King's title. Shrewsbury to Villiers, Sept. 8/18, 1697, in Coxe, p. 371.

the best that could be made in the circumstances.[1] Though he believed England could stand the strain of a prolongation of the war better than France could do, he was anxious that peace should be concluded as quickly as possible, provided the essential condition—the recognition by Louis of William as King of England—was secured.

Meanwhile residence in London had produced its usual result. In less than a month after his return he was again troubled with shortness of breath, though he had taken lodgings in the healthiest place he could find. Then came another attack of blood-spitting. "My distemper is returned upon me with such violence", he wrote to the Earl of Galway on August 14, "that I am forced to retire, and try if the same course and air, that did me good in the beginning of the summer, will set me up against winter".[2] Once more back at Eyford, he wrote to the King begging for permission to retire, and giving the most dolorous description of his symptoms. The hæmorrhage had now stopped, but he had such difficulty in breathing that he had to sit up in bed and so could get no rest. He dared not face the smoke and fogs of London. For nearly a twelve-month he had by the King's positive commands continued to hold a post of which he could not fulfil the duties; he was sure the King would not "think it reasonable or decent", that he should "any longer make a sinecure of a secretary's office".[3]

[1] Shrewsbury to William, July 20/30, July 27/Aug. 6, same to Portland, same date, and Aug. 18/28, Portland to Shrewsbury, Aug. 2/12, 1697, in Coxe, pp. 169–71, 354–5, 358–60, 363. See also *Letters of William III and Louis XIV* (ed. P. Grimblot, 2 vols. 1848), vol. I, pp. 84–7.

[2] *Buccleuch MSS.* vol. II, pt ii, p. 532. Bonet ascribed the relapse to Shrewsbury's working too hard (Aug. 13/23, in Add. MSS. 30,000, vol. A. f. 342). See L'Hermitage, same date, in Add. MSS. 17,677, vol. R.R. f. 417. Cf. *C.S.P.* (*Dom.*), 1697, p. 294, Vernon to Williamson, Aug. 10, "I am sorry to tell you the Duke of Shrewsbury's distemper has grown to the height it was last winter".

[3] Shrewsbury to William, Aug. 25/Sept. 4, 1697, in Coxe, p. 174.

Shrewsbury's anxiety to resign was increased by news which he received from London almost as soon as he had written his letter to the King, and which showed that not even yet had he heard the last of the Fenwick case. Even after Fenwick's execution the Secretary's office had still been kept busy with the importunities of adventurers anxious to give information of plots against the Government, some of them real, the majority imaginary. Towards the middle of August there came a lull, and the most harassed Under-Secretary wrote to his chief, "God be thanked, there is a cessation of discoveries".[1] Hardly had Shrewsbury received Vernon's letter than he heard that new informers, the most important of them named Price and Chaloner, were charging him with having endeavoured to contrive Fenwick's escape from justice.[2]

His informant offered to keep the matter dark in the meantime, but Shrewsbury, conscious that there was no truth whatever in this accusation at any rate, wrote confidently, insisting that the matter should be communicated to the Lords Justices without delay. "God be thanked", he wrote, "I am so perfectly innocent in this and all other matters where my fidelity to the Government can be charged, that I make it my most earnest request that this or any other information may be laid immediately before the Lords Justices."[3] He sent positive injunctions to Vernon to this effect. The accusation was treated with contempt by the Secretary's colleagues, both Somers and Tenison declaring that they were themselves in a position to prove the falsity of the charge and the anxiety which Shrewsbury had shewn to have Fenwick arrested. Before long Price and Chaloner, themselves under duress, were fully occupied in accusing

---

[1] Vernon to Shrewsbury, Aug. 21, 1697, in *Vernon Corr.* vol. II, p. 314.
[2] See *C.S.P.* (*Dom.*), 1697, pp. 337–41.
[3] *Buccleuch MSS.* vol. II, pt ii, pp. 541–2.

each other of counterfeiting exchequer bills and in trying to defend themselves against well-founded charges of contravening the act against coining.[1]

But though the story of Price and Chaloner carried no weight with Shrewsbury's friends it gave a new handle to his enemies, and the sensitive Secretary was more than ever determined to resign.[2] "I shall never be allowed to serve with advantage to your majesty, or with quiet to myself", he wrote in a new appeal to the King, "but be eternally embroiling your affairs with these sort of inquiries, and exposing myself to such an uneasiness as I am, of all mankind, the least fit, and the least able to bear."[3] Once again William proved adamant. Indeed, he was less inclined than ever to release Shrewsbury, for the choice of his successor was bound to create trouble. The Whigs considered that Wharton had an indisputable claim to the reversion of the office, while the King detested him personally as much as he liked Shrewsbury and was prepared to go to any lengths rather than entrust the seals to him. The Whig leaders for their part, conscious of this difficulty, preferred that Shrewsbury should retain his position, and they begged him to do so, insisting at the same time that the accusations of Price and his accomplices, having no foundation, afforded no ground for resignation, and that now the treaty of peace had been signed, there would be less for the Secretary to do.[4]

These appeals were fruitless. The utmost that Shrewsbury

[1] *Vernon Corr.* vol. I, pp. 314 *et seq.*; Coxe, pp. 486–8. For the information given against Shrewsbury see *Buccleuch MSS.* vol. II, pt ii, pp. 539–40.

[2] Shrewsbury was alarmed at the possibilities of forgery revealed by the claim made by the informers that they possessed the secret of "counterfeiting hands or washing out part of a writing and filling it up".

[3] Shrewsbury to William, Sept. 8/18, 1697, in Coxe, pp. 175–6.

[4] William to Shrewsbury, Sept. 23, Portland to same, Sept. 14/24, Somers, Orford, and Sunderland to same, Sept. 16/26, 1697, in Coxe, pp. 176–7, 491–4.

could be prevailed upon to do was to consent to deliver up the seals to the King in person instead of sending them to him as he had done in 1690.[1] With the intention of doing so he arrived at Kensington on November 2. A fortnight later the King returned, and Shrewsbury immediately waited upon him to tender his resignation. To his surprise and disgust William absolutely refused to accept it. But Shrewsbury would not yet take "No", and the personal interview having failed he once more had recourse to an imploring letter. He wished he could convey to his Majesty the distraction of his mind. Nothing could come of keeping up the struggle which his retention of office involved but the destruction of the poor remains of his life. Between ill-health, spleen, and the disgusts he had received and might reasonably expect to meet from the villainous attempts of those who by false witness or other base means sought to ruin his reputation, he had, he said, taken so violent an aversion to public business that he could not bear the thought of continuance in it. Since nothing but retirement could bring amendment to one of his humour and his constitution he begged the King in charity to release him.[2]

This letter brought some concession. The King agreed to allow Shrewsbury to resign as soon as circumstances permitted, but for the present he must retain his office, though he need not remain in London and was free to do as much or as little work as he felt able to perform. On these terms Shrewsbury returned to Eyford on November 30.[3] The King had postponed the troublesome problem of finding a

[1] Orford to Shrewsbury, Sept. 24/Oct. 4, Oct. 21/31, Somers to same, Sept. 25/Oct. 5, in Coxe, pp. 499–500, 502–3.
[2] Shrewsbury to William, Nov. 18/28, 1697, in Coxe, p. 179; C.S.P. (Dom.), 1697, p. 476; cf. same to Galway, Nov. 25, 1697, in *Buccleuch MSS.* vol. II, pt ii, p. 580: "I can be esteemed nothing but a corpse, half buried already, and expecting the consummation of that entire ceremony".
[3] Luttrell, Nov. 30, 1697, vol. IV, p. 313.

successor, and the Whigs avoided for the time being the loss of prestige which the Duke's retirement would mean to their party, especially if there was any prospect of a Tory succeeding him. Shrewsbury had secured a promise, however indefinite, of relief, and in the meantime the faithful Vernon transacted all his business for him.

But no sooner had the arrangement been made than it was upset. On the very day after Shrewsbury's departure, Sir William Trumbull, his colleague in the Secretary's office, suddenly resigned, complaining that he had been treated more like a footman than a Secretary of State. Before the Whigs realised what was happening Vernon had, regardless of his own protests, been appointed by the King to the vacant post. The news of this appointment which soon followed him to Eyford was most disconcerting to Shrewsbury. Portland's suggestion that Vernon could do the whole work of the Secretary's office did not commend itself, and once more he wished to resign. He was, however, prevailed upon by the King and Portland not to do so in the meantime, and the former threw out a hint of transfer to a less exacting post. But Shrewsbury promptly replied that he was unfit to fill any post at all. He had, he said, no relish for power or riches, and was convinced that none could be happy who set their hearts on either. He had grown fond of country retirement and country pursuits and had lost the inclinations that had formerly reconciled him to the town.[1]

It was not long before a vacancy occurred which was not of the King's making. The Whigs were furious at the appointment of Vernon to the post which they had earmarked for Wharton, and they attributed it to the influence of the already obnoxious Sunderland. Attacks were made upon him in both Houses, and being thoroughly alarmed, to his master's great annoyance he hastily resigned, hoping thus

[1] Shrewsbury to Sunderland, Dec. 11/21, 1697, in Coxe, pp. 507–8.

to avert formal proceedings.[1] Despite his refusal to consider the acceptance of another office Shrewsbury was immediately bombarded with appeals to take the vacant position of Lord Chamberlain.[2] The King pressed this suggestion in the hope that he would thereby be able to retain him in the Ministry; the Whigs because they counted upon him to use his influence in that position to secure the appointment of Wharton to the Secretaryship in his place.

While giving no encouragement to this proposal, Shrewsbury was prepared to undertake the rôle of mediator between William, Sunderland, and the Whigs which circumstances practically forced upon him. The task was practically hopeless. The Whigs were sore because the King had of late been more intimate with Sunderland than with them; the King was sore because they had fallen foul of his favourite; while Sunderland was not disposed to return to the uncomfortable position in which William's partiality had involved him. Shrewsbury had an interview with the King at Windsor early in March, but failed in his negotiation. He had personally no objection to terms being made with Sunderland—it was a matter of indifference to him whether the latter returned to Court or not—but he had to insist upon the King's acceptance of Wharton for the Secretaryship as an indispensable condition of securing the whole-hearted co-operation of the Whig party, and this condition William was still resolute not to accept.[3]

Any possibility of the renewal of the discussion was prevented by a recurrence of Shrewsbury's malady. Relying upon the good effects of his three months' stay at Eyford, he

---

[1] Sunderland recognised that his own colleagues would do nothing to defend him. Burnet, vol. II, pp. 207–8; *Vernon Corr.* vol. I, pp. 448–51.

[2] C.S.P. (*Dom.*), 1697, p. 538, Vernon to Williamson, Dec. 31.

[3] Luttrell, Jan. 1, 1697/8, vol. IV, p. 326; L'Hermitage, Jan. 4/14, 7/17, in Add. MSS. 17,677, vol. S.S. ff. 105, 109; Coxe, pp. 180–1, 509–10, 519–26; *Buccleuch MSS.* vol. II, pt ii, pp. 594–5.

joined the King at hunting, and the exertion brought on a very bad attack of blood-spitting. He retired to Wharton's house at Woburn. He stayed there a month without recovering and then once more went back to Eyford, having definitely declined to accept any other office. On hearing this, William wrote to Portland,

I fear he is worse to-day than ever. He has written a letter to Vernon, like a dying man, who is determined to think no more of any business whatever. Thus, I believe, we may already reckon him as dead to the world, which grieves me not a little and embarrasses me no less. Nobody here considers him dangerously ill, because, during the four days which he spent with me at Windsor, he seemed tolerably well, and went out hunting with me three times; nor was he taken ill till the night between Friday and Saturday, on which day he had resolved to come to London with me. I do not know what to make of it, but during those four days he appeared to me quite resolved to return to business, always paying me the compliment to say that it was only to please me and serve me, for, that if he followed his own inclinations, he would retire altogether from the world. This will cause a grand fracas among all parties, who will fear more than ever the return of Lord Sunderland.[1]

Notwithstanding all his previous failures William made one last attempt to win over Shrewsbury and through him to come to a better understanding with the Whigs. Vernon was sent to arrange a new meeting, which was to take place in Godolphin's house at Newmarket, and here on April 7 Shrewsbury came, though by no means perfectly recovered from his last attack.[2] The new discussions lasted several days, but they ended in the old *impasse*. The King would not have Wharton, and the Whigs would not have Sunderland. Shrewsbury gave up the problem in despair, and after another visit to Woburn once more returned to the solitude of Eyford. Godolphin wrote: "Wee have had the Duke of Shrewsbury

---

[1] William to Portland, Mar. 14/24, 1697/8, in Grimblot, vol. I, pp. 309–11. Cf. same to same, Mar. 21/April 1, in *ibid.* p. 327.
[2] *Vernon Corr.* vol. II, p. 31.

in my house, but in soe uncertain and I doubt, dangerous an estate of health that to mee there seems but little hopes of keeping him long which considering what other prospects wee have to supply the want of him, is a subject too disagreeable to speak of ".[1] Shrewsbury was willing to retain the seals till the end of the Parliamentary session; it had at last to be recognised that there was no chance of persuading him to continue after that.[2] William was anxious that the Duke's present seclusion and impending resignation should be attributed to his ill-health and not to the difficulty over Wharton, but it was impossible to disguise the fact that they were somehow connected with the breakdown of important negotiations with the Whigs.[3] Shrewsbury's visits to Wharton looked suspicious. Had he made Wharton's cause his own? Which was the ultimate and essential cause of his insistence on retirement—the weakness of his· health or the strength of his Whiggism?

William finally agreed to Shrewsbury's surrender of the seals in December 1698, and the Duke sent his "most sincere and humble thanks" for the King's compassion.[4] He did not formally relinquish his office till the following June. William's unwillingness to part with him was such that in September he pressed him to accept either the Lord Chamberlainship or even the Lord Treasurership, with the proviso that he would be allowed to transact all the business of this office by deputy.[5] Shrewsbury declined the great honour of the Lord Treasurership, but in October accepted the appointment in the Household. His secretary, Sir John Stanley, did all the work for him. His correspondence with

[1] Godolphin to Lonsdale, April 17, 1698, in *Lonsdale MSS.* (H.M.C.), Rept. XIII, app. pt vii, p. 109.
[2] Luttrell, April 7, 1698, vol. IV, p. 365; Grimblot, vol. I, p. 437.
[3] *Vernon Corr.* vol. II, pp. 61–3.
[4] Coxe, p. 181.
[5] See *Shrewsbury's Journal*, May 18, 1702, in *Buccleuch MSS.* vol. II, pt ii, p. 762.

the Duke relates to furniture for the Horse Guards, quilts for Yeomen of the Guard at Hampton Court, card tables at Kensington, Lenten preachers at Court, chinaware in the Queen's apartments at Kensington, the entertainment of the ambassador from Savoy, payment to Sir Godfrey Kneller for portraits, the appointment of a new groom porter, the livery for the rat-killer, the Maundy Thursday charity. Such were the weighty matters with which Shrewsbury was now concerned.[1]

In May 1700 the King offered him the Lord-Lieutenancy of Ireland, together with the office of Groom of the Stole. On the 10th he was informed that the King depended on his going to Ireland,[2] and next day Marlborough wrote to say that he had heard that if his health permitted, he was to have these two appointments, and that he wished both Shrewsbury and the King joy of them.[3] A week later the Earl of Galway wrote from Dublin, "J'ay apris avec beaucoup de joye, que vous estes resolu d'accepter le Gouvernement de ce Royaume".[4] But Galway was misinformed. Shrewsbury was resolved not to accept the offer. He was once again afflicted with hæmorrhage, and he was ascribing this relapse to "uneasiness of mind" produced by the King's wishes. William wrote with his usual kindness to calm him, "I will not press you in anything, but will leave you entirely at liberty, merely desiring you to attend to only the re-establishment of your health".[5] Shrewsbury seized upon this assurance not merely to decline the new offer but to resign the Lord Chamberlainship. William could not say he was well pleased with this renunciation of his employment, but he acquiesced in it, being satisfied of his integrity and affection.[6]

[1] *Buccleuch MSS.* vol. II, pt ii, pp. 629–52 *passim*.
[2] *Ibid.* p. 647.   [3] *Ibid.*   [4] *Ibid.* p. 647.
[5] William to Shrewsbury, May 22, 1700, in Coxe, p. 184.
[6] *Ibid.* p. 184.

CHAPTER VII

Travels Abroad, 1700–1705

Until the autumn Shrewsbury lingered on in England. He
had promised William to do his best to moderate the violence
of the Whigs, and he still remained in communication with
the party leaders, while in August he attended a party meeting
at Boughton. But as the King had expected and as he was
himself driven to acknowledge, the task was hopeless, its
only result being to lessen his credit with his friends. The
more extreme section of the party led by Wharton had hailed
his resignation with triumph as the result of their persuasions
and as an indication that he had finally broken with the King
and Sunderland.[1] They found, however, to their great annoyance, that their hopes of his now joining them in uncompromising opposition to the Tories were not going to be fulfilled.
They were disappointed in him. At a time when their
position was threatened and they stood in need of all the
support they could get he was abandoning them. As their
opposition to the Court became more and more pronounced,
he was drifting further and further away from them.[2] When
on July 30 the Princess Anne's only surviving child, the Duke
of Gloucester, died, and the problem of the succession was
thereby reopened, the party question threatened to become
particularly troublesome. The Tories, now led by the Earl
of Rochester, were ascendant in the King's confidence.[3]

[1] Vernon to Shrewsbury, in *Vernon Corr.* vol. III, p. 94; Bonet,
June 21/July 2, in Add. MSS. 30,000, vol. D. f. 207.
[2] Coxe, pp. 626–9.
[3] Rochester seems to have been making indirect attempts to
induce Shrewsbury to return to office. See *Vernon Corr.* vol. III,
p. 110.

With his own party discredited and refusing to listen to his counsels of moderation, Shrewsbury resolved to withdraw altogether from the confusion and to go abroad, as his physicians advised.

At the beginning of October he paid a visit to Sunderland at Althorpe;[1] on the 28th he had a prolonged audience with William at Hampton Court. Of what happened at that interview there is no record. The Whigs put the worst construction upon it, following as it did so soon upon his stay with the hated Sunderland. He was suspected of having assented to, if not actually advised, the recent changes in the Ministry.[2] But probably Shrewsbury's chief business with the King was merely to obtain the necessary permission to leave the kingdom.[3] On November 1 he left London for Dover; two days later he crossed to Calais, whence he made his way slowly by Abbeville and Amiens to Paris, which he reached on the 8th. He called upon our ambassador, the Earl of Manchester, and on the 23rd he was received by Louis XIV. "This morning", he wrote in his diary for the day,

the Ambassador called me before seven and we went to Versailes where I saluted the King, and he received me tolerably civilly, but the Court was in too great hurry and exultation upon their new K[ing] of Sp[ain] to admit much other thought. Nobody was so perfectly civil as my old acquaintance the Duke of Lozune [Lauzun], but perhaps it was not without design; for he began to

---

[1] *Portland MSS.* vol. III, p. 633; C. Cole, *Historical and Political Memoirs* (1735), p. 230.

[2] L'Hermitage, Nov. 1/11, in Add. MSS. 17,677, vol. U.U. f. 334; *Memoirs of Public Transactions*, pp. 37–8.

[3] "Le Duc de Shrewsbury, Chef des Whigs est prêt à partir pour Montpelier où il va pour retablir s'il peut sa santé ruinée. Il a demandé la permission à sa Majesté, selon la pratique ordinaire des Grands de ce Pays, lorsqu'ils veulent sortir du Royaume. On la lui a accordé assez facilement, ce qui fait penser que son absence ne fera pas de la peine" (Bonet, Oct. 31/Nov. 11, in Add. MSS. 30,000, vol. D. f. 309.)

tell me how kindly King James had always taken the distinguished civility I had shewed him when I was sent on the message, and was grounding upon this some further discourse, when I cut him short, and told him I confessed I had great compassion at that time for his circumstances, but desired that we might not discourse on that but on any other subject. An hour after he took occasion to commend the P[rince] of Wales, and wished that by any means I might have an opportunity of seeing so fine a youth. I told him I questioned not his merit, but had no great curiosity, but if I must see him, I would rather it were here than in England. This reply dashed all further discourse of this kind.[1]

It was natural no doubt for one of James's supporters to attribute Shrewsbury's recent resignation, apparent breach first with the King, then with the Whigs, and his subsequent visit to France to Jacobite sympathies, but if his replies to Lauzun were as unequivocal as his own record of them any such idea must have been speedily dispelled.

Soon after this Shrewsbury left Paris for Montpellier, staying a few days *en route* at Nîmes. Here he notes with reference to his experience of French hostelries, "In the inns of France you have often ill beds, always ill linen, generally ill chambers, and dirty and few attendance; but then the meat, drink, and cookery is [are] far beyond Eng[land]. I have come into villages where I have found turkeys, partridge of both kinds, hens, rabbits, leverets in the larder; and you will find nowhere so ill provided but you may have very good

---

[1] *Journal*, Nov. 1 (o.s.) to Nov. 23 (n.s.), in *Buccleuch MSS.* vol. II, pt ii, pp. 746–7. Cf. *Life and Character*, pp. 11–12. The author, who seems to be particularly well informed about Shrewsbury's visit to Versailles, says that he was received with great state, as if "to make mankind believe that he was upon a negotiation". He adds that Shrewsbury "took that care during the time he stay'd at Paris, as to avoid everybody belonging to that court [*i.e.* of St Germain], even the Earl of Middleton who was married to his mother's sister, and with whom he had for many years been in the most intimate and affectionate friendship, he would not see nor any belonging to him, not even his aunt, because he would not give the least suspicion of an inclination to that court".

mutton, a good second course ".[1] On December 8 he at last reached his destination, and he established himself in a small house outside the town, being unable to obtain accommodation in Montpellier itself as the Estates of Languedoc were then in session. Here he hoped to settle down in peace and quiet, undisturbed by the harassing cares of office, to recuperate his health. For a short time his hopes were realised. He lived very happily in the society of the few English people gathered in the district and of its leading French citizens, one of the latter, the Bishop of Lodève, proving to be an old school-fellow at the Navarre College.

But before long Shrewsbury felt obliged to leave French soil altogether. On November 1 (n.s.) death had at last taken Charles II of Spain the sufferer, and the male line of the Spanish Habsburgs was extinct. With a cynical disregard of his promises to William III and to Heinsius, the Grand Pensionary of Holland, Louis XIV had thrown over the Partition Treaty and acknowledged his grandson the Duke of Anjou as Philip V of Spain. Shrewsbury had found the French Court too much excited about this to give much thought to anything else.[2] A new European war seemed the probable outcome, and towards the end of February Shrewsbury had decided that it was desirable to be in neutral territory. The news that the Dutch had recognised the new King of Spain induced him to postpone his journey, but when a fortnight elapsed without any news of England's following their example, on March 17 he set out for Geneva.[3]

He was more secure in Geneva, but its climate did not suit him nearly so well. At Montpellier his health had considerably improved and he had been free of his old complaint, but the air of Geneva was too relaxing and "the fogs from the lake made his distemper grow upon him ".[4] He dosed

---

[1] *Buccleuch MSS.* vol. II, pt ii, p. 748.   [2] See *supra*, p. 144.
[3] *Buccleuch MSS.* vol. II, pt ii, p. 751.
[4] *Ibid.* p. 753; *Life and Character*, p. 12; *Vernon Corr.* vol. III, p. 145.

himself with "a vast quantity of vitriol". He had been considering the possibility of returning to England at no distant date, but his relapse put an end to ideas of that nature. Moreover, there was nothing in the political situation at home to tempt him to return. The death of Charles II and Louis' acceptance of the will had led to the discovery of the existence of the Partition Treaties, and since then the Tories had been busily engaged in making party capital out of this revelation by attacking the Whig ministers who had been in office when the negotiations were undertaken. Whilst they did their utmost to ruin Portland, Somers, Orford, and Halifax, they shewed no disposition to include Shrewsbury among their intended victims, and Vernon was able to write: "Your Grace has been treated with great distinction in all these enquiries where your name appeared".[1] Nevertheless, there was no point in unnecessarily venturing near the hornets' nest; Shrewsbury was ever prudent.

Not till June did he write to any one of those former colleagues upon whom their enemies had fallen, and even then his tone was more circumspect than cordial. In addressing Somers he excused himself for not having written before on the grounds that he had been expecting until his relapse to be returning to England shortly and that he had not dared at so great a distance to write all he wished to say. Caution, he said, still hindered him from expressing all that he wished to say. All that caution did allow him was to condole with Somers on his "mortification", and to comfort him with the pious reflection that "in a little time mankind will come to itself, and learn truth and justice". These events, he said, strengthened him, "with more weight than I ever expected", in his old hatred of office. He could only wonder "that a man can be found in England, who has bread, that will be concerned in public business. Had I a son, I would sooner

[1] Vernon to Shrewsbury, April 21, in *Vernon Corr.* vol. III, p. 144.

breed him a cobbler than a courtier, and a hangman than a statesman". He assured Somers that if he could be of service to him, to Halifax or to Orford by writing to any friends or by coming himself, there was nothing in his power that he would not be prepared to do, to shew his real concern and the value he placed upon Somers' friendship.[1]

Somers' original reply appears never to have reached its destination; a second letter, written more than two months later, was little more than a formal expression of thanks for Shrewsbury's offer of assistance, and a congratulation upon his good fortune in being able "to live remote from such a country as ours".[2]

By the time that he received this letter Shrewsbury was in Italy. On August 30 he had left Geneva in search of a more attractive climate south of the Alps. He made a brief stay at Turin and "slipped by without making my compliments at that Court"; found that in Genoa "most of the company was at their country houses but a few whom he had known in England were still there and shewed him what company was to be seen";[3] then, after visits to Pisa, Lucca, Leghorn, he arrived in Florence. He had had a long-standing offer from Blackwell, the envoy to the Grand Duke of Tuscany, of the use of his house,[4] and here he remained from September 29 to November 17. In Florence he visited the palaces and picture-galleries and the opera. "The scenes", he recorded, "were poor, the theatre little, no dancing, and not above two or three good voices, but the music pleased me much better than the French. It is always set to express the meaning of the words. They sing the dialogue much faster than the French; almost as fast as if it were spoke, which

[1] Shrewsbury to Somers, June 17, 1701, in Coxe, pp. 632–4.
[2] Somers to Shrewsbury, Aug. 24, in *Buccleuch MSS.* vol. II, pt ii, pp. 653–4.
[3] Add. MSS. 7121, f. 66.
[4] Blackwell to Shrewsbury, Dec. 15/25, 1699, in *Buccleuch MSS.* vol. II, pt ii, p. 631.

makes it less tedious. Their songs have many repetitions but many of them extreme fine." He deplored the absence of flutes and oboes in the orchestra.[1]

On October 17 he resumed his journey; proceeding by way of Siena and Viterbo, he reached Rome on the fourth day. He had had some idea of going on still further and sojourning in Naples.[2] Actually he remained in Rome for nearly three and a half years. His choice of residence afforded opportunity for his enemies to spread abroad the report that he had decided to return to his former faith and that he was seeking absolution from the Pope. But it was anxiety for his physical and not his spiritual health that had brought Shrewsbury to Rome. He at once prepared for a long stay, "to divert himself with the curiosities of that city",[3] and he took a very handsome palace near the Capitol, which belonged to the son of Salvator Rosa.[4] His diary during this period mainly consists of comments upon the society of Rome, of which he at once became a prominent member, of records of visits to churches, libraries and galleries. "He conversed indifferently with all sorts of people at Rome, especially the Literati and improved his knowledge in painting and architecture to which last he applied assiduously, and made a very good collection of the first."[5] His journal shews his particular interest in manuscripts in the Vatican Library and elsewhere, in the proceedings of the Holy Office, which he frequently discusses, and most of all in the Countess Adelaide, a widow, whose husband had been in the service of Queen Christina of Sweden. Her father was the Marquis Paleotti of Bologna, her

[1] *Journal*, Oct. 30, in *ibid*. p. 756.
[2] *Life and Character*, p. 13.
[3] Luttrell, Dec. 23, vol. v, p. 122.
[4] *Buccleuch MSS*. vol. ii, pt ii, p. 757; *Life and Character*, p. 13.
[5] *Ibid*. p. 15. His friends had a high opinion of his artistic judgment, and he executed a number of commissions for Somers and Halifax. Cf. *Buccleuch MSS*. vol. ii, pt ii, pp. 662, 695–6, 703; Coxe, pp. 643–6.

mother a daughter of "that eminent mathematician who lived at Florence", Sir Robert Dudley, and a lineal descendant of the father-in-law of Lady Jane Grey. To the Countess Adelaide Shrewsbury was introduced as soon as he arrived in Rome and he became an almost daily visitor to her house; "and as she had a great many engaging qualities and he of a generous as well as amorous temper there became a strict friendship between them".[1]

During his long sojourn in Rome Shrewsbury lost both his mother and his grandfather. Of the death of the former he records laconically on May 31, 1702, "Received letters from England that on the 19th April (o.s.) my mother died. I said nothing of it in my family till I enquired how I ought to mourn".[2] On August 29, 1703, he received "the melancholy news of the Earl of Cardigan's death".[3] The death of William III in March 1702 would seem to have caused him greater distress. When first he heard the report, he prayed God it might prove "as false as formerly". Next day "with affliction and a great cold" he kept his bed.[4] The accession of Queen Anne placed Marlborough and Godolphin in power. They were anxious to include Shrewsbury in the new Ministry, and it being generally supposed that he would speedily return to England the post of Master of the Horse was kept vacant for him. The day after the receipt of a letter from Godolphin offering him the post he wrote in his diary, "Now I have almost been offered all the great places of the kingdom; twice I quitted Secretary, once Chamberlain;[5] King William once offered me to be Lord Treasurer, often to be President and Privy Seal, to be governor to the Duke

[1] *Life and Character*, pp. 15–16.
[2] *Buccleuch MSS.* vol. II, pt ii, p. 762.
[3] *Ibid.* p. 771.
[4] *Journal*, April 4 and 5, in *ibid.* p. 761.
[5] This is misquoted in Coxe (p. 182, n.): "Now I have almost been offered all the great places of the Kingdom, since I quitted Secretary; once Chamberlain...".

of Gloucester, and last to be Lieutenant of Ireland and Groom of the Stole at the same time ".[1] Flattered as he may perhaps have been at this renewed proof that his influence was not regarded as extinct, Shrewsbury never contemplated acceptance. He wrote back to Godolphin heartily congratulating him on his new position—"You have long deserved the best employment in England", he said—but declining the honour offered to himself on account of "a certain incapacity, both of body and mind, never to engage more in a court life".[2] Still Godolphin and Marlborough hoped to obtain his support for their war policy when once he should come back to England, and of his early return there seemed some prospect at this time. During the summer his health had greatly improved, and although he was still subject to occasional attacks of bleeding, they were only slight and soon stopped of themselves without his having to have recourse to vitriol as had been necessary before.

But the expectations of his return to England in the winter of 1703/4 were unfulfilled. Either because his health grew worse or because he still shrank from being plunged again in the quarrels of parties he still lingered on in Rome. As the winter and the spring passed away and he did not appear, rumours began to be circulated that there were secret and sinister reasons for it. It was discovered that he had received a visit from a hermit who came from Cardinal Jansen, the French agent in Rome, with the connivance of the Pope, bringing vague tentative proposals for the opening of negotiations for peace to be transmitted by the Duke to the English Government. Shrewsbury had given a civil but determined answer that he would not meddle in the matter.[3]

[1] *Journal*, May 18, in *Buccleuch MSS.* vol. II, pt ii, p. 762.
[2] Shrewsbury to Godolphin, July 1, in Coxe, p. 635 (from the Blenheim collection).
[3] *Journal*, April 26, 29, 1703, in *Buccleuch MSS.* vol. II, pt ii, p. 778.

The fact that he had been approached in this way became known in England, but not the nature and manner of his reply. That he should have been regarded both by the Pope and the French agent as a fit channel for such a proposal was quite sufficient to prejudice him in some quarters.

There was the more serious rumour that he desired to be received back into the fellowship of the Roman Catholic Church which he had once abjured. Shrewsbury had done his utmost to avoid giving the slightest ground for such a report. While abroad he frequently gave assistance to poor Protestants, and on one occasion he helped forty Dutch seamen, who had been in prison in Naples and who came to beg from him, to reach Leghorn "that they might not here [*i.e.* in Rome] be debauched from serving their country and from their religion".[1] It is perfectly clear from the unflattering remarks in Shrewsbury's diary upon Roman Catholicism, particularly as it was practised in Rome, that there was never the slightest prospect of his recantation. When on January 24, 1703 there was an alarming earthquake in Rome and in consequence of it the churches were open, the priests hearing confession all night, he comments: "All run to confession, imagining that mumbling a few words to the priest, and the priest to them, their consciences are safe, without any real or firm purpose to amend their lives".[2] A few months later he writes, "I do profess to God I think the Roman Church full of ignorance, tricks, and error",[3] and, again, he throws contempt on "this wretched Court, which may be esteemed by those who take him [the Pope] to [be] God's vicegerent, but by us is not esteemed more than a D[uke] of Parma".[4] The author of the *Memoirs of Public*

[1] *Buccleuch MSS.* vol. II, pt ii, pp. 747–8, 779, 785.
[2] *Ibid.* p. 765.   [3] *Ibid.* p. 768.
[4] *Ibid.* p. 771. Cf. also p. 767: "Certainly nothing but interest and no religion can make a man of sense and learning embrace that sect in this country, where one sees nothing among them but pride, luxury, and ignorance".

Transactions asserts that he was so strict a Protestant that he refused to comply with rituals in the churches which other Protestant visitors would submit to "rather than not satisfye their curiosity", and he adds, "I have heard his Grace say frequently to live at Rome is to be confirm'd a Protestant". All Englishmen, he declared, ought to travel abroad in order to appreciate the value of their country's constitution and its religion. The same authority says that he particularly "abhorred the processions made to the Madonas and the worshipping of our Saviour Jesus Christ in the shape of a wafer".[1]

Nevertheless, several attempts were made by a certain Father Forbas to induce him to abjure. Shrewsbury told the priest on the first occasion that he "believed it more impossible" for him "to be a Papist than a Turk".[2] Forbas, however, persisted for a time till the Duke "appealed to God and used several imprecations" upon himself if he did not believe the Roman Church to be in error.[3] So far was Shrewsbury from contemplating abjuration while he was in Rome that he actually converted his cousin, the third Earl of Cardigan, to follow his example and abandon Popery for the Church of England.[4] The Pope, Clement XI, bore Shrewsbury no good will, and, suspecting him of being engaged in political intrigues, employed spies to watch his movements.[5] He discovered nothing, for there was nothing to discover, and when after Blenheim there seemed to be a prospect of the victorious troops descending upon Italy, he thought it politic to change his attitude to the English Duke. "A year ago", the latter wrote in his diary in August 1704, "I was so ill in the opinion of the Pope that it was thought a crime to go near me; now

[1] *Memoirs of Public Transactions*, pp. 56–7.
[2] *Journal*, Sept. 9, 1702, in *Buccleuch MSS.* vol. II, pt ii, p. 764.
[3] *Ibid.* April 16, 1703, in *ibid.* p. 768.
[4] *Life and Character*, pp. 13–15.
[5] *Journal*, Aug. 27, 1703, in *Buccleuch MSS.* vol. II, pt ii, p. 771.

that they fear the D[uke] of Marl[borough] and his red-coats should come into Italy, his Holiness does nothing but commend me".[1]

But though there was no ground for the suspicions which were circulating in England as to the reasons for Shrewsbury's sojourn in Rome, they gave uneasiness to some of his Whig friends, who were in any case perturbed by his correspondence with the Tory ministers. Somers in vague but meaningful terms recommended him, if he still found that his health detained him abroad not to "raise an expectation of his coming, because it always raises a new discourse, and every time more spiteful".[2] In his reply Shrewsbury asked for particulars as to the nature of the censures cast upon him in his absence, protesting that if the calumny was to the effect that he had changed his religion, he took care that nobody should be able to believe it in Rome. He thought that people should bear in mind what he had done "to preserve the liberty and religion" of his country, when "I ventured my life as freely, if not more than any body, my house being the place, where most of the considerable meetings were held, in order to call in his late majesty".[3]

In his response to this letter Somers dismissed the tale of Shrewsbury's conversion as palpably false, but he alluded more seriously to the rumour of his having been engaged in secret negotiations for peace.[4] Vernon wrote to suggest that Shrewsbury should compose a formal letter, which might be published, either to the Archbishop of Canterbury or to his relative William Talbot, the Bishop of Oxford, specifically denying the charge of reconversion; and he at the same time suggested that the Duke should leave Rome for Vienna or some other place further north to make trial by degrees of

[1] *Journal*, Aug. 4, 1704, in *Buccleuch MSS.* vol. II, pt ii, p. 782.
[2] Somers to Shrewsbury, June 1704, in Coxe, pp. 640–1.
[3] Shrewsbury to Somers, July 5, in *ibid.* pp. 642–3.
[4] Somers to Shrewsbury, July 21, in *ibid.* pp. 643–4.

how cooler climates agreed with him.[1] Shrewsbury assured Somers that he had had no share whatever in any political negotiations, and then, following Vernon's advice, he wrote to the Bishop of Oxford, solemnly asserting his attachment to the Church of England, and explaining his choice of Rome as a place of residence. It was his misfortune that "there is no where in Europe a Protestant country favoured with the warm sun". Had not Portugal been debarred by the length of the sea-voyage and France and Spain by the fact of the war he would never have come to Italy. As it was he had selected in Rome "the least Popish of any place in Italy", with the exception of Venice, where the moist air would not agree with him. He had supposed that his repudiation of Romanism in James II's reign would have rendered him less liable to imputations of an inclination to that religion than any man alive.

In my conduct and discourse I have constantly here endeavoured to convince every body of my steadiness. I never go to any of their churches, unless it be sometimes for a moment to look at a picture. In case I have, accidentally, been present at the Elevation of the Host, I have never bent a knee (a thing which many strangers make no scruple to do), the contrary being sometimes not without danger from the rudeness of the people. I have declined all intimacy with Prelates and Cardinals....I have never been with the Pope, though solicited to it by the offer of a treatment equal to if not more than any of my rank have ever had. In my discourse among my countrymen, I have never omitted to express the folly and superstition of this religion infinitely more ridiculous here than it is either in England or France; and to the Italians themselves I have done the same, as much as good breeding and the Inquisition allowed me to declare. Whoever is so stupid as to consider no farther in religion than outward show, will be in danger to be charmed by this practised here. Their churches, the musick, illuminations and scenes delight the ear and the eye beyond our operas. But whoever reflects that religion is intended for something more solid, will never be

[1] Vernon to same, Aug. 18, in *Vernon Corr.* vol. III, pp. 264–6.

satisfyed with this bigottry and superstition, calculated only for outward appearance, and not in the least to correct human passions, and make a man better.[1]

This letter fully answered the purpose for which it was designed. Its contents were soon widely known, and Somers was able to assure Shrewsbury that it "had a very good effect", and gave "great satisfaction to several who (without any reasonable ground) were under wrong impressions".[2] But if the letter eased matters for Shrewsbury in England it created difficulties for him in Rome. Such outspoken strictures upon the Roman Catholic religion as he had expressed in that manifesto were not politic in a resident in the Papal States. Accordingly he decided to go to Venice, which, as he had expressed it, was the only place in Italy less popish than Rome. His health had greatly improved during the past three years. "I have had that benefit, by this warm climate," he wrote to Hill, the English resident in Turin, "that every relapse has been less than the former; and the bleeding has these last two times stopped of itself, without any astringent remedies which it never would do in England."[3] His hope "that I should have heard no more of the illness of my breast" had not indeed been realised, but in a letter written to the same correspondent seven months later he was able to say, "I have been so well this summer and autumn, that I hope I shall be able to continue of returning home this spring".[4] It was not, however, until the end of April that he finally left Rome. The delay was partly due to a return of his old complaint, which lasted till the middle of March, and to reluctance to remove to a less kindly climate, but probably it was due still more to reluctance to leave the Countess Adelaide.

[1] Shrewsbury to Talbot, Bishop of Oxford, Sept. 27 (n.s.), 1704, in *Ballard MSS.* (Bodl.), vol. x, no. 181.

[2] Somers to Shrewsbury, Oct. 5, Dec. 1704, in Coxe, pp. 644–7.

[3] April 12, 1704, in *Corr. of Richard Hill* (ed. W. Blackley, 1845), pt ii, p. 737.   [4] Nov. 29, 1704, in *ibid.* p. 751.

That lady had had an offer of marriage from a Frenchman in October 1703, and Shrewsbury had advised her as a friend not to decline it.[1] Whether one reason for the Countess's refusal was that she even then entertained higher hopes, and when it was that Shrewsbury first fell in love with her, it is impossible to say. She was a Roman Catholic and had a daughter who had taken the veil. Evidently she and the Duke used to have religious discussions. One day she told him a story of how Lord Clermont, falling desperately ill and being converted to the Roman Church, received extreme unction and immediately afterwards began to make a wonderful recovery, "which worked so much on his father, Lord Middleton, that from a most inveterate heretic he turned good Catholic".[2] But Shrewsbury succeeded in converting the Countess to Protestantism some months before he proposed marriage to her, "upon my lending her a Bible in the vulgar tongue, where she was infinitely surprised to find so little of her old religion".[3] It was apparently on April 24, 1705, that he asked the Countess to marry him. Three days later he set out from Rome, following his cousin the Earl of Cardigan, who had left for Venice some months before. Travelling by way of Spoleto, Loretto, Ancona, Rimini, and Ravenna, he arrived at his destination on May 3.[4]

The change did not suit him. Within a week he was laid up with an attack of gout and threatened with a return of his old trouble. "I have been here but few days", he wrote despondingly to Stepney the English representative in Vienna, "and found so moist and cold climate that I am at present laid up with the gout in my knee and feel some so ugly symptoms in my breast, that if my legs were at liberty, I think I should be inclined to use them to get out of this

[1] *Journal*, Nov. 23, 1703, in *Buccleuch MSS.* vol. ii, pt ii, p. 773.
[2] *Ibid.*, April 13, 1703, in *ibid.* pp. 767–8.
[3] In *ibid.* p. 711.
[4] *Ibid.*, April 13, 1703, in *ibid.* pp. 788–9.

water-rat country."[1] Soon the threatened attack of hæmorrhage developed and proved the worst he had had since his arrival in Italy. Shrewsbury cordially detested Venice. "It is", he wrote in his journal, "the only city I was ever in where I declare I could not live, for there is no place to walk and take the air, and I think the air moist and unwholesome."[2] He stayed there during May and June, paying occasional visits to Padua and Vicenza. On July 5 he set out for Augsburg. Crossing the Venetian plain, he traversed the Tyrol as far as Trent, then turned north up the valley of the Etsch through Bozen and Brixen, and over the Brenner Pass to Innsbruck. Thence he made his way over the Bavarian highlands and down the valley of the Lech to his destination, which he reached eleven days after leaving Venice,[3] and lodged in the house where Marshal Marsin had stayed. At Augsburg he was more despondent than ever about his health.

"I have had a tedious journey of eleven days", he wrote to Hill, "being willing to try if that softly pace would agree better with me than the violenter motion of the post, to which some attributed my relapse at Venice; but it has proved all one; for as soon as I came into the mists and cold air of the Tyrol mountains, I began to bleed, and will stay here some days to patch up a crazy corpse I am so weary of, that I hardly think it worth the while any more to mend."[4]

As he put it in another letter, "The misty cold mountains of the Tirol had the same effect...as the stinking fogs of the marshes of Venice".[5] The next month was one of misery, the hæmorrhage being succeeded by gout, and the gout by

[1] May 9, 1705, R. Warner, *Epistolary Curiosities* (2nd series, Bath, 1818), p. 134.
[2] July 5, in *Buccleuch MSS.* vol. II, pt ii, p. 790. Cf. Warner, pp. 136–8; *Hill's Corr.* pt ii, p. 754.
[3] *Journal*, July 5–16, in *Buccleuch MSS.* vol. II, pt ii, pp. 790–1.
[4] *Hill's Corr.* pt ii, p. 755.
[5] Warner, p. 139.

another attack of hæmorrhage. He complained dismally that he was "spitting up his lungs, not to say his life".[1] Once more he was reduced to using spirits of vitriol, to which he had not had to have recourse for the last two years.

Despite his illness Shrewsbury was anxious to be married as soon as possible. Now that he was in a Protestant city there was no longer any obstacle. Accordingly on August 28 he wrote to the Countess asking her to join him. On September 18 she arrived in Augsburg. The following day she formally declared herself a Protestant before one of the senators of the city "in a manner that gave full satisfaction as to religion", and on the 20th, after she had made a similar statement to a Lutheran minister, the latter performed the marriage ceremony at Shrewsbury's lodging in the presence of the senator, two patricians, the owner of the house and the Duke's servants.[2] The next day Shrewsbury wrote to Marlborough informing him of his marriage. With the exception of his uncle Sir John Talbot, Marlborough was apparently the only one of his friends to whom he mentioned the matter. He told Talbot that he knew his wife's "being without fortune and a foreigner would make his choice censured by everybody". In a formal communication to Delafaye, a clerk in the office of the Secretary of State, he wrote in almost an apologetic tone about his marriage "to a widdow lady I was acquainted with at Rome, who tho an Italian I am throwly persuaded will be not only a good wife, but a good Protestant". He wished people would be contented not to judge "till they might do it upon grounds that were reasonable".[3] But this they were

[1] *Ibid.* p. 140.
[2] *Journal*, Aug. 28–Oct. 1, in *Buccleuch MSS.* vol. II, pt ii, pp. 791–2.
[3] Shrewsbury to Talbot, Sept. 21, Oct. 8, in *ibid.* pp. 710–11; same to Delafaye, Sept. 21, in Add. MSS. 32,686 (*Newcastle Papers*, vol. I), f. 6. A copy of this letter is printed in *Bath MSS.* vol. I, pp. 76–7, where it is described as being from Shrewsbury to Robert Harley, but it is clearly only a transcript of the letter to Delafaye.

not prepared to do. The news of the Duke's marriage roused equal surprise and curiosity, and the wildest stories were spread abroad in order to account for his extraordinary choice of a wife.[1]

On October 10, Shrewsbury and his bride left Augsburg for Frankfort. Crossing the Danube at Donauwörth, they visited the battlefield of Blenheim, and travelling slowly on through Nuremberg they reached Frankfort on the 16th. This time the journey was not followed by a relapse, and Shrewsbury decided to push on to Holland and so home to England. But his progress continued to be very leisurely, and it was a month before he started on the next stage. During the stay in Frankfort the Duchess received instruction from a French Calvinist minister and made a new recantation. At the beginning of November he received a visit from Marlborough, who had for some time past been anxious to see him in order to persuade him to accept some office on his return and to support the war policy of the Ministry.[2] It appears from a letter which Marlborough wrote to Godolphin that he was not unhopeful of persuading Shrewsbury, but he had to go to Vienna to arrange plans for the next campaign without having received a definite promise.[3]

On November 12, Shrewsbury and his wife sailed down the Main to Mainz; thence down the Rhine through Coblentz and Cologne, where they were joined by the Duchess's brother, the Marquis Paleotti, to Rotterdam and The Hague. In Holland they remained for several weeks, seeing much of Marlborough, who arrived on December 14. The two dukes constantly discussed the general political situation at home

---

[1] See Onslow's note to Burnet, vol. II, p. 546, where it is suggested that Shrewsbury was forced to marry the Countess "by a furious brother of hers, with whom the Duke did not care to quarrel". But Shrewsbury did not meet the brother till six weeks after his marriage. See *Life and Character*, pp. 16–18.

[2] *Journal*, Nov. 1, 1705, in *Buccleuch MSS.* vol. II, pt ii, p. 794.

[3] Coxe, p. 659.

and abroad, Shrewsbury receiving from the other much confidential information. Departure for England was delayed owing to its dependence on Marlborough's convenience, which governed the movements of the convoy. The fleet at length sailed on January 7, 1706, and reached Deptford three days later.[1] After an absence of just five years and two months Shrewsbury was once more upon his native soil.

[1] *Journal*, Jan. 1–7, 1705–6, in *Buccleuch MSS.* vol. II, pt ii, pp. 798–9.

CHAPTER VIII

Alliance with the Tories

At the time of Shrewsbury's reappearance in England, Queen Anne's Ministry was essentially a Tory Administration. It is true that Nottingham, the zealous High Church leader, had been displaced as Secretary of State for the Northern Department by the more moderate Robert Harley in May 1704, and that the Whig William Cowper had succeeded Sir Nathan Wright as Lord Keeper in October 1705; but the great Whig chiefs, the Junto, were excluded, despite the fact that there was stronger support for the war policy of the Government among the Whigs than among the Tories (the latter maintaining that we should have confined our energies to the sea and not entered the land war as a principal), and despite the fact that the General Election of 1705 had been a great success for the Whigs. It was after that event that Cowper had been introduced into the Ministry. At the same time Addison was made Under-Secretary of State. Godolphin was appreciating more and more his dependence upon Whig support, but he was still reluctant to admit into the Government the dominating personalities of the other camp.

Latterly Shrewsbury had been in communication with members of both parties. He had been in correspondence with Marlborough, who was of course a personal friend, since the battle of Blenheim,[1] and he had latterly been in personal touch with him. He had refused to commit himself to the suggestion that he should join the Administration, but he was thoroughly in sympathy with the Ministers' war policy.

---

[1] Cf. Coxe, pp. 636–9. See also letters to Godolphin, in Add. MSS. 28,056, ff. 17–22, 220–1.

"I think", he wrote in his journal just before leaving for England, "we in England can never be contented, and ought to spend to the last rather than lose our Mediterranean trade, and the West Indies also, if Philip remain King of them, though the French will promise a free trade".[1] Shrewsbury had also been in correspondence with Halifax. That redoubtable Whig stalwart had written to him in the previous July, when the tide had begun to turn in favour of the party, legitimately boasting that the storm was over—he was thinking particularly of the impeachment of the Junto at the end of the previous reign—the winds were beginning to fall and the heavens to clear up. Their vessels had proved sound, not full of leaks, as their enemies had maliciously pretended and their friends ridiculously believed. "Your grace", he went on, "is come at a time that even we are well used, and you may expect all the caresses and courtship that you can desire."[2] The tone of the letter suggests that Halifax regarded Shrewsbury as a fair-weather pilot only. Hence the stress laid on the present serenity of the elements. The caution of the reply which he received from Shrewsbury could only confirm him in his diagnosis. "As sunshine follows clouds", wrote the Duke with sage sententiousness, "so clouds do, in England, as surely succeed sunshine. It is a climate so inconstant, that whoever will be active in it, must provide against all weathers". He had not the strength either of mind or body to resist such hardships. "I beg my friends will permit me to be an insignificant cypher, rather than a bad figure."[3] Halifax was plainly disgusted by such faint-heartedness. He confessed that Shrewsbury's letter had put him out of humour.

"I am", he pursued, "quite out of conceit of England, since the air of the country, and the temper of the people, will not suffer

[1] *Buccleuch MSS.* vol. ii, pt ii, p. 796.
[2] Halifax to Shrewsbury, July 24, 1705, in Coxe, pp. 652–3.
[3] Shrewsbury to Halifax, Aug. 24, in *ibid.* pp. 653–4.

one to live here, that any other country would be proud of. I confess, I always thought that there was too much fine silver in your grace's temperament: had you been made of a coarser alloy, you had been better fitted for public use. Your mind is too tender, you lay too much weight on the rude, unmannerly treatment every body meets with in England, and you suffer too much from the idle, ill-natured stories you hear."[1]

Could Shrewsbury's constitutional reluctance to face the rough and tumble of politics be overcome now that he had had over five years' holiday from it? At first it seemed that it might; that he could be prevailed upon to accept the office of Lord Chamberlain. He was the friend of Marlborough, whose confidence carried with it that of the Lord Treasurer; he was personally most acceptable to the Queen, who was susceptible to such charm of manner as he admittedly possessed, and he was well received by her when he appeared at Court. Shrewsbury took a house near St James's and here he was soon visited by Godolphin and most of the other ministers.[2] But while the Lord Treasurer and his principal associates were anxious to have Shrewsbury as a colleague, the Whigs, whose views they realised more and more they must now consider, though they continued to "live in civilities" with him on his return, were very suspicious. They suspected him of having advised William III to transfer the balance of power in the Cabinet from them to the Tories; they suspected him of having left England in order to avoid any ill-consequences that might follow upon the publication of the Partition Treaties; and, according to the Duchess of Marlborough, they "thought that his long stay at Rome, and his strange marriage there, gave them good reason to be

[1] Halifax to Shrewsbury, undated, in Coxe, p. 655.
[2] Luttrell, Jan. 5, 1705/6, vol. VI, p. 2. One strong motive for visiting the Duke was curiosity to see his wife. Cf. Lady Pye to Abigail Harley, May 4: "She [a Mrs Key] told me a great deal of Lady Shrewsbury and such stories as made me very sick of her Grace. But with all that the ladies now begin to admire her and even the graver sort..." (*Portland MSS.* vol. IV, p. 300).

jealous of him, till he had been tried for some time, whether he still adhered to the principles of the Revolution". Marlborough and Godolphin "studied to overcome the jealousies that the Whigs had of him", but in vain.[1]

It was not long before Shrewsbury left London for his estates at Grafton and Eyford. Thence he paid a visit to Bath, after which he settled down on a new estate which he had bought in Oxfordshire—Heythrop—and watched the building there, on plans which he had brought with him from Italy, of "a most noble palace...which is certainly one of the best and noblest in England".[2] As Heythrop was near Woodstock, where Blenheim Palace was being built for Marlborough, Shrewsbury saw something of the latter whenever he happened to be in England. During the session of 1706–7 he entrusted Marlborough with his proxy in the House of Lords, observing that he could not recollect that they had ever differed.[3] Both were animated by antipathy to the Junto. Indeed three or four years later Harley informed Cowper "that the D. of Marlb. being at D. Shrews: house in Oxfordshire, soon after his comeing into Engl: had complain'd to D. Shrews: of his own and the Q. uneasiness at the tyranny of the Juncto,— desired the D. of Shrews: assistance, which he promised; that D. Shrews. self, Harct.[4] and St. John, etc. thereon went into proper measures".[5] Whatever the "proper measures" referred to may have been, they were not effective, and in June 1707 we find Marlborough writing to his wife about Shrewsbury and saying, "I do not think he can ever be of much use, but it is much better to have mankind pleased than angry; for a great many that can do no good, have it always

[1] Burnet, vol. II, p. 546; *Life and Character*, p. 18; *Private Correspondence of the Duchess of Marlborough* (2 vols. 1838), vol. II, p. 133.
[2] *Portland MSS.* vol. IV, p. 329; *Life and Character*, pp. 18–19.
[3] Dec. 26, 1706, in Coxe, p. 660.
[4] Sir Simon Harcourt, later Lord Chancellor.
[5] *Cowper's Diary*, Sept. 10, 1710, p. 43.

in their power to vex and do hurt".[1] Later on in the same year Shrewsbury was approached by John Sheffield, Duke of Buckinghamshire, who first as Earl of Mulgrave, then as Marquis of Normanby, had played an ambiguous part in the party conflicts of the previous reign, but had been mainly on the Tory side. Buckinghamshire now suggested that Shrewsbury should join with him in an attempt to effect an alliance between the moderate men of both factions. Shrewsbury in reply agreed that nothing was more desirable for the good of the people, but did not see how any one so retired from public life as he was[2] could be useful in bringing it about without changing the whole course of his life, with which he was so perfectly well contented as to be very unwilling to alter it.[3]

Two months later any chance of such a combination of moderates as Buckinghamshire had suggested and Shrewsbury approved entirely vanished. It was discovered that a clerk in Harley's employ in the Secretary of State's office, named William Greg, had been guilty of treasonable practices. Grave suspicions were thrown upon his master; these were proved to be without foundation, but Harley had certainly been guilty of gross carelessness and neglect, and so great was the scandal that he was forced to retire. With him there elected to go his brilliant friend, the hope of the Tory party, Henry St John, and Harcourt, the Attorney-General. These resignations drove Marlborough and Godolphin into the arms of the Junto. The successes of the Whigs at the polls

---

[1] *Corr. of Duchess of Marlborough,* vol. I, pp. 81–2.

[2] Shrewsbury had taken his seat in the Upper House on Jan. 8, 1706, and until the middle of March attended almost all the sittings, being placed on various Committees, and acting as one of the Managers for the Lords in a Conference with the Commons on the Militia Bill on Mar. 13. See *L.J.* vol. XVIII, pp. 60–159 (*passim*).

[3] Buckingham to Shrewsbury, Nov. 29 and Dec. 6, Shrewsbury to Buckingham, Dec. 8, 1707, in *Buccleuch MSS.* vol. II, pt ii, pp. 718–20.

in the General Election of the following May only served still further to increase their dependence upon their uncongenial allies. In the autumn Wharton became Lord-Lieutenant of Ireland and Somers Lord President of the Council. The triumph of the Junto was complete.[1]

Shrewsbury was not included in the reconstituted Ministry. His alienation from the Junto and Marlborough's and Godolphin's alliance with them meant that he was left isolated. The Ministerial crisis had the effect of rousing him to take action. In March he left Heythrop for London, and the result of the visit was a decision to throw in his lot with the disgraced Secretary of State. The Duchess of Marlborough suggested that he was dissatisfied with Godolphin because Lady Shrewsbury asked him for a pension for her husband and was refused it.[2] However that may be, Shrewsbury became more and more deeply involved in intrigues against the Government and those intrigues ended eventually in every Whig being driven out of office. He was valuable to the new Opposition. As the Duchess of Marlborough grudgingly admitted, he "had acquired a sort of reputation for wisdom which added a weight and reputation" to their proceedings.[3]

While in London Shrewsbury had frequent interviews with Harley, and he also saw Harcourt and Harley's other allies. When he returned to Heythrop Harley visited him there; in the winter of 1708-9 he was again in London, and in consultation with Harley. Hitherto since his return to England Shrewsbury had refrained from attendance at Court;[4] but now at Harley's desire he began to attend. Harley was anxious, as he afterwards expressed it, that the

[1] Burnet, vol. II, pp. 494-7, 515-16.
[2] *Corr. of Duchess of Marlborough*, vol. II, pp. 133-4.
[3] *Ibid.* p. 137.
[4] See *ibid.* pp. 247-8; Coxe, p. 662; Brit. Mus., *Egerton MSS.*, 1695, f. 41.

Duke should "give Mrs Morley right impressions", and he realised that Shrewsbury's charm of manner was likely to make him *persona grata* with the Queen. The task of giving Mrs Morley "right impressions" was not very difficult, for she was prepared to receive them. The domineering temper of the Duchess of Marlborough was at last overcoming the endurance of her long-suffering friend, and her place in the royal affections and the royal confidence was being usurped by Mrs Masham, the ally of Harley and the Opposition.

The Opposition was also being assisted by war weariness. The brilliant victories of Marlborough at Ramillies and of Eugene at Turin in 1706 had been followed by the disastrous defeat of our forces in Spain at the battle of Almanza on April 25, 1707. On July 11, 1708, Marlborough achieved one of his greatest triumphs at Oudenarde, and this was followed by the capture of the great fortress of Lille. But victories no longer produced the same popular enthusiasm as in the earlier stages of the war, and the financial burden was exceedingly heavy. The terrible losses sustained in the Pyrrhic victory at Malplaquet on September 11, 1709 and the absence of any tangible results apart from the fall of Mons reduced the value of Marlborough's prestige as an asset to the Ministry, while their peace negotiations in 1709 and 1710 were doomed to failure by their arrogant and preposterous insistence that Louis XIV should co-operate in driving his grandson Philip out of Spain.

Shrewsbury was convinced of the desirability of coming to terms with France. Ever "of a pacifick temper, no man of war",[1] he watched the progress of the war with nervous anxiety. It was clear that there was little chance of serious efforts for peace being made either by Godolphin and Marlborough or by the Whigs, and this fact brought Shrewsbury closer than ever to his new-found Tory allies, who stood for a peace policy. It is perhaps the key to his subsequent

[1] *Memoirs of Public Transactions*, p. 68.

conduct. He was convinced that "the generality of the nation long for peace", and equally convinced that in the present political situation they could not hope to get it.[1] Meanwhile the efforts of Harley and his supporters, aided by some discontented Whigs, notably the Dukes of Somerset and Argyll, the latter an inveterate foe of Marlborough, were unrelaxing. The part which was being played by Shrewsbury in these manœuvres received scant attention. The Whigs had long ceased to take any notice of his doings, and at first Marlborough and Godolphin were not disposed to attach much importance to his association with Harley.

But Shrewsbury's hostility to the Government was clearly revealed in the late autumn of 1709 by his ceasing to call upon Lady Marlborough, as he had been in the habit of doing frequently during his residences at Heythrop—according to her as often as twice a week. It became clear to him that if he was to retain his influence at Court and to assist Harley to obtain office he must sever connection with the discarded favourite.

"He did not, indeed, after this enter into the railing part", wrote that lady; "but still kept up the decorum of speaking well and civilly of the Duke and Duchess of Marlborough and Lord Godolphin. Yet his Duchess made court visibly to Mrs. Masham, and ran in with the popular cry of censuring and railing at the Duchess of Marlborough, as the most grateful topic at Court in this critical juncture. In the midst of which, she would sometimes in proper places run out in themes of high civility and compliment which were known too well to be such as the Duke had taught her in order to hide the part they both were acting."[2]

Still more convincing proof of Shrewsbury's present attitude was forthcoming when Parliament assembled. He had already agreed to give Harley his support in the House of Lords as soon as any question of importance should arise.

---

[1] Shrewsbury to Harley, Nov. 3, 1709, in *Bath MSS.* vol. I, p. 197.
[2] *Corr. of Duchess of Marlborough*, vol. II, pp. 134–7.

It was not long before it came. Shrewsbury arrived in London on December 2 for the Parliamentary session. A month before, on November 5, Dr Henry Sacheverell had preached his famous sermon in St Paul's Cathedral before the Lord Mayor and Aldermen of the City of London asserting the doctrine of non-resistance, violently attacking Latitudinarians and Dissenters, and "the crafty insidiousness of...crafty Volpones". Godolphin, being only too sensitively aware that his nickname was Volpone, was so stung by this affront as to insist, despite wiser counsels, upon the impeachment of the offending divine, and thereby played into the hands of his adversaries.

The trial opened on February 27, 1710. Already the London crowds as they surged round the Queen on her way to Westminster Hall in a sedan-chair, and round the accused on his way in his elaborate coach, had made their sentiments abundantly clear. The Government obtained a verdict of guilty by sixty-nine votes to fifty-two, but the extreme leniency of the sentence—merely suspension from preaching for three years—was virtually a confession of defeat. The Whigs incidentally secured a solemn and splendid re-affirmation of the doctrines underlying the Revolution in the speeches of Walpole, King, Lechmere and the other managers for the impeachment; but for Godolphin, who cared nothing for the principles of the Whigs, the result had not a single redeeming feature. The trial did but serve to reveal the strength of the Opposition. Shrewsbury came definitely into the open in voting in favour of Sacheverell. In debate on the all-important first article of the impeachment he declared that although he had taken as great a share as any in the Revolution and would go as far as any to vindicate the memory of the country's late defender, and although he personally considered the Church of England perfectly safe under her Majesty's administration, nevertheless he could not approve the making the contrary opinion a high crime

and misdemeanour.[1] To Marlborough Shrewsbury's conduct
was an unmistakable indication that the Queen's sympathies
were with the Opposition. His inveterate caution would not
have allowed him to do such a thing had he not known he
"made his court to the Queen" by the action he was taking.
Still he was amazed that Shrewsbury could think it possible
for the Tories to be strong enough to ruin the Whigs in
conjunction with the Lord Treasurer and himself.[2]

Events speedily shewed that Shrewsbury's appreciation of
the political situation was much more sagacious, or at least
much better informed, than Marlborough's. Emboldened
by the expressions of loyalty to the Crown and also to the
Church which the Sacheverell trial had evoked, Anne was
prepared to act strongly and Shrewsbury, whose reluctance
to take office had been completely overcome, was the medium
employed. On the prorogation of Parliament in April,
Godolphin retired to the congenial surroundings of his
racing-stables at Newmarket. Availing herself of the absence
of her two principal advisers—Marlborough was on the
Continent—the Queen on April 14 sent for the Marquis of
Kent and requested him to resign his place as Lord Chamberlain. Kent made no difficulty, his compliance being rewarded
with a dukedom. Shrewsbury was at once appointed in his
place.[3] The sole intimation vouchsafed to any of her Ministers
by the Queen was a curt note to Godolphin, written a few
hours before Shrewsbury's entrance upon his new duties, to
announce the *fait accompli*. Having heard, she said, of
Shrewsbury's willingness to serve her, she was very glad to

[1] Luttrell, Mar. 18, 1710, vol. VI, p. 558; Cobbett's *Parliamentary History*, vol. VI, col. 883.
[2] Marlborough to the Duchess of Marlborough, April 4, in Coxe, *Life of Marlborough* (3 vols. Bohn), vol. III, p. 27.
[3] Luttrell, April 15, May 23, vol. VI, pp. 570, 585; Burnet, vol. II, p. 546; A. Boyer, *Life and Reign of Queen Anne* (1722), pp. 470–1. Two days later he was sworn of the Privy Council (Doyle, *Official Baronage*, vol. III, p. 325).

accept him, "having a very good opinion of him, and believing he may be of great use in these troublesome times". She hoped the change would be approved by Godolphin.[1]

It met of course with his strongest disapprobation. Both the Queen's choice of her new Minister and the method of his appointment meant that the Lord Treasurer was being deliberately flouted. If this kind of thing could happen he no longer enjoyed the Queen's confidence, was no longer her chief adviser in anything but name. He at once wrote a strong protest in reply. While professing to have no personal ill-feeling against Shrewsbury—"there was no man", he said, "of whose capacity he had a better impression or with whom he had lived more easily for above twenty years"—he urged that the Duke's appointment would have a bad effect upon the allies and upon the progress of the war.[2] The day after he had written the letter he started off for London. On arrival he at once had an interview with the Queen. Her reception was not at all reassuring.[3] But Godolphin's love for office, for the routine of business as well as the direction of policy, was as great as Shrewsbury's aversion. He had no intention of resigning despite this second rebuff, and his determination to remain was only strengthened by interviews with his Whig colleagues. They were all resolved to retain office and, if possible, avert a dissolution until the existing Parliament had run its full course of three years.

The Whig Ministers disliked Shrewsbury's appointment at least as much as Godolphin did. He was, as Lady Marlborough quaintly expressed it, "a man that t'other day they would have thrown over the top of the house if anybody had

---

[1] Queen Anne to Godolphin, in Coxe, *Life of Marlborough*, vol. III, p. 61.
[2] Duchess of Marlborough's *Account of her Conduct*, pp. 248–53; Boyer, *op. cit.* pp. 470–1.
[3] Godolphin to Duchess of Marlborough, in Coxe, *Life of Marlborough*, vol. III, p. 63.

proposed his coming into employment".[1] Curiously enough, they were unable at first to credit that the appointment could have been made entirely without Godolphin's concurrence, and they suspected the Lord Treasurer of having connived at the introduction into the Ministry of one whom they regarded as a traitor to the Whig cause. Probably the leaders were soon disabused of this complete misconception, but it was a long time before the rank and file were disillusioned.[2]

Shrewsbury's appointment took everybody excepting Harley and his associates completely by surprise. It "astonished the whole nation, stocks fell, the Duke of Marlborough abroad, everything in confusion".[3] Burnet's comment that it "gave a great alarm" is an altogether inadequate description of the sensation which it created, and if Ministers themselves were blind as to what it betokened, the general impression was that "a total change of the Ministry would quickly follow". Some assumed that it was intended to give Shrewsbury the chief place in the Cabinet. Here they were mistaken, but they were quite right in attributing the appointment to "a secret management between him and Harley with the new favourite".[4]

Meanwhile the cause of all this disturbance was pursuing a course of action which made confusion in the Ministerial camp worse confounded. Partly because he was perturbed by the storm he had raised and at the fall in the price of stocks, which was a very unflattering comment upon his appointment, and partly because he wished to allay the suspicions of his colleagues, Shrewsbury was profuse in assurances to Godolphin of his adherence to the principles he had always

---

[1] *Corr. of Duchess of Marlborough*, vol. i, p. 324.

[2] Sunderland to Duchess of Marlborough, April 1710, in *Corr. of Duchess of Marlborough*, vol. i, p. 301; Count Maffei to Marlborough, in Coxe, *Life of Marlborough*, vol. iii, p. 64.

[3] *Life and Character*, p. 20.

[4] Burnet, vol. ii, p. 546; Foxcroft, *Supplement to Burnet*, p. 427.

professed.[1] Soon after the latter returned to town he received a visit from the Duke. He wrote at once to acquaint Marlborough of the substance of their conversation. Marlborough had been amazed at the courage of Shrewsbury in rushing into a certain storm in company with "the greatest knaves in the nation". He was now informed that Shrewsbury had been "extremely full of professions" to him, to Lady Marlborough, and to Godolphin.

"By whatever door he came in", Godolphin reported him as saying, "it was always with an intention and a desire to live well with us three, and not only so, but with all others we would have him live with, not doubting, he added, that it would have been done much sooner, if you and I had been entirely masters of it; and that, perhaps, it was as well for us that it had happened in this manner, considering the jealous humour of the Whigs." "His grace", went on Godolphin, "protested most solemnly to me that he never had spoken one word to Abigail in his life; and then he said the only sore place was the difference betwixt Lady Marlborough and the Queen, and that all the rest might presently be set right. This, he said, was going a great way, for the first conversation, but that he desired to use all freedom with me."[2]

This was only the first of a long series of interviews with the Lord Treasurer at which Shrewsbury put forward the same arguments.[3] He also wrote personally to Marlborough what the recipient described as a "very kind" letter.[4] At the

[1] Maynwaring, a correspondent of the Duchess of Marlborough, writes to her on April 21: "You are certainly in the right that 28 (Shrewsbury) will never be true to the Whigs....I think if he declare himself a Tory, there are so many secret arrows that may be shot at him, that he will soon be beaten down, and if he pretends to act with the Whigs, it will be so insincere and awkward an alliance that it will not last; so that in either case his reign will be but short..." (*Corr. of Duchess of Marlborough*, vol. I, pp. 305–6).

[2] Godolphin to Marlborough, April 20, 1710, in *Corr. of Duchess of Marlborough*, vol. II, pp. 421–2; Coxe, *Life of Marlborough*, vol. III, pp. 66–7.

[3] *Ibid.* p. 70.

[4] Marlborough to Godolphin, May 5/16, in *Corr. of Duchess of Marlborough*, vol. II, p. 440.

same time he continued to assure the Whigs that "whatever reasons he had to come into the Ministry then he would never depart from his principles as an Englishman and an asserter of the rights and liberties of the country ".[1] No doubt Shrewsbury honestly conceived that his political principles were the same as they had always been, but general assurances to this effect did not explain his equivocal conduct in acting with Harley. When he was told soon after his appointment that it was generally said that he was opening the door for a Tory Ministry he retorted peevishly that "he opened no door but what he could shut when he pleased". Marlborough shrewdly commented on this that in Holland if a man cut a dyke he did not know how much water he might not let in and he certainly could not stop it if he would.[2]

When Shrewsbury had been in office for a few weeks and nothing further happened of an ominous nature both Marlborough and Godolphin were inclined to take heart. Marlborough ventured to believe that Shrewsbury's natural temper would lead him to give moderate counsels at any rate for a time,[3] and Godolphin was persuaded "Shrewsbury's inclination goes with us".[4] But while they were able to express such views about Shrewsbury himself they could not help being apprehensive about the forces behind him, could not help suspecting that Harley and his allies were responsible for the appointment and that the step would never have been taken had they not been "ready to go into all the extravagances imaginable".[5]

[1] Sunderland to Duchess of Marlborough, April 27, in *ibid.* vol. I, p. 309; *Life and Character*, p. 21.
[2] *Life and Character*, p. 21.
[3] Marlborough to Godolphin, May 5 (n.s.), in Coxe, *Life of Marlborough*, vol. III, p. 68.
[4] Godolphin to Marlborough, April 17, May 16, in *ibid.* pp. 66, 69.
[5] Marlborough to Godolphin, May 5 (n.s.), in *ibid.* p. 68.

That these apprehensions were only too well justified was proved only a few days later when Shrewsbury gave Godolphin very clearly to understand that his friends had begun to press for further alterations in the Ministry, and in particular for the removal of the Earl of Sunderland, who had been Secretary of State for the Southern Department since December 1706. Sunderland, the son of the statesman who had played so ambiguous a part at the time of the Revolution and who had succeeded in obtaining so much influence with William III, was the youngest member of the Whig Junto, but, if only owing to the fact that he was son-in-law to Marlborough, by no means the least influential. His blatancy in airing his republican ideas, and perhaps still more his want of courtly consideration for her made him anathema to Queen Anne. Godolphin was greatly taken aback by a suggestion which certainly did mean the break-up of the whole Ministry, and said that it would be quite intolerable to both Marlborough and himself. Shrewsbury apparently had not anticipated so positive a reply, though it is difficult to understand why he should have been surprised by it, and he hastened to say that for his part he would never press for anything that would be disagreeable to the Duke of Marlborough, and that he could live much better with Sunderland than with some of his friends, by which Godolphin understood him to refer to Orford, or possibly to Somers.[1]

For a month Godolphin and his Whig supporters were kept in suspense while the Queen and her secret advisers were searching for a satisfactory successor to Sunderland. The former were of opinion that only by securing Shrewsbury's support could they avert the threatened catastrophe. Some of them were under the impression that his influence was all-powerful with the Queen, and Walpole went so far as to

[1] Godolphin to Marlborough, May 12, in *Corr. of Duchess of Marlborough*, vol. II, p. 433; Marlborough to the Duchess, in Coxe, *Life of Marlborough*, vol. III, pp. 76–7.

term him "the only visible minister".[1] Godolphin, believing that it was only Shrewsbury's consideration for Marlborough which prevented the immediate execution of the plan, suggested that the latter should write to the Lord Chamberlain and make a strong bid for his assistance. Marlborough promptly complied. He endeavoured to persuade Shrewsbury of the bad effects which a Ministerial crisis in England would have upon our allies, and begged him "to reflect seriously on the present situation", and to give a "helping hand to prevent the mischiefs that are threatening us". He made a personal appeal, "I expect particularly, from your friendship to me, that you will be a support to Lord Sunderland, and from your zeal for the Queen's service and the public, that you will use your endeavours that the Parliament may die its natural death".[2]

Walpole saw more clearly than Godolphin the realities of the situation—namely, that whatever Shrewsbury's personal inclinations might be, it was Harley and not he that had the commanding influence with Anne. For himself he declined to believe that the Duke differed from Harley as much as he pretended, if he differed from him at all.[3] At last on June 13 the blow fell; Sunderland was dismissed. Harley and his associates had had some difficulty in finding a successor, but on the 15th Lord Dartmouth, a strong Tory, received the seals.

Not even yet were Godolphin and Marlborough convinced of the inevitability of their own downfall. They still hung on; they still hoped to be able to prevent a dissolution of Parliament;[4] they still looked to Shrewsbury, "the most reasonable

[1] Walpole to Marlborough, June 6, 1710, in Coxe, *Life of Marlborough*, vol. III, p. 86.
[2] Marlborough to Shrewsbury, June 19 (n.s.), in *ibid*. pp. 81–2.
[3] Walpole to Marlborough, June 2, in *ibid*. pp. 85–6.
[4] There was a general impression that Sunderland's dismissal would be followed by an early dissolution. Cf. *Wentworth Papers* (ed. J. J. Cartwright, 1875), p. 117.

of them all ", who had " so much credit with Mrs Morley ", to help them in this. But on June 17 Godolphin writes that Shrewsbury is pretty mysterious. Like the Jacobite Melfort who had been able to report "nothing of positiv " about the Duke, so Godolphin now could get nothing definite out of him. He was still engaged in the futile task of trying to reconcile Shrewsbury's protestations and his own pathetic persuasion of his attachment to himself with his conduct ever since the Sacheverell trial. Marlborough, on the other hand, had come to the conclusion that the only way in which to obtain any assistance from Shrewsbury was, as he put it, to " manage " him—that is to say, to play upon his " timorous nature ".[1] It was a useless suggestion, for there was now nothing for Shrewsbury to fear. Indeed he and Harley felt so sure of their ground that they were ready to proceed to their next and decisive step, the dismissal of the Lord Treasurer.

The Queen had very readily assented to the dismissal of Sunderland, but she had considerable scruples as to parting with the man who had controlled the national finances ever since her accession. She did not like his associates, but Godolphin had been a firm rock of security for Anne as well as for the nation and the allies. Could the country get on without him and could his place be adequately filled? In the preliminary discussions Shrewsbury took a prominent part. His lodgings as Lord Chamberlain were convenient for securing Harley secret access to the Queen—there were useful backstairs—and here also Shrewsbury himself had numerous clandestine interviews with prominent politicians in the second fortnight of July and the first week of August.[2]

[1] Letters of Godolphin, Marlborough, and the Duchess of Marlborough, June–August, in Coxe, *Life of Marlborough*, vol. III, pp. 83–4, 94–6, 117–18.

[2] Duke of Somerset to Harley, July 26, 30, in *Portland MSS.* vol. IV, pp. 552, 553; Peter Wentworth to Lord Raby, Aug. 4, in *Wentworth Papers*, pp. 128–9.

According to his biographer, before the Queen consented to the change[1] Shrewsbury was requested to give his opinion on three questions: whether the public credit could be maintained in the event of the retirement of Marlborough and Godolphin; whether the schemes proposed could be carried through without a dissolution or, alternatively, a dissolution take place without danger to the state, and a new Parliament be obtained "with due dispositions for the purposes laid down"; whether negotiations for peace could be opened without danger to the Government and with honour to her Majesty and her allies. "It is said the Duke answer'd all these in the affirmative and reason'd so clearly upon them to her Majesty, as gave her particular satisfaction, and was the great support to her mind in the distractions which follow'd."[2]

It was suggested that in the event of Anne's consenting to Godolphin's dismissal the Treasury should be put in commission and that Shrewsbury should be made First Commissioner. The Duke hastened to dissipate this idea. "I have", he wrote to Harley, "ten reasons, every one strong enough to hinder my doing it." He had no understanding of Treasury matters and no head for them.[3] Eventually it was decided that the position of First Commissioner should be taken by Earl Poulett, while Harley took the second place as Chancellor of the Exchequer. But to all intents and purposes the latter was head of the Commission and of the Administration. The formal dismissal of Godolphin took place on August 7.

[1] Both the Emperor and the Directors of the Bank of England brought strong pressure to bear upon her not to agree.

[2] *Memoirs of Public Transactions*, pp. 49–50.

[3] Shrewsbury to Harley, July 22, in *Bath MSS.* vol. 1, p. 198. Cf. Swift to Archbishop King, Sept. 9, in *Swift's Corr.* (ed. F. E. Ball, 6 vols. 1910–14), vol. 1, p. 195: "Mr Harley is looked upon as first Minister, and not my Lord Shrewsbury, and his Grace helps on the opinion, whether out of policy or truth".

For more than a month after this Harley and Shrewsbury held their hands. They had gone as far as they had originally intended to go and were anxious to retain several of the Whigs who still held office, in particular Somers, Cowper, and Walpole. Harley, when urging Cowper to remain, assured him that "a Whig game" was "intended at bottom". But in September it became apparent that they had reached a point at which it was impossible to halt. The Whigs were suspicious of the new leaders and anticipated that the forthcoming General Election would result in favour of themselves. The orthodox Tories, such as Atterbury, strongly objected to these overtures and the delay they occasioned, being anxious for a speedy dissolution which they were convinced would be to their advantage. For Harley and his associates the choice, therefore, seemed to be between satisfying the Tories and leaving themselves at the mercy of the Whigs. Once having come to this conclusion, they acted with a boldness which surprised even their own supporters. By the end of the year, as the result either of voluntary resignation or of dismissal, practically every Whig Minister had been displaced. In the room of Somers, Devonshire, Cowper, there entered Tories such as Rochester, Buckinghamshire, and St John. As Sunderland put it, Harley and Shrewsbury had in the end proved "determined to make thorough business of it".[1] But "as the Duke himself often said, not the Queen herself ever proposed, either to have carried the measures which they intended to pursue to such a length, or to have so generally and indeed universally changed hands from the Whigs to the Tories".[2] When he first started caballing with Harley, Shrewsbury himself certainly cannot have contemplated so complete a trans-

[1] Sunderland to Marlborough (n.d.), in Coxe, *Life of Marlborough*, vol. III, p. 137.
[2] *Memoirs of Public Transactions*, pp. 51–2; cf. Burnet, vol. II, pp. 553–4, and notes by Dartmouth.

formation. The fact remained that the man who had at one time been reckoned the Prince of the Whigs had been largely instrumental in bringing about the triumph of their enemies.[1]

[1] Cf. Maynwaring to Duchess of Marlborough (n.d.) (*Corr. of Duchess of Marlborough*, vol. I, p. 390). He refers elegantly to the "stinking ugly chambermaid, that has betrayed her only friend to a papist [Shrewsbury] in masquerade, that went to Italy to marry a common strumpet, and to the most arrant tricky knave [Harley] in all Britain, that no man alive believes any more than an Oates or a Fuller; to have all this plainly designed, and actually transacting, is what I will defy the Bishop of Salisbury, or whoever is best read in history, to show any parallel for".

CHAPTER IX

The Paris Embassy and the Irish Lord-Lieutenancy

After the ministerial crisis of 1710 we hear little of Shrews-bury for a time, and although it was possible for a French observer in January 1711 to speak of England being governed by Harley and Shrewsbury,[1] it appears that the latter allowed statesmen of more forceful personality such as Harley and St John to take the lead, and was content to fall into the background. There were, indeed, speculations as to the relative strength of coteries within the Ministry; suggestions that Harley and Shrewsbury led one and Rochester another,[2] that Sir Simon Harcourt, who became Lord Keeper on October 19, 1710, was a "creature" of Shrewsbury's;[3] and rumours in May 1711 that the Duke was to be made Master of the Horse and President of the Council. He remained, however, simply Lord Chamberlain.

The Duchess had hopes of being made a Lady of the Bed-chamber, but months passed and still her ambition was not gratified. The Dukes of Shrewsbury and Buckingham, writes Lord Berkeley of Stratton in March 1712, have been "of late much out of order...sick with fretting for their Ladies being refus'd to be of the bedchamber".[4] The Duchess was still exciting a great deal of interest and a great deal of scandal. In a little character-sketch of Shrewsbury, written shortly

[1] *Journal inédit de Jean-Baptiste Colbert, Marquis de Torcy* (ed. J. F. Masson, Paris, 1884), p. 348.
[2] But if so, says Peter Wentworth, Lord Raby's brother, Rochester seems "to be very great" with Shrewsbury and they often dine together (*Wentworth Papers*, p. 152).
[3] *Journal de Torcy*, Mar. 31, 1711, pp. 416–17.
[4] *Wentworth Papers*, pp. 174, 275.

before this by Lord Raby, the future Earl of Strafford, he speaks of him as having "married a Lady very poor and of an indifferent reputation; which lost him his credit amongst his old friends".[1] Indeed, to London society the marriage had seemed inexplicable before the Duchess appeared in London, and it seemed even more inexplicable afterwards. Her lack of education and her unconventional foreign ways made her seem very odd indeed. But if she was criticised she was not neglected, and when she established a *salon* it was a great success and excited the envy of the Duchess of Marlborough, who was dismissed from the royal household in January 1711. The latter, we are told in the following November, "intends to set up an assembly to out do the Duchess of Shrewsbury's".[2] Still, the language and conduct of the queer Italian offended against decorum. She scandalised society by talking openly about her bunions. She is, writes Lady Strafford after paying a visit to her Grace at this time, "more rediculouse in her talk than ever. She told all the company as they cam in that she was very much out of humour for she had things growing upon her tooes like thumbs that made her so lame she could not stirr".[3] But two days later Lady Strafford has a more serious story to tell. "Her Grace of Shrewsbury is now very coquet with Lord Ashburnham, and I think rather more so with Lord Starrs for she pull'd him about so in the Queen's lodging 'twas a shame to see her."[4] The same authority informs us a few months later how a friend of the Duchess's named Colonel Murray arrived in town from Scotland and how her Grace, espying him in the drawing-room, "ran to everybody she knew. 'Oh,' says she, 'here is Coll. Murry, the town says

[1] *Ibid.* p. 134. *Diary of Lady Cowper* (ed. S. Cowper, 1864), p. 8: "All the world knowing that her Brother had forced the Duke to marry her after an Intrigue together".
[2] *Wentworth Papers*, p. 208.
[3] Nov. 25, 1711, in *ibid.* p. 213.
[4] *Ibid.* p. 214.

I have an intreague with him, so I should not give him any of my pretty kind eyes, but I will and smile upon him two [*sic*]'".[1] The Duchess's behaviour was probably more seemly than that of a number of the censorious ladies who affected to be shocked by the levity of her tongue. She was good-humouredly content to be made a figure of fun. The story about herself which she liked best was one told shortly after the creation of the twelve new Tory Peers to serve party purposes at the opening of 1712. It ran that in conversation with Lady Oxford one day the Duchess remarked, "Madam, I and my Lord are so weary of talking Politicks, what are you and your lord?" Lady Oxford sighed and said she knew no Lord but the Lord Jehovah. "Oh dear! Madam," exclaimed the Duchess, "who is that? I believe 'tis one of the new titles, for I never heard of him before."[2] Queen Anne found the eccentricities of the Duchess of Shrewsbury highly diverting; no one since her husband's death had been able to make her laugh so much.[3] The Duchess "had a wonderful Art at entertaining and diverting People", admits Lady Cowper, though she adds that "she would sometimes excel the Bounds of Decency". She admits too that "she had a great Memory, had read a good deal, and spoke three Languages to Perfection".[4]

The all-consuming desire of the Tory ministers on their accession to office was the conclusion of peace with France. There is no doubt that one of Shrewsbury's principal motives in joining with the Tories was his anxiety that the war should be brought to a speedy termination. Informal feelers were put forward through the medium of the Abbé Gaultier, a French priest who was chaplain to Lady Jersey, and who had

[1] April 4, 1712, in *Wentworth Papers*, p. 283.
[2] Feb. 25, 1712, in *ibid.* p. 263.
[3] *MSS. of the Duke of Sutherland* (H.M.C. Rept. v), p. 190.
[4] *Lady Cowper's Diary*, pp. 8–9. Another reservation follows: "With all her Prate and Noise, she was a most cunning, designing Woman alive".

already been acting as a secret agent for the French Government in England. In July 1710 we find Louis XIV's great minister, the Marquis de Torcy, instructing Gaultier to get into touch with Shrewsbury as his protection will be very useful to him in London.[1] Before long Gaultier found himself able to report that Shrewsbury and Harley, who at present governed England, had agreed with Jersey that he (the Abbé) should be sent to Torcy to inform him "qu'ils etoient absolument resolus de finir promptement la guerre et de travailler sincerement de bonne foy et efficacement a faire la paix". He added that "pour des raisons d'etat et pour leur propre sureté ils n'osaient commencer aucun traité en Angleterre", and the Court of France was desired to renew peace conferences in Holland.[2] In this message we see the commencement of those clandestine negotiations behind the backs of our Dutch allies which have thrown so much discredit upon the Oxford Administration. There were indeed overt conferences in Holland which culminated in the Peace of Utrecht; but, so far as Great Britain was concerned, the all-important discussions were those conducted between London and Paris. Towards the Dutch the Government showed definite hostility; one of the main objects of Swift's brilliant defence of the peace policy of the Ministry, *The Conduct of the Allies*, was to throw odium upon them. The climax came, after the dismissal of Marlborough, in the celebrated "restraining orders" of May 1712 to his successor in command of our forces in Flanders, the Duke of Ormonde, which immobilised them and rendered it possible for Villars to recover the ground which he had lost to Marlborough in the previous campaign.

[1] *Mackintosh Collection*, in Add. MSS. 34,493, vol. VII, ff. 1, 2.
[2] *Mackintosh Coll.* in Add. MSS. 34,493, vol. VII, f. 48, Gaultier to Torcy, n.d. But the letter is clearly that of Dec. 23/Jan. 3, 1710/11, *Aff. Etr. Angl.* 230. See L. G. Wickham Legg, *Matthew Prior* (Cambridge, 1921), p. 146.

How far, if at all, Shrewsbury was implicated in the less creditable proceedings of the Government in their peace policy it is not possible to say. It was known abroad that he was keenly desirous of peace. Robethon, then Hanoverian envoy at The Hague, wrote in March 1711 to Bernstorff on the subject of the desire of the extreme Tories of the October Club that England should return to her former policy of detachment from Continental affairs, to say that all in England were weary of taxes and anxious for a speedy peace; that the Queen's ministers were of the same mind, and among them Shrewsbury.[1] While Marlborough was conducting the remarkable campaign of 1711, in which he drove a breach through Villars's vaunted *non plus ultra* lines, Shrewsbury was in correspondence with him, but we do not possess the replies which he made to the General's discussions of the European situation.[2] When Prince Eugene visited England as representative of the Court of Vienna to discuss military plans for the ensuing campaign, he arrived at a most inauspicious moment. The very day before he landed, January 1, 1712, the Ministry had completed the reinforcement of their party in the House of Lords by twelve new peers, with whose support they hoped to secure the approval of the peace preliminaries in that Chamber. The Prince's visit was most embarrassing to the ministers, who converted it into a mere social event. He attended the Duchess of Shrewsbury's assembly and dined more than once with the Duke.[3]

Ere this Shrewsbury had begun to entertain serious misgivings about the peace negotiations. These are expressed in a letter which he wrote to St John, now Viscount Bolingbroke, on August 25, 1711. "I continue still to mistrust the

[1] Robethon to Bernstorff, Mar. 21, 1711, in O. Klopp, *Der Fall des Hauses Stuart*, vol. XIV, p. 673.

[2] Marlborough's *Letters and Despatches, 1702–12* (ed. Sir G. Murray, 5 vols. 1845), vol. V, pp. 330–1, 420, 518.

[3] *Wentworth Papers*, pp. 246–7; Luttrell, vol. VI, p. 723.

sincerity of the French", he said. He feared that their proposals were "nothing but arts to sow division among us". The preliminaries in so far as they concerned our allies were so inequitable, he argued, that their publication would inevitably create serious trouble.

> Though we know her Majesty has a fair and just intention, with relation to the allies, yet in these papers little notice having been taken of their interests, neither in general words nor in particular, it may look suspiciously, as if her party had had no consideration but of what concerns Britain; and, having settled that with France, would leave her friends to shift for themselves at a general treaty, in which her partiality might be liable to suspicion, since she had beforehand stipulated for herself: this, as it is far from her design, so in all the papers that pass, a more than ordinary care should be taken to explain that to the world.

Some of the French proposals seemed to him "so dis-advantageous to the allies" that he thought no notice should be taken of them. "Looking over the papers again", he concluded, "I am more of opinion there is something in them looks so like bargaining for yourselves apart, and leaving your friends to shift at a general treaty, that I am confirmed the exposing such a paper...may create great jealousy and complaint from the allies."[1] This weighty pronouncement seems to have been efficacious, for something was done to make the suggested terms relating to the allies more acceptable.[2]

But Shrewsbury's disquietude does not appear to have been entirely allayed. Though he had been nominated as one of the plenipotentiaries for the signing of the preliminaries, they were actually signed by the two Secretaries of State only, St John and Lord Dartmouth. This in itself may mean nothing, but when the time arrived for the formal peace conferences to be opened at Utrecht he declined the suggestion

[1] *Bolingbroke's Corr.* vol. I, pp. 335–7.
[2] See Legg, *op. cit.* pp. 164, 166.

that he should be one of the plenipotentiaries there.[1] It is, moreover, significant that when the protracted peace negotiations were at last nearing their conclusion, and the Duc d'Aumont was accredited ambassador-extraordinary to the Court of St James's in November 1712, his instructions informed him that while Shrewsbury desired to see the end of the war his natural timidity, under the guise of prudence, often discovered to him imaginary dangers, and that the principal difficulties of this negotiation had had for their foundation the Duke's distrust of the clearest proposals made by the King of France, and that the more clearly they seemed to be advantageous to England the more thoroughly he thought they ought to be examined.[2]

While the Congress at Utrecht was in session, secret negotiations between England and France continued to be transacted in Paris, at one period (in August 1712) by St John himself, who had been raised to the Peerage on August 7 as Viscount Bolingbroke, but for most of the time by Matthew Prior, poet and diplomat, whom Bolingbroke took with him to Paris as secretary and left behind him to deal with such weighty questions as those of the compensation to be made to the Elector of Bavaria for the losses he had sustained in the Bourbon cause, and the disposal of Tournai.

In November the Duke of Hamilton was nominated ambassador-extraordinary to bring to a conclusion the negotiations with the Court of France which had now been in progress for over two years. On the 15th, on the eve of his departure for Paris, he was killed in the duel with Lord Mohun immortalised in *Esmond*. On the 23rd Shrewsbury was appointed in his stead. He was instructed that pending his assumption of the character of ambassador-extraordinary on the actual signing of peace, he was to "cultivate a sincere friendship" between the two Courts of France and England

---

[1] Oldmixon, *History of England*, p. 476.
[2] *Mackintosh Coll.* in Add. MSS. 34,493, vol. VII, f. 88.

and in particular to direct his attention to the still outstanding question of the renunciation by the Dukes of Berri and Orleans and other members of the Bourbon house of any pretensions to the Spanish throne, Philip V having already renounced his contingent claim to the French throne, to the question of the possession of the island of Cape Breton, and of the French pretension to fishing rights off the coast of Newfoundland, the cession of which island to England had already been settled.[1] These problems, together with that of the projected commercial treaty between England and France, were to prove Shrewsbury's chief preoccupations when he reached Paris.

Lord Berkeley of Stratton at first got the impression that Shrewsbury did not take very kindly to his appointment. "He seem'd not much pleas'd with it, spoke of the expense it would be to him, and how likely it was to keep him longer than he wisht, for he must stay till the peace was made if it was made."[2] However, a fortnight later the same writer thinks he must have been mistaken. "I perceive it was only a copy of his countenance for he is extreamly pleas'd with it."[3] The Duke was delayed a long time by contrary winds on his journey to France. Setting sail from the Thames, he was compelled to land at Margate on December 15. For a week he remained there. He then went on by land to Dover, whence he wrote to Bolingbroke lamenting the continuation of his enforced inactivity. "I presume it cannot be imagined I would willingly remaine in these disagreeable sea towns one moment after the wind permits me to sail."[4] It was not till January 4 that he landed at Calais. Next day he went on to

---

[1] P.R.O. *Foreign Entry Book*, xxvi. Full powers for Shrewsbury, pp. 72–3; instructions, pp. 76–80; credentials, pp. 86–8. See also Boyer, *Political State of Great Britain* (2nd ed. 1718), vol. IV, p. 339.

[2] *Wentworth Papers*, p. 305.

[3] *Ibid.* p. 308.

[4] L'Hermitage, *Dispatches*, in Add. MSS. 17,677, vol. G.G.G. ff. 7, 13; P.R.O. *State Papers, France*, cliv, f. 207.

Boulogne, being met a league outside the town by seventy or eighty gentlemen, all the noblesse of the district, who conducted him to its gates. On January 12 he arrived at Paris, where he was accommodated in the splendid mansion of the Duc de Soissons, which had been placed at his disposal by the King.[1] He had a preliminary discussion with Torcy about the Catalans and about the Newfoundland fisheries, on which the latter shewed himself very unyielding.[2] On the 17th he had an audience of Louis XIV at Marly, and after having enjoyed the privilege of watching the King dine in his accustomed solitary state, he himself dined with Torcy, the other guests being the three marshals, Tallard, Villars, and Villeroy.[3]

Shrewsbury found himself at once confronted by the questions of the Newfoundland fishing rights and the commercial treaty, and he discovered that they were closely connected. Prior had ere this intimated the willingness of the English Government to agree to the French claim to be allowed to continue to fish off the coast of Newfoundland and to dry their cod on its shores. But Shrewsbury was instructed that if France was to have Cape Breton she must abandon her claim to the fishing rights. He discovered in the French minister "more stiffness than I imagined not to go beyond what Mr. Prior sent over on that head, alleging that to quit entirely the fishery of Newfoundland would beggar three of their Provinces".[4] He wrote both to Oxford[5] and to Bolingbroke protesting against his being "so straightly tied up" on the Newfoundland question, "that I have no power to hearken to any expedient upon this point; it naturally leads them to suspect some trick, or that I am more stiff than I need to be, and, what is worst of all, discovers our irresolution, and so weakens all that can be said".[6]

[1] Boyer, *Political State*, vol. v, pp. 17–18.
[2] P.R.O. *State Papers, France*, clvii, ff. 1, 2.   [3] *Ibid.* f. 11.
[4] *Bath MSS.* vol. I, pp. 228–9.
[5] Harley became Earl of Oxford, May 23, 1711.
[6] *Bolingbroke's Corr.* vol. III, p. 333.

Bolingbroke's reply (on January 25) was that the stiffer attitude of her Majesty's Government regarding the fishing rights was due to the French having "created unreasonable and unexpected difficulties on the article of commerce".[1] He had already in a lengthy letter of instructions to Shrewsbury alleged that the French were now offering better commercial terms to the United Provinces than to Great Britain, which was a "direct violation of faith". He suggested that when the Duke next saw the French ministers about it, he would "not think fit to give it a much softer term". They were to be given to understand that they were removing a corner-stone of the peace settlement.[2]

Shrewsbury expressed the utmost diffidence as to his capacity to deal with the matter of the commercial treaty at all. Before the receipt of Bolingbroke's letter of the 25th he had already written to Oxford urging that it was necessary to send either to Paris or Utrecht "some person well versed in trade, who can debate, and knows something of the state of their commerce as well as ours, for to one so ignorant as I am they affirm some facts and deny others that defeat all the arguments I could be master of in the small time I had to be informed upon a subject I had never thought on in my life". On this Bolingbroke commented: "Odd confession for a Secretary of State who was in office at the treaty of Ryswick".[3] No doubt the details of the commercial treaty were complicated, for Prior remarks in a letter to Bolingbroke some months later, that the *mélange* of letters, replies, and explanations "and my endeavouring to understand it, had like to make me run mad, if the Duke of Shrewsbury's extreme good sense, and Monsieur de Torcy's not only honest, but right understanding, had not redressed us".[4]

[1] *Bolingbroke's Corr.* vol. III, p. 336.   [2] Jan. 19, in *ibid.* pp. 306–24.
[3] *Bath MSS.* vol. I, p. 229. He made the same suggestion in a letter to Bolingbroke, Feb. 4 (n.s.) (*Bolingbroke's Corr.* vol. III, p. 368).   [4] *Bolingbroke's Corr.* vol. IV, pp. 106–7.

Shrewsbury was soon convinced of the sincerity of the wish for peace in France. "All in this country, great and small, desire the peace and want it, the officers of the army I think as much or more than any", he reported to Oxford.[1] Nevertheless, it continued to be exceedingly difficult to bring the tedious and prolix negotiations to an end. Shrewsbury became impatient and recommended Bolingbroke to deal firmly with the French Court. He wrote on February 22 (n.s.): "I confess myself at a loss to guess what her Majesty will say at the opening of this session, when we have neither peace nor war....I think it is time to speak clearly, and tell this Court what you expect for your allies and what for yourselves, with assurance, that what you ask being granted, you are ready to sign, and to invite the others to do the same".[2] The English ministers had already lost patience, and Bolingbroke dispatched to the Duke two papers, containing the Government's demands concerning the articles appertaining to ourselves as yet unsettled and the general treaties respectively, instructing him to offer these as the Queen's *ultimatum*.[3] This plain threat to renew hostilities failing apt compliance by the French Government proved speedily efficacious. The Commercial Treaty was concluded to the satisfaction of the English Administration, and that being so the French right to fish off the coast of Newfoundland was conceded.[4]

Shrewsbury's attention now became centred upon nice details of form and etiquette, which seem to have held an exaggerated importance in his eyes. Should the renunciation of their claims to the throne of Spain by the Dukes of Berri

[1] *Bath MSS.* vol. I, p. 229. He wrote in very similar terms to Dartmouth, P.R.O. *State Papers, France*, clvii, f. 5.

[2] *Bolingbroke's Corr.* vol. III, pp. 414–15.

[3] *Ibid.* pp. 417–39, esp. 426–7.

[4] "The Duke of Shrewsbury executed this important commission with that speed and success, which could only be expected from an able minister." Swift, *History of the Four Last Years of the Queen* (*Works*, Temple Scott ed. vol. x), p. 186.

and Anjou come in the body of the treaty, or should it follow the signing of the treaty, before its ratification?[1] Should the speech of congratulation upon the conclusion of peace which he would have to make at an audience of the King of France be delivered in Latin, French, or English? There were precedents for the selection of Latin, but he thought that the use of that language on the forthcoming occasion would be "a little impracticable".[2] The audience took place on April 17.

Peace having been signed, Shrewsbury made his state entry into Paris in his new capacity as ambassador-extraordinary on June 11.[3] At about noon on that day a procession consisting of English nobility and gentry was marshalled just outside the Porte S. Antoine. The Duke then received the formal congratulations of the Princes and Princesses of the blood and of the other foreign ministers residing in Paris, after which he was solemnly conducted to the Hôtel des Ambassadeurs. On the 13th he paid a formal visit to Versailles.

"We had", wrote one member of his suite, with obvious satisfaction, "many thousands of spectators, the houses and streets were crowded in such a manner, the like has not been seen these many years; His Excellency's coaches and livery were indeed gloriously fine and rich, *et de bon goût*, very much admired. The British Nobility and Gentry that accompanied his Excellency being about 50 made a great show, being all in rich cloaths much for the honour of the Queen and their country."[4]

The Duke, for his part, confessed himself "very much fatigued with the compliments, ceremony and feasting of three days".[5] He was apparently delighted to receive a summons to return home. "He is very weary of us here",

[1] P.R.O. *State Papers, France*, clvii, ff. 56–8.
[2] *Ibid.* ff. 86–7, 105–8.
[3] *Ibid.* ff. 170–1.
[4] *Ibid.* f. 180.
[5] *Ibid.* ff. 172, 173.

wrote Prior to Bolingbroke on August 11.[1] Shrewsbury also stated that his wife had "never known a week's health" in France.[2] The Duchess had, however, according to one account, been "mightily liked", though the Jacobite Earl of Newcastle has a story of her being at a fair and of the crowd running after her to get a sight of her, and then running faster away as soon as they saw her, calling her *la villen beste*.[3] On August 23 the Duke and his wife embarked at Calais; they landed the following day at Dover. On the 26th the Duke was very graciously received by the Queen at Windsor.[4]

Shrewsbury seems to have accomplished all that was required of him at Paris with ability and success, and he possessed the presence, the dignity, the suavity, all that is implied by the "grand manner", which were of very real importance in a representative at the court of France in the resplendent days of Versailles. But in the transaction of practical business he owed much to Prior, who had held the threads of the Anglo-French negotiations in his fingers ever since July 1711. The peace was "Mat's Peace", not Shrewsbury's. Robethon gave it as his opinion that the Ministry sent the latter "merely to keep him at a distance from business, since everything is transacted by the means of Mr. Prior".[5] The critical Earl of Newcastle suggested that Shrewsbury treated his subordinate with *hauteur*. "Your gracious nephew", he writes to Middleton, "has not much the hearts of the people even Prior I am tould cant indure him, the truth ont is hee keeps him very much under for he dares not so much as to sitt down where he is without being bid, though

[1] *Bolingbroke's Corr.* vol. IV, p. 230.
[2] *Bath MSS.* vol. I, p. 233.
[3] Feb. 20, 1713, in *Wentworth Papers*, p. 321; Newcastle to Middleton, Paris, Feb. 12, 1713, in *Carte MSS.* (Bodl.), vol. CCXI, ff. 220–1.
[4] *Bath MSS.* vol. I, p. 238; Boyer, *Political State*, vol. VI, p. 124.
[5] Macpherson, vol. II, pp. 479–80.

the french my lord him att every word."[1] But the tone of Prior's references to Shrewsbury in his private as well as in his formal correspondence is always warm and appreciative; and that Shrewsbury, on his side, fully recognised the great value of Prior's assistance is also clear. "The Duke of Shrewsbury", Prior informs Bolingbroke, always does him the honour to let him "always assist him at the writing his letter".[2] Immediately on his return to England the Duke exerted himself on the poet's behalf.[3]

Shortly before Shrewsbury's departure from France Prior had written to Bolingbroke to say, "he will not, I think, be much pleased with most of you on that side".[4] And indeed the situation of the Ministry at this time was most unsatisfactory. The Whigs, who had opposed the Government's peace policy from the first, attacked the Commercial Treaty with particular venom, the whole manufacturing interest in the country being up in arms against the eighth and ninth articles which established reciprocal most-favoured-nation treatment between France and England. On this issue the very influential Tory Sir Thomas Hanmer went over to the enemy. This was a serious blow to the Government, for owing to the defection of Hanmer's following the all-important articles were rejected by the House of Commons. Still more serious was the ever-increasing antagonism between Oxford and Bolingbroke. The former was in bad health. On July 25 the Secretary had reported to Shrewsbury that "the Treasurer is again extremely ill, and I doubt his health is so shattered by frequent returns of illness, as to be little depended upon".[5] Certainly Oxford's unhappy tendency to procrastination was growing, and Bolingbroke's impatience

[1] *Carte MSS.* vol. CCXI, ff. 220-1.
[2] *Bolingbroke's Corr.* vol. III, p. 393.
[3] *Ibid.* vol. IV, p. 273.
[4] *Ibid.* p. 230.
[5] *Ibid.* p. 207.

with his unbusinesslike methods and apprehensions of their ill-effect upon the fortunes of the Ministry were only too well-founded. Expressing great satisfaction at the prospect of Shrewsbury's imminent return to England, Bolingbroke assured him in his letter of the 25th that no measure would be fixed on until his arrival. On the same day the Duke sent Bolingbroke a typical letter counselling caution. "Allow me for the present only to recommend temper and moderation, and to beg of you to do nothing hastily that may be deferred."[1] D'Aumont, the French Ambassador in London, wrote on August 7, with reference to the Tory disunion, "Cette situation rend de plus en plus la presence du Duc de Shrewsbury necessaire dans ce pays-cy. C'est le seul homme capable de ramener le Comte d'Oxford ou de balancer son credit dans l'esprit de la Reyne...",[2] and again, "J'ai beaucoup d'impatience du retour du Duc de Shrewsbury qui est fort capable d'achever une reconciliation...".[3]

What counsel Shrewsbury gave his colleagues on his return to England one does not know. He remained in the country but a short time, being appointed Lord-Lieutenant of Ireland in September in succession to the Duke of Ormonde. Rumours that he would go to Ireland had been current from time to time ever since the Ministerial crisis of 1710.[4] They had been strong in January 1712 when Swift had viewed the prospect with favour, his Grace being "a very great and excellent person".[5] In March Lord Berkeley of Stratton reported, "the Duke of Shrewsbury certainly goes to Ireland, after long aspiring to it";[6] and Swift was again sure that his appointment would take place. "My Lord Duke of Shrewsbury", he wrote on March 27, "will come here

[1] *Bolingbroke's Corr.* vol. IV, p. 205.
[2] *Mackintosh Collection*, in Add. MSS. 34,494, vol. VIII, f. 40.
[3] *Ibid.* f. 44.
[4] Cf. *Wentworth Papers*, pp. 144, 145; Luttrell, vol. VI, pp. 709–10.
[5] *Wentworth Papers*, p. 243; Swift's *Corr.* vol. I, p. 315.
[6] *Wentworth Papers*, pp. 281–2.

with great advantage, the generality being possessed with a very great opinion of his probity and capacity, and besides they have reckoned his Grace to be a friend to this country".[1] In the following May he was once more anticipating the Duke's appointment and pronouncing encomiums upon his character.[2]

Why was Shrewsbury sent to Ireland in 1713? To get rid of him, was one answer. The Duke of Argyll, being "of opinion that the Duke of Shrewsbury is the only one whose word is to be relyed upon", also wondered "he's so over seen as to be sent into Ireland".[3] The Jacobites found a very different answer, the wish no doubt being father to the thought. "The Duke of Shrewsbury", writes one of them, "goes to Ireland to call a Parliament and put that Kingdom into honest hands".[4]

On October 12 Shrewsbury left Windsor after seeing the Queen. At Holyhead he was delayed for a week by adverse winds, but on the 27th he landed at Kingstown. In an address of welcome which was presented by the Lord Mayor and aldermen of the City of Dublin his appointment was described as "accomplishing, at this juncture, the desires of all who endeavour to unite and strengthen the Protestant interest in Ireland". Magniloquent allusion was made to his distinguished ancestry, and to its illustriousness in almost every period of English history. But it was "below the dignity of great and eminent persons to adorn their character only with the borrowed graces of their ancestors—especially, while in their own persons, all wealth and merit outshines the glories of former ages". Shrewsbury's services to the Revolution settlement were specially alluded to, and the address concluded with expressions of the hearty affection

[1] Swift's *Corr.* vol. I, p. 321.
[2] *Ibid.* pp. 325-6.
[3] *Wentworth Papers*, p. 355.
[4] Macpherson, vol. II, p. 439. Cf. p. 446.

felt by the City of Dublin for "the constitution in Church and State, and the Protestant succession in the illustrious house of Hanover".[1]

Apparently, just before leaving England Shrewsbury had expressed the view that "there is no difference in Ireland but protestant and papist"—on which Lord Berkeley of Stratton sagaciously commented: "I wish he could bring it to that, but the truth is they are to the full as much divided as here".[2] Indeed Shrewsbury had a troublesome and difficult task before him in his new appointment, and his ease came to an end with the "Illuminations, Bonefires, Ringing of Bells and all other demonstrations of Joy", which brought his first day in Dublin to a conclusion. For party feeling in Ireland was running exceedingly high. The Whigs believed, or affected to believe, that ever since the departure of Lord Wharton, who had been Lord-Lieutenant from 1708 to 1710, the government of the country had been under Jacobite control. They also alleged that the Irish papists had been encouraged by the Chancellor, Sir Constantine Phipps, who in the interval between the departure of Ormonde and the arrival of Shrewsbury had, as the predominating personality among the Lords Justices to whom the administration of the country had been entrusted, been the virtual ruler of Ireland. His practice at the Bar had been largely among Jacobites; he had made his name as one of the counsel for Sacheverell. A masterful man and obviously the chief driving-force in the country, Phipps was regarded by the Irish Whigs almost as a second Tyrconnel.[3]

It was subsequently claimed by the Whigs that from the

[1] See Boyer, *Political State*, vol. VI, pp. 243–5.
[2] See *Wentworth Papers*, p. 356.
[3] See Oldmixon, *History of England during the reigns of William and Mary, Anne, and George I* (1735), p. 532; J. R. O'Flanagan, *Lives of the Lord Chancellors of Ireland* (2 vols. 1870), vol. I, pp. 536–54, and *D.N.B.* vol. XIX, pp. 310–17 (for Phipps); R. H. Murray, *Revolutionary Ireland and its Settlement* (1911), pp. 372–3.

very outset of his lord-lieutenancy, Shrewsbury definitely ranged himself on their side. The Whig annalist, Abel Boyer, writes: "When the Duke of Shrewsbury came to Dublin he quickly perceiv'd the Pretender's friends had receiv'd no small encouragement from Sir Constantine Phipps, Lord Chancellor, and took hold of all occasions to give a check to that spirit of rebellion which the countenance of Phipps had fomented". Boyer cites in particular the Duke's conduct on the occasion of the anniversary of William III's birthday, November 4, when he declared that he was still the same as he had been in the year 1688 and publicly drank to the glorious memory of King William—"a notable reproof of the disaffection of the Bishop of Cork, who preach'd against drinking that health, pretending that drinking to the dead was like praying for the dead".[1]

Shrewsbury's two chief sources of trouble when he first took the helm in Ireland were municipal and parliamentary elections, these being closely connected. Before his arrival in Dublin great excitement had already been aroused in that city over the question of the election of a new Lord Mayor. Seventeen aldermen, who regarded the existing Lord Mayor, Sir Samuel Cook, as the tool of Phipps, had met together and chosen one of their own number. Cook protested against this proceeding as invalid and the matter was referred to the Irish Privy Council, in which the Lord Chancellor was all-powerful. The Privy Council sustained Cook's objection and affirmed that the Lord Mayor for the time being had the right of nominating three aldermen to be put forward for election. When a meeting was held in accordance with the Privy Council's orders, twenty aldermen challenged the Lord Mayor's right to nominate, and a deadlock was created. Confronted with this problem at the very outset of his term of office, Shrewsbury reported to the Lord Treasurer on November 23 that he found "in this place a disposition more

[1] A. Boyer, *Life and Reign of Queen Anne*, p. 651.

obstinate than I had expected". When a petition was presented to him desiring him to take interim action on the ground that owing to the municipal *impasse* the courts in Dublin could not be held and no criminals could be tried, he made the proposal that the Mayor should proceed to a new election, and that he should withdraw one of his three nominees and substitute some one more likely to be acceptable to the City. Phipps at first approved of this scheme, but almost immediately afterwards declared that the Privy Council regarded it as derogatory to their dignity. Shrewsbury could not see that their dignity was in any way involved. He plainly regarded the attitude of the Privy Council as singularly stupid and ill-advised, the desirability of settling "this ridiculous dispute" at the earliest moment being so obvious. The prospects of "an easy session" of Parliament were otherwise exceptionably favourable, but the continuance of this agitation in Dublin would spoil all. It could be "nothing but the excess of folly, heat, or malice for any of her Majesty's servants to keep up this dispute". In these terms he expressed an oblique but decided censure upon Phipps. The repudiation of his policy by the Privy Council riled him; though a member of a Tory Administration he found himself already denounced as a Whig. As usual when public business worried him he was unwell. "I have been very ill since I came and the vexation of this usage has made me worse", he complained.[1]

Excitement in Dublin increased when the parliamentary election took place. There was a serious collision between the mob and the soldiery, one man being killed and several wounded. Both parties complained to the Lord-Lieutenant who instituted a committee of inquiry into the cause of the late disturbances, and also instructed the sheriffs to take the poll at two different booths in order "to prevent the meeting and clashing of the two contending parties". Being in-

[1] *Bath MSS.* vol. I, pp. 241-2.

formed that Papists and Jacobites were the chief promoters of the riot, he "caus'd several Popish chapels in Dublin to be shut up, which wonderfully endear'd him to all Protestants".[1] On November 17 the two Whig candidates were returned by large majorities.

When the Parliament assembled it was apparent that the party situation at Westminster was reversed in the Irish Legislature; for there was a Tory majority in the Upper House, a strong Whig majority in the Commons. On the 25th the session opened with the Lord-Lieutenant's speech, in which the most striking phrase was that "her Majesty having procured a safe and honourable peace had nothing more to wish but that her subjects might enjoy the benefits and advantages of it". The following day the Commons proceeded to the election of their Speaker, the Tory candidate being Sir Richard Levinz and the Whig candidate Alan Brodrick, the future Viscount Midleton. One of the reasons why Shrewsbury deplored the non-settlement of the municipal dispute was that he thereby lost the help of a number of Whigs who had promised him to vote for Levinz on condition that they were satisfied in the other matter.[2] As it was, Brodrick went about enlisting votes for himself by assuring members of the Lower House that he had the Lord-Lieutenant's approval; then upon Shrewsbury's making known the Queen's pleasure that Levinz should be chosen it was bruited abroad that the Crown was endeavouring to limit the liberties of the people by nominating the Speaker.[3] All this trouble would have been saved, Shrewsbury saw, had the Privy Council shewn rather more sense and less sensibility. In despite of the Lord-Lieutenant's intimation of the wishes of the Crown Brodrick was elected Speaker by four votes.

[1] Oldmixon, p. 532.
[2] *Bath MSS.* vol. I, p. 245.
[3] Swift's *Corr.* vol. II, p. 91. See also *ibid.* p. 81; *Corr. of Sir T. Hanmer* (ed. Sir H. Bunbury, 1838), p. 153.

The Whig House of Commons at once shewed its aggressive zeal by the introduction of a Bill attainting the Pretender and all his adherents of high treason and offering a reward to any one who should produce the Pretender dead or alive, and by enquiring into the recent action of the Government regarding the publication of a book entitled *Memoirs of the Chevalier de St George*, and regarding a theatre riot in Dublin which had followed upon the pronouncement of a eulogy on William III which an actor named Dudley Moore had included in a prologue to the play *Tamerlane*.[1] The printer of the book had been prosecuted, but the Government had intervened with a *nolle prosequi*, Phipps taking the view, probably with justification, that there was no seditious intent whatever in the publication. The House of Commons on December 18 voted that the work was a seditious and treasonable libel, and also that the Lord Chancellor's action gave great encouragement to the friends of the Pretender and was "contrary to his duty and to the Protestant interest". It also censured a speech which Phipps had made to the corporation of Dublin on the disturbed condition of the city, in which he made special reference to Moore and assumed his responsibility for the theatre riot. The Commons' resentment was due partly to their belief that the riot had been started by disloyal members of the audience, but also to the reasonable objection that as Moore was awaiting his trial at the time the speech was made the Lord Chancellor had been guilty of gross impropriety in prejudging an untried case. The attack upon Phipps in the Lower House culminated in the resolution to present an address to the Queen praying for his removal "for the peace and safety of her Protestant subjects of this Kingdom".[2] The members next turned their attention

[1] See Oldmixon, p. 533.

[2] The House of Lords, on the contrary, voted that Phipps "had in the several stations wherein he had served her Majesty acquitted himself with honour and integrity". It also censured a lawyer named Luttrell for having called him a canary-bird and a villain

to the chaotic condition of local government in Dublin, but their new deliberations only led to a fresh onslaught on the Chancellor, who was accused of having deliberately attempted to subvert the constitution of the city. As a challenging demonstration of their hostility to Tory Government and as a palpable strategic move towards securing the dismissal of the abhorred Phipps they next refused to grant supplies for any longer than three months.

Shrewsbury wrote in dismal tones to both Oxford and Bolingbroke. He was sure that nothing good was to be hoped from the present session or indeed from the present Parliament, and he held out no hopes of salvation in a dissolution; a new Parliament would be no better. He declared himself to be temperamentally unfit to deal with the situation and hoped for his recall and the substitution of some other governor better qualified for "this tempestuous station". He complained that the fact of its being generally understood that his tenure of office was to be brief had rendered him impotent, a mere "figure of a Viceroy in a Play". He had just one piece of advice to give—that the Government should try to shew its independence of the Irish House of Commons by cutting down establishments and subsisting on its non-parliamentary revenue.[1] Evidently a little after this he had some reason for suspecting that the Government contemplated an attempt to tax Ireland direct from Westminster, for he wrote to Oxford on February 2, 1713/14, expressing his satisfaction at finding his apprehensions on this score allayed.[2]

The Queen's reply to the address desiring the dismissal of Phipps was a frosty reminder that she was the best judge of whom she should employ in her service. When this message arrived Shrewsbury sent privately for the Speaker and seven or eight of the Whig leaders in the Lower House,

who had set the kingdom by the ears and ought to be hanged. *Bolingbroke's Corr.* vol. IV, p. 394.

[1] *Bath MSS.* vol. I, pp. 243-4. [2] *Ibid.* p. 245.

and informed them that Parliament was to be prorogued in order to give the Commons time to come to their senses, and that if they persisted in their vendetta against Phipps, Parliament would be dissolved. He hinted that it might be found possible to do without the Irish Parliament altogether. These threats produced no impression whatever, the members merely affirming their determination to grant no more supplies until the Chancellor had been removed.[1] Such recalcitrance foreshadowed a dissolution; in the meantime Parliament was prorogued till August 10.

Long ere that Shrewsbury had returned to England. He had been neither well nor happy in Ireland; he had naturally found his ambiguous position galling. As Boyer puts it, "He had not been long in Dublin before he found, that he was little more than the pageant of the Government of Ireland, of which the mainsprings were in the Lord Chancellor's hands".[2] The Duke himself complained that as soon as the compromise which he had suggested in the municipal controversy had been rejected, "from that time it was the public discourse here that it signified little what opinion I was of, since little regard would be had to it in England".[3] Phipps clearly retained the complete confidence of the Ministry, and his word carried greater weight than that of the Lord-Lieutenant. It particularly hurt Shrewsbury's pride that when he recommended his kinsman, the Bishop of Oxford, for the vacant Archbishopric of Armagh, the Lord Chancellor's nominee the Bishop of Raphoe was preferred.[4]

It may appear that Shrewsbury's record in Ireland was one merely of frustration and impotence; it is not, however, so insignificant as it seems at first sight.[5] While he tried to

[1] *Dispatches of L'Hermitage*, in Add. MSS. 17,677, vol. H.H.H. ff. 25, 35. [2] *History of Queen Anne*, p. 655.
[3] Shrewsbury to Oxford, Feb. 2, 1713/14, in *Bath MSS.* vol. I, p. 245. [4] *Mackintosh Transcripts*, in Add. MSS. 22,237, ff. 163-4.
[5] According to the fourth Earl of Chesterfield, Shrewsbury once said that the Lord-Lieutenancy of Ireland was "a place wherein a

divert the Whigs in the Irish House of Commons from their onslaught upon Phipps, it was well understood that the Lord-Lieutenant and the Lord Chancellor were not in accord. While the conduct of the latter gave occasion for his enemies to accuse him of disloyalty to the Hanoverian succession and partiality to Papists the former's attitude was quite unequivocal. His marked behaviour on the anniversary of the late King's birthday did not stand alone. He tightened up the administration of the penal laws against Roman Catholics which had grown lax, and finding that a number of priests had established chapels without having taken the oath of abjuration he had them imprisoned.[1] It being discovered that one or two Roman Catholics, notably a lieutenant in Lord Galway's regiment named Toby Butler, had been enlisting men for the Pretender's service, some 400–500 being discovered ready to embark, Shrewsbury took vigorous measures, leading to a number of arrests and to twenty-four executions for treason.[2] Contemporary Whig historians—Boyer and Oldmixon—record with great satisfaction the part which he played in Ireland, while Swift accuses him of " acting a part directly opposite to the court, which he had sagacity enough to foresee might quickly turn to account ".[3] Perhaps we are justified in regarding Shrewsbury's conduct at this period of his career as an instance of his prescience, a foreshadowing of his decisive action in the crisis of Queen Anne's last illness and death.

man had business enough to hinder him from falling asleep; and not so much as to keep him awake ".

[1] *Dispatches of L'Hermitage*, in Add. MSS. 17,677, vol. H.H.H. f. 35.

[2] Oldmixon, p. 535; Boyer, *History of Queen Anne*, p. 707. Cf. Shrewsbury to Prior, July 1st, in *Portland MSS.* vol. v, p. 469: " I may affirm that in Ireland not less than 4 or 5,000 men have been listed, some pretend 50,000, with promise to serve the Pretender, and hopes given them they shall soon return triumphant to enjoy their ancient claims in Ireland ".

[3] "Behaviour of the Queen's last Ministry", in *Historical and Political Tracts* (*Works*, ed. Temple Scott), vol. v, p. 453.

CHAPTER X

The Hanoverian Succession

During Shrewsbury's absence in Ireland the Ministerial situation became more and more critical. At the opening of 1714 the Queen was seriously ill and the Tories were greatly alarmed. During the spring the Whig attack both in the Press and in Parliament, particularly in the Upper House, was vigorous, sustained, and damaging, especially on the subject of our abandonment of the Catalans. The Duke of Argyll accused the Government of endangering the Protestant succession by combing out the Whig officers in the army and subsidising Jacobite clans in the Highlands. On April 3 a motion in the Lords that the Hanoverian succession was not in danger was carried by twelve votes only, owing to the defection of the Earl of Anglesey and several other Tory peers, who now played a part analogous to that of Hanmer and his "whimsical" followers in the House of Commons. Meanwhile the rift between Oxford and Bolingbroke continued to widen. When Shrewsbury was once more in England after a long delay in making his return from Ireland, due apparently to his not liking the weather in the Irish Sea,[1] there was much speculation as to which of the two rivals he would favour. Swift in his pamphlet, *The Behaviour of the Queen's last Ministry*, ranks him together with Harcourt and Windham as a supporter of the Secretary;[2] Boyer, in all probability more justly, declares that "finding those about the Queen jarring and disjointed, his Grace resolv'd to act a cautious and reserv'd part; and not to side with either of the contending parties, but as soon as a proper occasion

---

[1] Swift, *Corr.* vol. II, p. 138.   [2] *Works*, vol. v, p. 448.

(which he judg'd could not be far off) offer'd it self, to put himself at the head of the well affected to the protestant succession".[1]

Shrewsbury once more took his seat in the House of Lords on June 14.[2] The following day, when the Schism Bill passed in that House by seventy-seven to seventy-two, he was absent.[3] That measure, whose object was the destruction of the Dissenters' schools, had been devised by Bolingbroke as an appeal to the High Church interest and as an embarrassment to Oxford, who posed as a protector of the Nonconformists. The Bill was indeed, as Defoe puts it, "a mine dug to blow up the White Staff". Shrewsbury spoke strongly against Bolingbroke's motion that the measure should be given the same force in Ireland as in England, arguing that the Papists in that kingdom were growing stronger and stronger and that it would be dangerous, therefore, to create division in the ranks of the Protestants.[4] The resolution was, however, carried. To this extent he ranged himself against Bolingbroke. When, however, Oxford sharply retaliated by lending his support to the demand for an inquiry into the negotiations relating to the commercial treaty with Spain, it having been alleged that a share in the profits of the lucrative *Asiento* contract had been corruptly reserved for Lady Masham, Bolingbroke, and his friend Arthur Moore, on a motion for papers in the Upper House, Shrewsbury "was one of eight or nine lords, that stood by my Lord Bolingbroke...and spoke with a good deal of spirit".[5] Again, when on July 5 (n.s.) the Lords offered an address to the Queen desiring her to renew her instances for having the Pretender

[1] *History of Queen Anne*, p. 707.
[2] *L.J.* vol. XIX, p. 715.
[3] *Ibid.* p. 717.
[4] *Dispatches of L'Hermitage*, in Add. MSS. 16,777, vol. H.H.H. f. 262.
[5] Ford to Swift, July 6, in Swift's *Corr.* vol. II, p. 171.

removed from Lorraine, to issue a proclamation against Papists and Non-jurors, and to offer a reward for the apprehension of any who enlisted men for the Pretender, a correspondent of Robethon, the Elector's secretary, ascribed the action of the House to the influence of Oxford and Shrewsbury.[1]

In the second half of July there were renewed rumours that the Duke had "undertaken a general reconcilement", and would mediate between the Treasurer and the Secretary.[2] On the other hand, Arbuthnot has a story of how in a conversation with him, Oxford and Shrewsbury meanwhile walking up and down together nearby, Bolingbroke said, "I know how I stand with that man (pointing to the dragon),[3] but as to the other, I cannot tell".[4] On July 20 Ford writes to Swift: "A reconcilement is impossible....The Duke of Shrewsbury declares against him (Bolingbroke) in private conversation; I suppose because he is against every chief minister, for it is known he has no kindness for the Colonel" [Oxford].[5] On the 16th Shrewsbury had given a dinner party to all members of the Cabinet, but Oxford had excused himself from attendance.[6]

To the question whether Bolingbroke was at this time planning a Jacobite restoration it will probably never be possible to give more than a conjectural answer. The evidence in favour of the view that he was comes mainly from Jacobite sources and is similar in character to that which can be brought against nearly all the leading statesmen of the period, irrespective of party, at one time or another between 1688 and 1715. There are indeed some circumstantial letters from Gaultier and from d'Iberville,[7] who was French ambassador

---

[1] Macpherson, vol. II, pp. 630–1.
[2] *E.g.* Swift's *Corr.* vol. II, pp. 179, 187.   [3] *I.e.* Oxford.
[4] Swift's *Corr.* vol. II, p. 185.   [5] *Ibid.* p. 189.
[6] D'Iberville to Louis XIV, July 19, to Torcy, July 22, in Add. MSS. 34,497, ff. 33, 34.
[7] See *E.H.R.* vol. XXX, pp. 501–18; Legg, *Matthew Prior*, pp. 245–56.

in London in succession to D'Aumont, but these are as incriminating to Oxford as to Bolingbroke, and while they record that Oxford said he would never consent to England being ruled by a German, they also record Bolingbroke's conviction: "Better a Turk than a Papist"[1]—and the Pretender categorically refused to purchase the throne by a recantation. But was the party policy which Bolingbroke was deliberately following in July 1714 compatible with the succession of the House of Hanover? He had nothing but contempt for Oxford's "trimming" methods; he was intent upon strengthening the Tory party upon a High Church foundation; he knew, as he confessed in later days in his *Letter to Sir William Windham*, that in addition to the suspicions felt for the Tory party at the Electoral Court, "particular prejudices" were entertained against him. Yet he continued to work for the aggrandisement of the Tory right wing. As he put it, "I resolved not to abandon my party by turning whig, or, *which is a great deal worse*, whimsical".[2]

Shrewsbury had kept sedulously aloof from the Jacobites since the Fenwick case, and one of his earliest proceedings after re-entering office in 1710 had been to get into touch with the Electoral Court. In two letters of August 18 and October 20 to the Elector he protested his "faithful and inviolable attachment" to him and his family, and declared that he felt there was no way in which he could serve the Queen better than by contributing to the good understanding between the courts of St James's and Hanover, and by helping to destroy the cabals of those who aimed at disturbing the Hanoverian succession.[3] "I entreat your Electoral Highness to do me the justice to believe", he wrote a year later, "that you have not either in England or in any other part of the

[1] *Stuart Papers at Windsor Castle* (H.M.C.), vol. I, introd. pp. xlvii–lii.
[2] *Works of Bolingbroke* (ed. D. Mallet, 5 vols. 1777), vol. I, pp. 27–8.
[3] See Macpherson, vol. II, pp. 185–6, 196.

world any one who is more entirely devoted to you".[1] During his embassy in Paris he had been most circumspect in avoiding members of the Court of St Germain who desired to visit him.[2] The Earl of Newcastle wrote to Middleton in January 1713, "As to my Lord Srosbery, I can give you but very litel account of him, for I find he is resolved to keepe himselfe out of the way of any of us and he has as good as declared himselfe upon that point".[3] In Ireland, as we have seen, Shrewsbury had appeared as a champion of the Protestant succession. It is indeed in that capacity that he has secured a permanent place in English history. The crisis of 1714 proved the truth of his assertion in Ireland on November 4, 1713 that he was still the same as he had been in the other great crisis of 1688.

The tense days of crisis in 1714 began with the Council meeting on July 27, at which Bolingbroke had the satisfaction of seeing Oxford ousted from the Treasurership; the hour of his own triumph seemed at hand. But his hopes were short-lived indeed. The Council meeting was stormy. Oxford indulged in an angry invective against his enemies; the Queen in an equally angry denunciation of him. From the agitation of that scene Anne never recovered. On Thursday, July 29, she suffered from violent pains in the head, but she obtained some relief before night. Next morning, however, she was much worse; she lay "speechless, motionless, and unsensible". News of the Queen's condition was sent by the Duchess of Ormonde to the meeting of the Privy Council, which was assembled at the Cockpit in Whitehall. The Ministers at once adjourned to Kensington. Two of Boling-

---

[1] Oct. 3, 1711, in Macpherson, vol. II, p. 255. To these advances the Elector replied in suitable terms, Oct. 16, 1710, *ibid.* pp. 194–5; Nov. 7, 1711, *ibid.* p. 264.

[2] *Bolingbroke's Corr.* vol. III, p. 374. He met the Duke of Berwick at dinner at the Duc de Noailles, but would not receive him in his own lodgings (*ibid.* p. 373).

[3] *Carte MSS.* vol. CCXI, f. 208. Cf. Macpherson, vol. II, p. 373.

broke's chief supporters, Buckinghamshire and Windham, were absent; Shrewsbury was presiding. The story of this meeting, as commonly told, suggests that it was a Cabinet meeting, and that the Dukes of Somerset and Argyll broke in upon its deliberations not only without summons but also without warrant. Their appearance had probably been already arranged by Shrewsbury, who rose to thank them for "their readiness to give the Council their assistance in that nice juncture".[1] The co-operation of the three great Dukes, whose common action had been so important in ushering in the ministerial changes of 1710, is significant; it appears to have quite daunted Bolingbroke, to have convinced him instantaneously that his plan—whatever its nature may have been —was ruined. Some one representing how necessary it was that a new Lord Treasurer should be appointed, Shrewsbury was proposed for the position—it is said by Bolingbroke himself— and unanimously approved.[2] The Queen having regained consciousness, Shrewsbury, together with several others of the Lords, was admitted to her bedside. She then entrusted him with the White Staff, saying that "they could not recommend a person she liked better", and bidding him use it for the good of the nation.[3] Such was her weakness that the Lord Chancellor had to hold and direct her hand towards the Duke as she conferred upon him the symbol of the highest office in the state. Shrewsbury was now at one and the same time Lord Chamberlain, Lord-Lieutenant of Ireland, and Lord Treasurer.

Boyer writes: "His Grace's advancement to the post of Lord Treasurer, immediately changed the face of affairs; dash'd the towering ambition of the Lord Bolingbroke;

---

[1] Boyer, *History of Queen Anne*, p. 714; I. S. Leadam, Longmans' *Political History of England*, vol. IX, 1702–60, p. 220.

[2] Ford to Swift, Aug. 5, 1714, in Swift's *Corr.* vol. II, p. 207.

[3] Peter Wentworth to Strafford, July 30, in *Wentworth Papers*, p. 408.

baffled his undigested schemes; alarm'd the friends of the Pretender; and wonderfully reviv'd the drooping spirits of the well-affected to the Hanoverian succession".[1] Or, as a correspondent of Swift's writing on July 31 put it laconically,[2] "My Lord Shrewsbury is made Lord Treasurer, and everything is ready for proclaiming the Duke of Brunswick King of England". It is noteworthy that Thomas Hearne commenting on Shrewsbury's appointment refers to him as "a very great whigg".[3] The Lord Treasurer and the other Peers who were now in the ascendant acted with vigour. There being a slight run on the Bank of England, Shrewsbury sent to enquire what condition it was in and to give an assurance of assistance to the utmost of his power in case of need.[4] As the result of the proposal made by Argyll and Somerset that all privy councillors without exception who lived in or near London should be called upon to attend, Somers and several other supporters of the House of Hanover attended the meetings of the Council on the 30th. On the 31st orders were dispatched to the troops in Flanders to return to England, and the heralds were ordered to be in readiness to proclaim the new King. The Hanoverian resident was instructed to be in attendance with the black box, which, in accordance with the stipulations of the Regency Act of 1705,[5] contained the names of those who had been designated by the Elector to act as Lords Justices on the demise of the Queen. At about 7 a.m. on Sunday, August 1, Queen Anne died. The terms of the Regency Act, whose existence proved of incalculable value to the House of Hanover, were then carried out to the letter. When the list of Peers nominated by George I to act as Lords Justices was read it was found that the only minister

[1] *History of Queen Anne*, p. 714.
[2] Swift's *Corr.* vol. II, p. 205.
[3] *Remarks and Collections of Thomas Hearne* (ed. Doble, Rannie and Salter, Oxford 1884–1918), vol. IV, p. 388.
[4] Boyer, *Political State*, vol. VIII, p. 633.
[5] Re-enacted, after the legislative Union with Scotland, in 1707.

among them was Shrewsbury. He thus became "doubly one of the Lords Regents of Great Britain; a circumstance hardly to be parallel'd in our history; and which adds a new lustre to the Family of the Talbots, so illustrious for so many ages ".[1]

The rapid rise in stocks, which was really due to the confidence engendered in the financial world by the realisation that the Hanoverian succession was going to be effected without serious trouble, was ascribed by Swift's friend Charles Ford to "the hatred of the old treasurer and the popularity of the new one".[2] Shrewsbury was for a brief period the most powerful and the most sought-after man in the country. "The Duke of Shrewsbury has so many flocking about him that there's no speaking to him now ", writes Peter Wentworth to Lord Strafford on August 20.[3] But in a week or two, and even before the arrival of George I, we once more hear the old story of his being in bad health and wishing to be relieved of his responsibilities. It is very certain, writes d'Iberville on September 4, that the Duke of Shrewsbury is "passionately anxious" to relinquish the Treasurership.[4] In later letters he says that the Duke appears to him to be prostrated (*fort abattu*), and that he cannot stand the strain of his various employments.[5] Bothmer, who as Hanoverian envoy held a position of great influence pending his master's arrival in London, notes on the 10th that Shrewsbury "begins to be sick", but hints that the illness is not genuine.[6] The King landed in England on the 18th, and a new Administration was speedily constituted. Shrewsbury ceased to be Lord Treasurer on October 11. He was the last that ever held the post, the Treasury having ever since remained in commission. He was succeeded as Lord-

[1] Boyer, *Political State*, p. 630. [2] Swift's *Corr.* vol. II, p. 215.
[3] *Wentworth Papers*, p. 416. [4] Add. MSS. 34,494, f. 83.
[5] *Ibid.* ff. 118, 119.
[6] Bothmer to Robethon, in Macpherson, vol. II, p. 653.

Lieutenant by Sunderland. There were rumours that he would be deprived of the office of Lord Chamberlain, but to this he was reappointed on October 17.[1] He had already, on September 26, accepted the posts of Groom of the Stole and Keeper of the Privy Purse. Rumour was busy during these weeks. One said that Shrewsbury had no desire to retain the Viceroyalty of Ireland; another that he had been deprived of it unceremoniously. One attributed his slight delay in accepting the post of Groom of the Stole to pique that the Keepership of the Privy Purse was not immediately offered with it; another to continued affection for the Tory party, which was being so thoroughly dispossessed with the accession of the new Sovereign.[2]

The position of Shrewsbury was by no means easy. George I was personally well affected towards him, but he was unable to resist the pressure of the predominant faction who clamoured for the ostracism of all but out-and-out Whigs. He had not liked the Whigs "driving on so fast" and making such rapid changes.[3] Shrewsbury was "amphibious" and revealed himself in that character at the General Election of November 1714 by recommending a Whig as candidate for one borough in which he had interest, and a Tory for another.[4] He did not sit in the Cabinet, and d'Iberville reports on October 8 that since the King's arrival he has had the gout or has pretended to and has not appeared at Court; he cannot have any influence there in any case, because of his old quarrel with the Whigs who are now predominant.[5] Certainly the days of Shrewsbury's power in 1714 were short-lived. In January 1715 he was once more suffering from gout

[1] Boyer, *Political State*, vol. VIII, p. 273.

[2] G. E. C. *Complete Peerage* (8 vols. Exeter, 1887–98), vol. VII, p. 143; Add. MSS. 34,496, ff. 15, 21–2, 140.

[3] Peter Wentworth to Strafford, in *Wentworth Papers*, Sept. 21, 1714, p. 420.

[4] Add. MSS. 34,496, ff. 84, 172.

[5] *Ibid.* f. 15.

and was thinking of resignation, but the Duchess dissuaded him, while she was loud in assurances to the King that he had no more faithful servant than her husband.[1] But the resignation was delayed only till the following July. Oxford, Bolingbroke, Ormonde and Strafford, were all impeached at this time for their several parts in carrying out the peace policy of the late Administration—Bolingbroke, in anticipation of such a move, had already fled the country.[2] There were suggestions that Shrewsbury should be impeached as well. D'Iberville reported on July 17 that the reigning ministers were determined to remove the one man among them capable of giving moderate counsels, and that they were using the threat of impeachment to force him from office. Only if he resigned would they guarantee him immunity. The King, it was said, had been reluctant to part with him, but at last agreed to advise the Duke to retire voluntarily. One story runs that some of his friends had counselled him to postpone resignation till he had re-established his credit with the Tories, but that his wife had this time brought pressure upon him to retire at once.[3] "The Duke of Shrewsbury gave up his stick last night very unwillingly", recorded the old Duchess of Marlborough in the postscript to a letter begun on the 8th.[4] He never held office again.

[1] D'Iberville to Torcy, Jan. 31, 1715, in Add. MSS. 34,498, f. 10; April 25, f. 51.

[2] Oxford, on the other hand, elected to stand his trial. He was committed to the Tower on July 16, 1715. He remained there for nearly two years. In May 1717 some of his friends in the House of Lords put forward the view that his impeachment had automatically lapsed with the prorogation of 1716, and that he ought to be discharged. Shrewsbury was one of the large majority (eighty-eight to forty-four) who voted against this. When the case did come on in June 1717 it provoked a quarrel between the Houses, and the Commons not appearing on July 1, the day fixed for the trial, the Lords unanimously declared Oxford acquitted.

[3] D'Iberville to Louis XIV, in Add. MSS. 34,498, ff. 86, 88; *Unpublished Letters of Dean Swift* (ed. G. G. B. Hill, 1899), p. 52.

[4] *Letters of Sarah, Duchess of Marlborough*, pp. 119–20.

The influence of the Duchess of Shrewsbury survived that of her husband. Appointed Lady of the Bedchamber to Caroline of Anspach, the Princess of Wales, Adelaide enjoyed a brilliant success in the early years of George I which quite eclipsed her earlier glories. The King found her very entertaining, as his predecessor had done. Other ladies were very jealous of the favour she enjoyed. Lady Cowper tells us that her appointment to the Bedchamber was not of the Princess's choice; that she only agreed to it after the King had importuned her three times for it.[1] The Duchess, it was alleged, would not allow anyone else to speak with the new monarch. "I believe", writes Lady Strafford on November 11, 1714, "the Duchess of Shrewsbery will devour the King".[2] In Lady Mary Wortley Montagu's *Roxana, or the Drawing-room*, the Duchess figures as Coquetilla, and is there denounced with great venom.

> Yet Coquetilla's artifice prevails
> When all my merit and my duty fails;
> That Coquetilla, whose deluding airs
> Corrupt our virgins, still our youth ensnares;
> So sunk her character, so lost her fame,
> Scarce visited before your highness came:
> Yet for the bedchamber 'tis her you choose,
> When zeal and fame and virtue you refuse.
> Ah! worthy choice! not one of all your train
> Whom censure blasts not, and dishonours stain![3]

While Shrewsbury sank into comparative obscurity after 1714, he made one or two noteworthy appearances in the House of Lords. When Parliament assembled in March 1715 Bolingbroke took exception to some of the terms of the loyal

[1] *Diary of Lady Cowper*, p. 8.
[2] *Wentworth Papers*, p. 439.
[3] *Letters and Works of Lady Mary Wortley Montagu* (ed. Lord Wharncliffe, 3rd ed. 2 vols. 1861), vol. II, p. 434. For identification of Coquetilla see *Letters of Horace Walpole* (ed. Messrs Paget Toynbee, Oxford, 16 vols. 1903–5), vol. XIII, p. 442; H. Walpole to Lady Ossory, Feb. 1, 1787.

address moved in the Upper House, wherein the late peace settlement was disparaged and an assurance was expressed that his Majesty "would recover the reputation of this Kingdom in foreign parts". This phrase was deliberately inserted by the Whigs on the present occasion in retaliation for the similar reflection on William III which the Tories had made on the accession of Queen Anne. Bolingbroke moved the amendment to the address by the substitution of the word "maintain" for "recover", and the omission of the remainder of the sentence which asserted that the loss of reputation was "by no means to be imputed to the nation in general". Shrewsbury supported the amendment on the ground that that House ought on all occasions to be particularly tender of the honour and dignity of the Crown, and he reminded his hearers that he had opposed the similar motion of 1702.[1]

He again sided with the Tories—with Nottingham, Atterbury, Buckinghamshire, Abingdon and Paulet, in opposition to the Septennial Bill when it was introduced into the House of Lords in April 1716; and spoke "vehemently" against it. It was in frequent not in long parliaments that this champion of the triennial system believed. Against the argument that the measure would reduce parliamentary corruption and the expenditure of money on elections, he made the witty and pertinent rejoinder that "as to the saving of money, he could not see that, for he believed everybody knew that an annuity of seven years costs dearer than an annuity of three".[2] His name appears among the thirty-one signatories of a protest against the committing of the Bill on April 14, mainly on the grounds that frequent parliaments were required by the fundamental constitution of the kingdom and that this

[1] *Parl. Hist.* vol. VII, p. 46.
[2] *Stuart MSS.* vol. II, p. 123; N. Tindal, *Continuation of Rapin's History of England*, 1757–63, vol. XIX (VII of Continuation), p. 12.

measure would rather increase corruption than prevent it.[1]
He also protested, together with twenty-three others, against
the passing of the Bill on the 17th.[2]

What was the attitude of Shrewsbury to the Court and
Government at this time? He supported the dynasty during
the 1715 rebellion despite the assurance of Bolingbroke, now
acting as Secretary of State at the Jacobite Court, made to
the Pretender on August 20, that "the Duke of Shrewsbury
is frankly engaged, and was the last time I heard of him, very
sanguine".[3] A year later, when the Duke of Argyll was very
influential with the Prince of Wales and strongly upholding
him in his inveterate hostility to his father, it was stated that
the former had introduced Shrewsbury "into his royal
highness's favour and intimacy".[4] On the pretext of his
wife being a Lady of the Bedchamber Shrewsbury has made
himself an inhabitant of the Prince's residence, "which by
all accounts, his publick as well as private reception and
conferences with both prince and princess sufficiently encourage". So writes Walpole to Stanhope in August 1716.[5]
Argyll, Islay, Rochester, Shrewsbury, their wives, and other
Tories are constant attendants at Hampton Court, which
"does not a little animate the Tories", he noted a little
before.[6] All having country houses within about fifteen miles
distance, these Lords, and one or two others mentioned in a
subsequent letter, have excellent opportunities for caballing.[7]

While caballing with the Opposition at home, Shrewsbury

[1] Rogers, *Complete Protests*, vol. I, pp. 227–30.
[2] *Parl. Hist.* vol. VII, pp. 307–8.
[3] W. Michael, *Englische Geschichte im achtzehnten Jahrhundert* (2 vols. Berlin and Leipzig, 1921), vol. I, p. 508; Lord Mahon, *Hist. of England*, 1713–83 (7 vols. 1858), vol. I, app. p. xix.
[4] W. Coxe, *Memoirs of Sir R. Walpole* (3 vols. 1798), vol. II, p. 66: S. Poyntz to Stanhope, Aug. 10/21, 1716.
[5] *Ibid.* p. 64; Walpole to Stanhope, Aug. 9/20.
[6] *Ibid.* p. 61; same to same, Aug. 7/18.
[7] W. Coxe, *Memoirs of Sir R. Walpole*, vol. II, p. 78; same to same, Aug. 30/Sept. 10.

was once again in these latter days in touch with the Jacobites abroad. In July 1716 he sends his humble respects to Avignon, to ask if there is "any determinate scheme in hand for making another attempt within some tolerable compass of time". He intimates in conversation with the intermediary that there is no prospect of success unless "a regular and considerable force be brought into the kingdom"—a prospect which, after the failure of the rising of the previous year, he probably thought negligible.[1] In October 1717 Mar (now a Duke in the Jacobite peerage) writes to J. Menzies, the chief Jacobite agent in England, for news of Shrewsbury, of whom he has heard little for a long while.[2] Presumably in answer to this letter Menzies reports on November 4 (n.s.) that he has had an interview with Shrewsbury, "who is right and true notwithstanding late and close temptations and who is also your real friend".[3] In a letter of December 16 he refers to the Duke as "a prodigy of clear sound sense, worth a thousand friends, and has done more real service".[4] Such statements do not necessarily mean more than that Shrewsbury allowed the Jacobite agent to pay him one or two surreptitious visits and indulged in a few polite and non-committal assurances. But he seems to have gone further than this. The annexation of Bremen and Verden by George I in his capacity as Elector of Hanover in 1715 involved Great Britain in an anti-Swedish policy on behalf of interests not her own. Any such complication afforded an opportunity for the exiled house of Stuart, and advantage was taken of this one, as the English Government soon found reason to suspect. Early in 1717, in defiance of the law of nations, Count Gyllenborg, the Swedish ambassador at St James's, was arrested in his own house and his papers seized; three weeks later, Baron Görz, the Swedish ambassador at The

[1] *Stuart MSS.* vol. IV, pp. 55–6.
[2] *Ibid.* vol. v, p. 126.   [3] *Ibid.* p. 177.   [4] *Ibid.* p. 325.

Hague, was, at the request of the English monarch, also apprehended. These arbitrary proceedings were morally justified by the evidence which was thus discovered that both ambassadors had been in negotiation with St Germain for a new Jacobite attack upon the reigning dynasty in England, to be assisted with 12,000 Swedish troops. Shrewsbury seems to have been implicated in the plot, though this the British Government never learnt. Gyllenborg had asked that the Jacobites should raise the sum of £50,000 in support of the enterprise; an undertaking was given to supply £20,000. The Bishop of Rochester agreed to contribute £5,000; he had hopes that Shrewsbury and the Earl of Portmore would also contribute liberally.[1] It appears that Shrewsbury was "in no intimacy" at this time with Atterbury,[2] who was by far the most zealous and vigorous of the English Jacobites, so that Atterbury's expectations of financial support from him would not by themselves be incriminating; but Menzies (writing, as it happened, actually after Shrewsbury's death), declared that "nobody certainly wishes better to the...Company" than the Duke and Portmore,[3] and, although the language of the Jacobite letters relating to these financial transactions is inevitably obscure, they certainly seem to indicate that some money passed from Menzies to Gyllenborg through Shrewsbury's hands. The letters in question are a year later in date than the arrest of Gyllenborg and refer to the disappearance of some of the money. Menzies is anxious that Shrewsbury should be questioned "whether he did not give it to Gyllenborg. There is no question but orders were sent to him...to deliver what could be had to Gyllenborg".[4] Shrewsbury could be asked to clear up the

[1] *Stuart Papers*, vol. v, pp. 528–9.
[2] Mar to Maj.-General Dillon, Feb. 12, 1718, in *ibid.* p. 463.
[3] Mar to Menzies, Feb. 15, in *ibid.* p. 478.
[4] L. Inese to Mar, Jan. 17, in *Stuart Papers*, vol. v, pp. 391–2. Cf. Menzies to Inese, Jan. 6/17, *ibid.* p. 393. Cf. however, two cryptic letters, the Pretender to Mar, June 20, 1717, and Mar to the

matter being "still alive". Probably the suggestion came too late. The Duke was dangerously ill, and did not recover.

Shrewsbury who had suffered from asthma of late, fell ill with inflammation of the lungs about the middle of January 1717/18.[1] After his life had been despaired of he rallied, but almost immediately afterwards he had a relapse.[2] "The poor Duke has a wonderful escape if he recovers," wrote Dr William Stratford on February 1, "I should have thought the prescriptions he has had surer than any draughts his lady ever mingled in her own country."[3] That same day Shrewsbury died, succumbing at the age of fifty-eight to the weakness of the lungs which had been his bane ever since early manhood.

With his death the Dukedom of Shrewsbury and Marquisate of Alton became extinct, but the Earldoms of Shrewsbury and Waterford devolved upon his first cousin Gilbert Talbot. The Duchess survived her husband for nine years. A fortnight after the Duke's death her brother the Marquis of Paleotti was committed to Newgate for murdering his servant in the street. A month later, after she had vainly solicited the King (who had no power to grant the request) that he might be beheaded rather than hanged, Paleotti was executed.[4] With the death of her husband and the scandal of her brother's end the triumphs of Coquetilla were ended.

Pretender, July 16, *ibid.* vol. IV, pp. 368–9, 456, which suggest Shrewsbury's aloofness.

[1] *Stuart Papers*, vol. V, p. 393.
[2] *Ballard MSS.* (Bodl.), vol. XX, f. 96: Dr G. Clarke, Jan. 30.
[3] *Portland MSS.* vol. VII, p. 233.
[4] *MSS. of Lord Polwarth* (H.M.C. 1911), pp. 444, 462.

CHAPTER XI

Conclusion

In the foregoing pages the story of Shrewsbury's career has been told with as little of comment and conjecture as possible. It is well to propound the puzzle completely before attempting its solution. A puzzle the Duke's career certainly is, for it is full of apparent contradictions. At one time he acts with notable courage and determination; at another he is so cautious and circumspect as to lay himself open to the charge of timidity or even cowardice. He is one of the prime movers in bringing about the accession of William of Orange; before long he is engaged in Jacobite intrigue, or at least gives grounds for grave suspicion that this is so: he is one of the prime movers in bringing about the peaceful accession of George I; three or four years later he has resumed his connection with the Jacobites, and almost the last thing one hears of him is that he is supporting a dangerous plot against the Hanoverian Sovereign. He has a great reputation for equal charm and integrity, and he wins general esteem; yet there are times when he is deeply suspect to his associates. For many years he is a close friend and confidant of the Marlboroughs, and he stands by them when they are in disgrace with William III; but he turns against them in 1710, and they complain most fiercely alike of his "sophistries" and of his insulting behaviour to them.[1] Prior to the termination of his second Secretaryship he is reckoned as one of the great princes of the Whigs, and he is closely associated with the other prominent leaders of the party; but later on he becomes an object of suspicion to them, in the first place because of his intimacy with Sunderland, still more when he leaves the

[1] Coxe, *Life of Marlborough*, vol. III, pp. 118–19.

[222]

country on the eve of the impeachment of the Junto on the
score of the Partition Treaties, in which he was implicated
as well as they. When he returns to England and to public
life he becomes a member of a Tory Administration; Harley
"tampers with him",[1] uses him as a convenient instrument
for the attainment of his own ambitions. But does Shrewsbury remain a mere instrument? What are his relations with
the two allies and rivals in the Tory camp? One of them at
all events—Bolingbroke—for all his cleverness cannot tell.
He is no sooner in office than he wants to be relieved of it—
"he went out of the Great Offices", says Macky, "with as
much ease as he shifted his cloaths"[2]—yet is he as indifferent
to power as his constant railings against the cares of administration would suggest? Is his first resignation of the Secretaryship to be accounted for, not by reluctance to remain in
power, but by chagrin that one of his colleagues is more
powerful than he? The reasons that Shrewsbury himself
gives are incapacity and ill-health. Repeatedly he alleges
illness as the explanation of his inactivity, of his flights from
Westminster and Whitehall into the sequestered wilds of
Gloucestershire or to climes still more remote. Are his
illnesses genuine or are they merely evasions of difficulty?

Such are some of the puzzles which render Shrewsbury
something of an enigma. In endeavouring to solve them let
us start with facts about which there is little or no dispute.
In the first place there is unanimous testimony as to his
charm of appearance (despite his loss of one eye) and of
manner, his graciousness and courtliness. "If he dies",
writes the Jacobite agent Menzies with reference to the
Duke's serious illness in January 1718, "the best head and
the politest gentleman in England falls".[3] John Macky
speaks of him as "a Great Man, attended with a sweetness

[1] Coxe, *Life of Marlborough*, p. 57.
[2] *Memoirs of Secret Service* (1733), p. 14.
[3] *Stuart Papers*, vol. v, p. 393.

of Behaviour, and easiness of Conversation, which charms all who come near him. Nothing of the stiffness of a statesman, yet the capacity and knowledge of a piercing Wit".[1] Burnet speaks in similar terms. "He is so far from haughtiness and impatience of spirit, which are the common frailties of young men that are above the common level of mankind, that during his ministry I never heard that the indiscretion of those who came to him, especially of importunate suitors, drew one passionate answer from him."[2] No man could win the title of "King of Hearts" as his sobriquet without possessing that genuine kindliness of disposition which is the source of courtesy and urbanity when they are lavished upon all, whatever their character and station.[3] Clearly he inspired affection. He gave William frequent cause for annoyance, by his insistence upon resignation at the most inconvenient moments, by his reluctance to serve when most needed: yet the patience and forbearance of the King were well-nigh illimitable. This may be partly due to the fact that the great Whig peer was at those times almost indispensable for party reasons. But there is a warmth of tone in the letters which the King writes to Shrewsbury on these occasions, and still more in those relating to Fenwick's accusations, which surely betokens real personal feeling on the part of one who was normally little disposed to give outward manifestation of any. Clearly also Queen Anne found him attractive, and his value to Harley during the negotiations of 1710 was largely due to his being *persona grata* with the Queen. Macky

[1] *Memoirs*, p. 15.
[2] *History of His Own Time*, vol. i, pp. 762–3; Foxcroft's *Supplement to Burnet*, p. 288. It has been suggested with, to say the least of it, considerable plausibility, that Macky purloined his characters from the pages of Burnet. See *Times Literary Supplement*, June 14, 21, 1928. The resemblance is not so close in the case of Shrewsbury as in some other instances, but there is some similarity.
[3] Cf. Strafford's description of Shrewsbury as "a man of great parts...very affable and obliging in his behaviour". *Wentworth Papers*, p. 134.

speaks of Shrewsbury with his "very charming Countenance" as being "the most generally beloved by the Ladies of any Gentleman of his Time".[1] There is, perhaps, a hint of libertinage in the description, and Shrewsbury's good name in this respect is not unsullied: the remonstrance addressed to him at the time of his conversion by Tillotson can have but one meaning.[2] On the other hand, we can confidently dismiss the ill-natured stories about an intrigue with the Countess Adelaide prior to his engagement to her as the half-malicious, half-puzzled gossip of a set of people who, while little troubled by the conventions of morality, found their social conventions outraged by the marriage of a great English duke to an obscure Italian countess. The truth is that, considering the deplorable initial drawback of his mother's vicious life and character, and the generally low moral standard of the society in which he moved, Shrewsbury's reputation has suffered remarkably little damage. Courtly manners are welcomed in the drawing-room and it is only cynicism that suspects them on this account. They are welcome also in the palace. Shrewsbury had a full sense of his own dignity, as the episode of his encounter with Berkeley at Paris indicated even in his earliest manhood.[3] For the purely formal side of an ambassador's duties no one could have been more admirably equipped; amid all the "pomp and circumstance" of Versailles he moved at his ease. He had indeed the happy capacity of being able to ingratiate himself both with Kings and Commoners. "He has ever been the favourite of the nation", wrote Swift, "being possessed of all the amiable qualities that can accompany a great man."[4]

If there is general agreement about Shrewsbury's attractiveness, so is there also as to his accomplishments. He was

---

[1] *Memoirs*, p. 15.   [2] Cf. *supra*, p. 16.   [3] *Supra*, p. 12.
[4] *Contributions to the Examiner* (*Works*, Temple Scott ed.), vol. IX, pp. 171-2.

"a man of great parts", says Strafford, and Burnet speaks of his possessing "no ordinary measure of learning" and "a correct judgment".[1] He was not an insular Englishman. He not only knew other languages and other countries besides his own, but he could make himself at home in them. His opposition to the censorship of the press in 1693 on the score that the system subjected "all learning and true information to the arbitrary will and pleasure of a mercenary, and, perhaps, ignorant licenser", does credit to his enlightenment. His journal shews a keen interest in letters and art, and his friends regarded him as a connoisseur[2]. They may have had an exaggerated idea of the excellence of his taste and artistic judgment. He was a dilettante rather than a scholar or skilled critic, but certainly he was a man of culture and refinement. Obviously too a retired private life, with the opportunity to indulge his love for his books and his paintings and for a quiet country-side, had a compelling attraction for him. His repeated diatribes against the drudgery of a statesman's existence do not spring solely from the vexations or embarrassments of the moment; they indicate a constitutional aversion. Born into another station or born in less critical times he might have been able to enjoy in undisturbed and undistinguished repose the sequestered existence which so strongly appealed to him.

But Shrewsbury could not evade the responsibilities of peerage, and his lifetime coincided with a very disturbed period of his country's history, a period of plot and counter-plot, of war and invasion, of unstable dynasties, of crisis upon crisis. Amid such conditions it was difficult for one born to greatness to remain in a cloistered obscurity. But happy was the man, who having to pursue his course before the eyes of the nation, was able to pursue it without hesitancy or deviation. There were few if any at all who did. None

[1] *History of His Own Time*, vol. I, p. 763.
[2] *Supra*, p. 149.

succeeded in escaping censure. Shrewsbury changed his religion at a time when the recent exclusion of Roman Catholics from public office and from Parliament rendered conversion materially advantageous: so this step was at once attributed to interested motives solely. But the decision was taken but a short time after the Earl had been serving in Flanders in the suite of the Duke of York, who as the only member of the royal family with whom the young man had been brought into close contact was most likely to advance his fortunes, and who was heir to the throne. If renunciation of Roman Catholicism was profitable in 1680, it required no great prescience at that date to foresee that before long it might easily prove to have been, from an utilitarian point of view, a great blunder. And so indeed on the accession of James II it was found to be. The evidence is quite insufficient to convict Shrewsbury of mere time-serving and religious insincerity. His conduct in Rome, and his references to Roman Catholicism in his journal, seem to indicate that his Protestantism was stalwart enough. Burnet lamented quite another kind of infidelity. "Some thought", he wrote—and when Burnet said "some" he usually meant the Bishop of Salisbury—"that, though he had forsaken popery, he was too sceptical, and too little fixed in the points of religion".[1] An anonymous informant relates that one, Pope, "said that the Duke of Shrewsbury told him he was of the same religion he was at fourteen and had never altered. Now, he being older than that when Tillotson converted him to the Protestant religion, and dying as he did in the same outward profession, Pope believed he was likewise a Deist".[2]

As it is possible to attribute the first decisive action of Shrewsbury's life—his conversion—to mere time-serving, so may the second—his strenuous support of William of Orange's enterprise—be ascribed to pique at James II's treatment of

[1] *History of His Own Time*, vol. I, p. 762.
[2] *MSS. of the Earl of Egmont* (H.M.C. Rept. VII), app. p. 244.

him, and more particularly at his loss of all his appointments. But such a view ignores the important fact that his fall from the royal favour was due to his firm refusal to revert to his old religion and to carry out the King's instructions that he should use his influence as Lord-Lieutenant to return members to Parliament subservient to James's will. Had Shrewsbury's conduct after 1689 always been as bold and straightforward as it was prior to that date there would have been little legitimate cause for criticism.

But when he came into power he seemed quite unable to stand the strain of responsibility. The resolute conspirator of 1688 developed into the singularly irresolute minister of 1689. The zealous champion of the claims of Whiggism and of William of Orange became rapidly discontented with his own party and his new King. The statesman whom William especially commended to Mary as one in whom she could implicitly trust insisted upon resigning office at the most inopportune moment. This proceeding seemed incomprehensible to many of his contemporaries, and at first sight the story that the Secretary resigned the seals in obedience to the exiled King's instructions seems to offer at least a plausible explanation. It has been said that "Shrewsbury's conduct throughout William's reign is inexplicable unless the fact that he was involved in Jacobite intrigues be accepted".[1] That he was engaged in correspondence with the Jacobites there can be no question. On his own admission at the time of the Fenwick discoveries he was in communication with his relative Middleton, and, even accepting his own assertion that his letters were purely private in nature, it was an improper proceeding for the Secretary of State to the King of England to have intercourse with the Secretary of the deposed monarch. Shrewsbury's letters written to his master at this time, reveal, as we have already seen, great distress of

[1] G. Davies, "James Macpherson and the Nairne Papers", in *E.H.R.* 1920, pp. 369–70.

mind if not remorse. And in the view of a less corrupt age it appears that well they might, for in modern eyes such double-dealing seems very odious. But, as has already been pointed out, the Jacobite agents were never able to report much that was positive about Shrewsbury, and, the wish being clearly father to the thought with most of the Jacobites overseas, we have to discount a good deal of what they assert regarding politicians at home. There is really nothing to shew that in keeping in touch with St Germain, Shrewsbury was doing anything more than that which the majority of his colleagues were doing, namely, taking out an insurance policy on the off-chance that James II might after all, as the result of French aid, succeed in recovering the throne. There is no reason to suppose that Shrewsbury ever had the slightest desire to witness another Stuart restoration; indeed, as has already been argued in these pages, there is every reason to suppose the contrary. He was too deeply implicated in the Revolution settlement as one of the ringleaders in 1688 to expect any favour from a restored James II. He was no fool and he was eminently cautious. Only a rash fool could have felt safe with a potentate who had abundantly revealed himself as obstinate in his prejudices, resentful of injuries, and implacable to his foes. Moreover, it should not be forgotten that Shrewsbury had a heavy financial interest in the maintenance of the Protestant succession. He had contributed £12,000 to the cost of the Prince of Orange's expedition; he advanced £10,000 to the Bank of England when it was founded. Overt actions speak louder than clandestine correspondence. Unmistakably in 1714, first in Ireland, then at the final crisis of the reign of Queen Anne, Shrewsbury exerted himself for the maintenance of the Protestant Succession.

His career is a strange mixture of occasional moments of certitude and resolute action and other periods of weakness and hesitancy. His constitutional caution looks very much like timidity. "If he were somewhat more active and less timorous in business, no man would be thought comparable to him", writes Swift in 1712.[1] The man who boldly risked all in 1688 came to be regarded as singularly lacking in spirit. His frequent illnesses have commonly been looked upon as convenient subterfuges for escaping from awkward predicaments. "Indeed", says a recent writer, "he had a most adroit way of avoiding political responsibility by quitting office at critical moments upon a plea of illness."[2] It is a natural view to take. Circumstances more than once made Shrewsbury's ill-health look highly suspicious, especially at the time of the Fenwick revelations. Was there anything more seriously amiss with him than the pricks of a bad conscience and a cowardly unwillingness to emerge from his rural shelter and face accusation in London? But the riding accident was no pretence, and the damage done to Shrewsbury's lungs as the result of it was permanent. It is indeed impossible to read all the evidence and not be convinced of the reality of his malady. The evidence comes from other sources besides Shrewsbury himself, and it is by no means true that his illnesses always coincided with times of political trouble. While his health was much better in Rome than it had been in England, he was frequently unwell even when abroad and entirely free from the cares and anxieties of public life. Never were his lamentations concerning his ill-health more bitter than when he was staying in Venice or travelling through the Tyrol, trying to patch up the "crazy corpse" of which he was so weary. Many complaints it is easy to simulate, but not the one from which Shrewsbury suffered— hæmorrhage of the lungs.

But to recognise the genuineness of Shrewsbury's physical infirmity is not necessarily to admit that the invalid was always as ill as he said he was or thought he was. Despite the

---

[1] *Corr.* vol. 1, p. 326.
[2] W. T. Morgan, *English Political Parties and Leaders in the Reign of Queen Anne*, 1702–10 (Yale U.P. 1920), p. 50.

constant lung trouble he succeeded in reaching the respectable age of fifty-eight. There can be no question that he was essentially a hypochondriac. His preoccupation with his symptoms, his everlasting wailing about his condition are deplorable in their unmanliness. It is impossible to read his pitiful appeals to William to be released from the not very exacting labours of office and not be impressed by the strong contrast between the behaviour of these two men, who suffered from somewhat similar ailments—the one fighting his life-long battle against physical disabilities with heroic stoicism and unflinchingly enduring the unceasing ardours of a harassed and strenuous career not merely in the council-chamber, but also on the battlefield; the other without any stoicism at all petulantly declaring at the first distressing symptom that only complete rest and retirement into the heart of the country can preserve his life. Shrewsbury's maladies were of the mind and spirit as well as of the body. When he begged to be relieved of the Secretaryship in September 1689 this young man, still under thirty, thought it no shame to speak of his health and strength as already decaying. He was in bed with fever. There is no reason to doubt the reality of the fever. Fever of mind had produced a fever of the blood, and each heightened the other. Of a morbid sensitiveness, he knew no peace of mind when events occurred to mar the even tenor of his way. Brooding over his own grievances, unkindly criticisms of his conduct openly expressed or (perhaps just as disturbing) merely imagined by himself, over his own failings as an administrator and his own disloyalties (though worse turpitude caused Marlborough and Russell not a qualm), he was a sick man indeed, wearied sometimes, one suspects, as much of himself as of the "crazy corpse", of which he so bitterly complained. To this sorry state was the gallant and resplendent young hero of the Whigs, as he had been in 1688, speedily reduced by even a very brief experience of the rough and tumble of political life, of the petty jarring irritations, the unkindnesses of friends, the animosities of enemies, the thwartings and disappointments, which are part and parcel of the honourable task of carrying on the business of the state. There is no hint of weakness in the early glimpses which we get of Shrewsbury, of the boy who knows his own mind when his uncle and guardian is inclined to be dictatorial, who enjoys his first and only experience of soldiering, who refuses to do James II's bidding in his capacity as Lord-Lieutenant, who from its inception takes so big a part in organising the expedition of William of Orange. But the crucible of public service, so much less obvious, yet so much more severe a test, than the stirring events of 1688, revealed the inherent weaknesses of Shrewsbury not only to others but to himself. Handsome, attractive, and even noble as is the face portrayed for us in Lely's picture in the Charterhouse, it lacks power.

Since he was so self-depreciatory, so often anxious to slink away from London and affairs of state into remoteness and obscurity it may seem a paradox to assert that he was ambitious of influence; but the contradiction is more apparent than real. Self-depreciation and even self-distrust are by no means incompatible with self-esteem. Unquestionably, chagrin at finding Carmarthen so often preferred to himself in the royal closet was the paramount cause of the fevers of the autumn of 1689. Again, contradictory though it may appear, Shrewsbury's defects as a politician were conjoined with a certain political suppleness. Failure to allow for this led to a serious misapprehension of the situation by Godolphin and Marlborough in 1710. Their conviction of Shrewsbury's inherent caution, and even timidity, caused them seriously to underestimate his importance.

Despite all his failings Shrewsbury possessed two valuable qualities, which sometimes rendered him more effective than the obvious flaws of his character and temperament suggested. The first was the product of his essential kindliness and good nature. "King William was used to say that the Duke of Shrewsbury was the only Man the Whigs and Tories both spoke well of."[1] Recognised as a man of conciliatory temper, tactful, discreet and sympathetic, he seemed to be cut out for the rôle of mediator. Thus when the Whigs fell foul of Sunderland in 1698 he was called in as the only likely reconciler. Again, when Oxford and Bolingbroke became utterly alienated in 1714 it was to Shrewsbury that observers looked to heal the estrangement. Thus, too, when Harley preached the gospel of moderation and compromise in 1710 it was to Shrewsbury he turned as the most effective instrument for the accomplishment of his designs. It is true that in his early days Shrewsbury acted as a zealous Whig and that he endeavoured to dissuade William from his policy of mixed Administrations; but he was temperamentally averse from extreme partisanship. He was of an entirely different type from such party "managers" as Wharton and the other members of the Junto. Being neither manager nor extremist, he could act with the moderate Tories in 1710 without doing violence to his convictions.

The second valuable quality which Shrewsbury possessed was political sagacity. On the major issues of politics he was usually right. Possessed neither of executive ability nor of driving force, he could yet exert influence apparently disproportionate to his powers, because he had a sure instinct as to the nation's needs and its truest welfare. He gave his support to the vigorous prosecution of the war with France during the reign of William III and also during the reign of Anne; but a natural astuteness as well as a naturally pacific inclination made him keenly aware when the national exhaustion and public opinion called for peace. Hence his urgent arguments addressed to William in July 1696, immediately he heard of the secession of the Duke of Savoy,

[1] Macky, *op. cit.* p. 13.

advocating the commencement of negotiations with France on the grounds that this event rendered decisive military success unlikely and that the country could not afford the financial strain of an indefinite prolongation of hostilities when there was no gain commensurate with the cost in prospect.[1] The letters in which Shrewsbury put forward this reasoning were eminently statesmanlike, and though William refused at the time to admit their cogency, he had before long to bow before the force of the circumstances upon which Shrewsbury based his arguments. So again, it is certain, as we have already seen, that one of Shrewsbury's strongest motives in joining the Tory Administration of 1710 was his sympathy with the principal article of their policy, which was the conclusion of peace. Ever since the disastrous failures of the allies in Spain, the deplorable breakdown of the Gertruydenberg conference, and the terrible losses of Malplaquet, the trend of public opinion and the character of the military situation indicated the advisability of an early peace. But Shrewsbury was no advocate of peace at any price. He protested vigorously against the inadequacy of the terms which we were asking for our allies, against the glaring discrepancy between what we insisted upon for ourselves and what we were content to secure for the Dutch.[2] Still more noteworthy is the prescience which is surely to be discerned in his conduct during the last few months of the reign of Anne. Without openly breaking with Bolingbroke as Oxford did, he does not seem to have approved of his policy. In Ireland, while endeavouring to keep peace and concord between the contending factions, he opposed the intransigent methods of Sir Constantine Phipps, and shewed himself unmistakably on the side of the Protestant Succession, alike by his public utterances and by his proceedings against the Jacobite recruiters. So, too, in the final crisis of August he took the principal part

[1] *Supra*, pp. 94–7.   [2] *Supra*, pp. 168–9.

in accomplishing the peaceful accession of George I. On that great occasion he once more "stood forth the Shrewsbury of 1688".

Macaulay adds the words, "Scarcely anything in history is more melancholy than that late and solitary gleam, lighting up the close of a life which had dawned so splendidly, and which had so early become hopelessly troubled and gloomy".[1] If the gleam be melancholy because of what went before, it is still more melancholy because of what followed. Macaulay could not forgive Shrewsbury for having gone over to the Tories; his recent conduct, prior to 1714, had not really been discreditable to him, as Macaulay's words suggest. On the other hand, the last days of Shrewsbury certainly are depressing. The gleam was so very brief; then once again, as of yore, follow weariness of business, dissatisfaction with his position, futile intriguing with the exiled royal house, the old enemy of ill-health, this time at least no counterfeit, bringing with it death. Thus unsatisfactorily closes a career in which there had been much that was unsatisfactory; and yet, if the interest of Shrewsbury's life is at times a melancholy interest, it also has its attractiveness, and something of the charm of the man who in his own day was, despite all his weaknesses, the "King of Hearts" still lingers on in the pages of history.

[1] *History of England*, vol. VI, p. 2686.

BIBLIOGRAPHY

There are three collections containing portions of Shrewsbury's correspondence:

Shrewsbury's Correspondence, ed. W. Coxe, 1821. The first part contains correspondence with William III for the periods of the first secretaryship, the ineffectual negotiations of 1693, and the years 1694–1700. The second part includes correspondence with Russell during his command in the Mediterranean; with Galway in 1695 and 1696, and with Portland, Jersey, and Williamson, during the peace negotiations which terminated in the Treaty of Ryswick. The third part consists of correspondence with the members of the Whig Junto during the years 1695–1704. Referred to as Coxe.

Letters illustrative of the reign of William III, 1696–1704, addressed to the Duke of Shrewsbury by James Vernon, ed. G. P. R. James, 3 vols. 1841. A valuable collection poorly edited. Referred to as *Vernon Corr.*

MSS. of the Duke of Buccleuch at Montagu House, vol. II (H.M.C.). Contains a number of the letters printed by Coxe and James and a great many more. Part i covers the period 1674—Sept. 1696; Part ii the period Sept. 1696—July 1708. The latter includes also the Duke's Journal of his travels abroad between 1700 and 1706. The letters for the reign of Anne are relatively few. Referred to as *Buccleuch MSS.*

MANUSCRIPT SOURCES

British Museum

Add. MSS. 15,895. *Hyde Papers and Correspondence*, 1688–1709, vol. IV. A few letters of 1696 and 1697.

Add. MSS. 17,677. L'Hermitage, *State Correspondence between England and the Netherlands*. Vols. N.N. (1693), O.O. (1694), P.P. (1695–6), Q.Q. (1696), R.R. (1697), S.S. (1698), T.T. (1699), V.V. (1700), contain numerous allusions to Shrewsbury.

Add. MSS. 25,377. *Correspondence of Francesco Terriesi*, vol. XX. For 1688–9 and 1690.

Add. MSS. 30,000. *Dispatches of F. L. Bonet*, esp. vol. A (1696, 1697).

Add. MSS. 34,493, 34,496, 34,498, 34,502, 34,514, 34,515. *Mackintosh Collection.* These transcripts are invaluable for the general history of the reign of William III; the volumes enumerated being particularly useful for Shrewsbury's career.

Add. MSS. 7,121, 32,686. *Newcastle Papers,* vol. I; *Egerton MSS.* 1695. Occasional references.

Bodleian

Ballard MSS. vol. X; *Carte MSS.* vol. CCXXXIII. Occasional references.

Public Record Office

Foreign Entry Book XXVI (*passim*); *State Papers, France,* vols. CLIV, CLVII (*passim*), for Shrewsbury's embassy to Paris.

PUBLICATIONS OF THE HISTORICAL MANUSCRIPTS COMMISSION

(In addition to *Buccleuch MSS.* at Montagu House, vol. II)

MSS. of the Earl of Ancaster (Rept. XIII, app. pt vi).
Marquis of Bath at Longleat, vols. I and III (Prior Papers).
Duke of Buccleuch at Drumlanrig, vol. I.
Earl of Denbigh (Rept. VIII). For News-letters of 1686–93.
S. H. le Fleming (Rept. XII, app. pt vii).
Sir F. Graham (Rept. VII).
Lord Kenyon (Rept. XIV, app. pt iv).
Earl of Lonsdale (Rept. XIII, app. pt vii).
Earl of Marchmont (Rept. XIV, app. pt iii).
Lord Polwarth (1911).
Duke of Portland, vols. II, III, IV, V, VII.
Duke of Rutland (Rept. XII, app. pt v).
Duke of Somerset (Rept. XV, app. pt vii).
H.M. the King (Stuart Papers at Windsor Castle, vols. I–v).
Duke of Sutherland (Rept. v).

CALENDARS OF STATE PAPERS. DOMESTIC

Reign of Charles II: vol. VIII, 1667–8; vol. XVI, 1673–5. A few references.

Reign of William III: vol. I, 1689–90; vol. IV, 1693; vol. V, 1694–5; vol. VI, 1695; vol. VII, 1696; vol. VIII, 1697. Numerous relevant papers.

BIBLIOGRAPHY

PEERAGES

G. E. C(okayne). *Complete Peerage.* 8 vols. Exeter, 1887–98. The new edition has been consulted as far as possible. It has reached H in vol. VI.

A. Collins. *Complete Peerage.* Ed. Sir F. Brydges. 9 vols. 1812.

J. E. Doyle. *Official Baronage of England.* 3 vols. 1806.

OTHER PRINTED AUTHORITIES

(i) ORIGINAL

Ailesbury, Memoirs of Thomas Bruce, Earl of. 2 vols. Roxburghe Club. 1890.

Barozzi e Berchet. *Relazioni degli Stati Europei, nel Secolo* XVII. Serie IV. Inghilterra. Venice, 1865.

Blackmore, Sir R. *A True and Impartial History of the Conspiracy against the Person and Government of King William III,* 1723.

Bolingbroke's Correspondence: J. H. St John, Viscount. 4 vols. 1798.

Bonet, Friedrich. *Reports.* In Ranke, *History of England* (Eng. trans., 6 vols. Oxford, 1875), vol. VI, app. pp. 144–274.

Boyer, Abel. *Histoire de Guillaume III.* Amsterdam, 1703. Also *History of King William III.* 3 vols. 1702–3.

—— *Life and Reign of Queen Anne.* 1722.

—— *The Political State of Great Britain.* 60 vols. 1711–40, esp. vol. VI.

Bramston, Autobiography of Sir John. Ed. Lord Braybrooke. Camden Soc. 1845.

Buckinghamshire, John Sheffield, Duke of. *Works.* 2 vols. 1729.

Burnet, Gilbert. *History of His Own Time.* 2 vols., folio. 1724–34.

Clarendon's Diary. In Correspondence of Henry Hyde, Earl of Clarendon, and Laurence Hyde, Earl of Rochester. Ed. S. W. Singer. 2 vols. 1828.

Clarke, J. S. *Life of James II.* 2 vols. 1816.

Cole, Christian. *Historical and Political Memoirs.* 1735.

Cowper, Diary of Lady. Ed. S. Cowper. 1864.

Dalrymple, Sir J. *Memoirs of Great Britain and Ireland.* 2 vols. 1771–3. Vol. II contains documents.

Dumont de Bostaquet, Mémoires de. Ed. C. Read and F. Wadington. 1864.

Ellis Correspondence. Ed. Hon. G. A. Ellis. 2 vols. 1829.

Essex Papers. Ed. O. Airy. Camden Soc. 1890.

BIBLIOGRAPHY

Evelyn, Diary of John. Ed. W. Bray. 2 vols. 1827.

Foxcroft, H. C. *Supplement to Burnet's History of His Own Time.* 1902.

Grimblot, P. *Letters of William III and Louis XIV.* 2 vols. 1848.

Hamilton, Comte A. *Mémoires du Comte de Grammont.* La Haye, 1741.

Hanmer, Correspondence of Sir Thomas. Ed. Sir H. Bunbury. 1838.

Hatton Correspondence. Ed. Sir E. Maunde Thompson. 2 vols. Camden Soc. 1878.

Hearne, Remarks and Collections of Thomas. Ed. Doble, Rannie and Salter. 11 vols. Oxford, 1884–1918.

Hill, Correspondence of Richard. Ed. W. Blackley. 1845.

Kennet, White. *Complete History of England...to William III.* 2nd ed. 3 vols. 1719.

Lexington Papers. Ed. H. M. Sutton. 1851.

Lords, Journals of the House of. Vols. XII–XX (*passim*).

Luttrell, Narcissus. *Brief Historical Relation of State Affairs.* 6 vols. Oxford, 1857.

Macky, John. *Memoirs of Secret Services.* 1733.

Macpherson, James. *Original Papers containing the secret history of Great Britain.* 2 vols. 1775.

Marchmont Papers. Ed. Sir G. H. Rose. 3 vols. 1831.

Marlborough, Account of the Conduct of the Duchess of. 1742.

Marlborough, Correspondence of Sarah, Duchess of. 2 vols. 1838.

Marlborough, Letters and Dispatches of John Churchill, Duke of, 1702–12. Ed. Sir G. Murray. 5 vols. 1845.

Mary II, Memoirs of. Ed. R. Doebner. Leipzig and London. 1886.

Montagu, Letters and Works of Lady Mary Wortley. Ed. Lord Wharncliffe. 3rd ed. 2 vols. 1861.

Oldmixon, John. *History of England during the reigns of William and Mary, Anne, and George I.* 1735.

Parliamentary History (Cobbett's). Vols. V, VI, VII.

Pepys' Diary. Ed. H. B. Wheatley. 9 vols. 1893–9.

Poems, Collection of...relating to the Time. 1689.

Poems on Affairs of State. 2 vols. 1716.

Prideaux, H. *Letters to John Ellis, 1674–1722.* Ed. Sir E. Maunde Thompson, Camden Soc. 1875.

Reresby, Memoirs of Sir John. Ed. J. Cartwright. 1875.

Rogers, J. E. Thorold. *Complete Protests of the Lords.* 3 vols. Oxford, 1875.

Savile Correspondence. Ed. W. D. Cooper. Camden Soc. 1858.

Shrewsbury, Life and Character of the Duke of. 1718.

Shrewsbury, Memoirs of Public Transactions in the Life and Character of. 1718.

Sidney, Diary of Henry. Ed. R. W. Blencowe. 2 vols. 1843.

Swift, Jonathan. *Correspondence.* Ed. F. Ebrington Ball. 6 vols. 1910–14.

—— *Unpublished Letters.* Ed. G. G. Hill. 1899.

—— *Works.* Ed. Temple Scott. 12 vols. 1897–1908. Esp. vol. v, *Historical and Political Writings*, and vol. x, for *The Four Last Years of the Queen.*

Torcy, Journal inédit de Jean Baptiste Colbert, Marquis de. Ed. J. F. Masson. Paris, 1884.

Warner, R. *Epistolary Curiosities.* 2nd series. Bath, 1818.

Wentworth Papers. Ed. J. J. Cartwright. 1875.

Williamson, Letters to Sir Joseph. Ed. W. D. Christie. 2 vols. Camden Soc. 1874.

Wood, Life and Times of Anthony. 5 vols. Oxford, 1817.

(ii) SECONDARY

Atkinson, C. T. *Marlborough and the Rise of the British Army.* 2nd ed. 1924.

Birch, T. *Life of Tillotson.* 2nd ed. 1753.

Biscoe, A. C. *The Earls of Middleton.* 1876.

Burghclere, Lady. *George Villiers, 2nd Duke of Buckingham.* 1903.

Cartwright, Julia. *Madame.* 1900.

Coxe, W. *Life of Marlborough.* 3 vols. (Bohn), 1847–8.

—— *Memoirs of Sir Robert Walpole.* 3 vols. 1798.

Cunningham, A. *History of Great Britain.* 2 vols. 1787.

Davies, G. "James Macpherson and the Nairne Papers", in *E.H.R.* vol. xxxv (1920).

Dictionary of National Biography, for articles on Abbot Montagu, Sir J. Trenchard, Sir J. Montgomery, Shrewsbury, etc.

Foxcroft, H. C. *Life of George Savile, Marquis of Halifax.* 2 vols. 1898.

Hunter, J. *History of Hallamshire.* Ed. Gatty. 1869.

Klopp, Onno. *Der Fall des Hauses Stuart.* 14 vols. Vienna, 1875–88.

Leadam, I. S. *Political History of England* (Longmans), vol. IX.

Legg, L. G. Wickham. *Matthew Prior*. Cambridge, 1921.

Lodge, Sir Richard. *Political History of England* (Longmans), vol. VIII.

Longueville, T. *Rochester and other Literary Rakes*. 1902.

Macaulay, Lord. *History of England*. Ed. Sir C. H. Firth. 6 vols. 1913–15.

Mahon, Lord. *History of England, 1713–83*. 7 vols. 1858.

Michael, Wolfram. *Englische Geschichte im achtzehnten Jahrhundert*. 2 vols. Berlin and Leipzig, 1921.

Murray, R. H. *Revolutionary Ireland and its Settlement*. 1911.

O'Flanagan, J. R. *Lives of the Lord Chancellors of Ireland*. 2 vols. 1870.

Paget, J. *Paradoxes and Puzzles: Historical, Judicial and Literary*. Edinburgh, 1874.

Parnell, Col. Hon. A. "James Macpherson and the Nairne Papers", in *E.H.R.*, vol. XII (1897).

Ranke, L. von. *History of England mainly in the Seventeenth Century*. 6 vols. Oxford, 1875.

Tindal, N. *Continuation of Rapin's History of England*. 1757–63. Vols. XIV–XXI are by Tindal.

Turberville, A. S. *The House of Lords in the Reign of William III*. Oxford, 1913.

Wolseley, Viscount. *Life of John Churchill, Duke of Marlborough*. 2 vols. 1894.

Stanley Weyman wrote a novel *Shrewsbury* (1898), which is based on the Assassination plot of 1696 and the Fenwick case.

ABBREVIATIONS USED

Add. MSS. Additional Manuscripts in the British Museum.

Bodl. Bodleian Manuscripts.

C.J. Journals of the House of Commons.

C.S.P. (Dom.). Calendars of State Papers, Domestic Series.

D.N.B. Dictionary of National Biography.

H.L. MSS. Manuscripts of the House of Lords.

H.M.C. Historical Manuscripts Commission.

L.J. Journals of the House of Lords.

Parl. Hist. Parliamentary History (Cobbett's).

INDEX

Abjuration Bill (1690), Shrewsbury's support of, 46–8; (1692), 59

Addison, Joseph, 162

Adelaide, the Countess. *See* Shrewsbury, Adelaide, Duchess of

Ailesbury, Thomas Bruce, second Earl of, ascribes Shrewsbury's action in the Revolution to pique, 28; on Shrewsbury's gentleness to James II, 32; criticises Shrewsbury's conduct as Secretary of State, 34–5; amused at Shrewsbury's attitude to Treason Bill, 98; and Jacobite plots of 1696, 99 n., 115, 127 n. Also mentioned, 51, 90, 111 n.

Anglesey, Arthur Annesley, fifth Earl of, 206

Anne, Princess; later Queen of England, intrigues with the Churchills, 43, 56–7; makes her peace with William III, 89; her accession, 150; grows tired of the Duchess of Marlborough, 168; and trial of Sacheverell, 170; her antipathy to Sunderland, 176; finds the Duchess of Shrewsbury entertaining, 184; is ill early in 1714, 206; her fatal illness, 210; appoints Shrewsbury Lord Treasurer, 211; death of, 212. Also mentioned, 92, 143, 197, 224

Arbuthnot, John, quoted, 208

Argyll, John Campbell, second Duke of, 169, 197, 206, 211, 212, 218

Ashby, Admiral Sir John, 54

Asiento contract, the, 207

Association, the, for the defence of King William's person and government, 100–1

Atterbury, Francis, Bishop of Rochester, 180, 220

Auersperg, Count, 90 n.

Augsburg, Shrewsbury married in, 158–60

Bank of England, establishment of the, 82, 84

Beachy Head, battle of, 52–4

Berkeley of Stratton, William, fourth Baron, quoted, 182, 189, 196, 198

Bernstorff, Baron A. G. von, 186

Berwick, James Fitzjames, Duke of, 210 n.

Bill of Rights, the, 37

Bishops, the Seven, and their trial, 25–6

Blathwayt, William, 78, 84, 93, 94

Bolingbroke, Henry St John, Viscount, accompanies Harley into retirement (1706), 166; conducts peace negotiations, 171–2, 187–9; quarrels with Oxford, 195, 206; author of the Schism Bill, 207; despises Oxford's trimming methods, 208–9; failure of his schemes, 210–11; impeached, 215; moves amendment to Address (March, 1715), 216–17; Secretary of State at Jacobite Court, 218; cannot fathom Shrewsbury, 223. Also mentioned, 165, 180, 182, 186, 194, 233–4

Bothmer, Count H. C. von, 213

Boyer, Abel, quoted, 199, 204–5, 206, 211–12

Boyne, battle of the, 52

Brest, unsuccessful attack upon (1694), 79–80, 82, 111

Bridges, George Rodney, marries Countess of Shrewsbury, 14

[242]

Bristol, occupied by Shrewsbury (December, 1688), 29
Brodrick, Alan (later Viscount Midleton), 201
Buckingham, George Villiers, second Duke of, 2–8
Buckinghamshire, John Sheffield, first Duke of (previously Earl of Mulgrave, and Marquis of Normanby), in opposition, 58; and Land Tax (1692), 59; and Triennial Bill (1693), 60; accused of corruption, 91 n.; his negotiations with Shrewsbury (1706), 166. Also mentioned, 88, 180, 182, 211
Burne-Elmes, duel between Buckingham and Shrewsbury's father fought at, 4
Burnet, Gilbert, Bishop of Salisbury, on Shrewsbury's conversion, 19; on his appointment as Secretary of State, 34; tries to dissuade Shrewsbury from relinquishing office (1690), 47, 49 n.; on the royal veto, 61; on Shrewsbury's appointment as Lord Chamberlain (1710), 173; on Shrewsbury's character, 224 and n.; on Shrewsbury's "infidelity", 227. Otherwise quoted or referred to, 30 n., 38, 45–6, 55, 63, 84, 90, 92, 97
Butler, Toby (Jacobite), 205

Camaret Bay. See Brest
Cardigan, George Brudenell, third Earl of, 153
Cardigan, Thomas Brudenell, second Earl of, 2, 7, 8, 150
Carmarthen, Marquis of. See Leeds, Duke of
Caroline of Anspach, Princess of Wales, 216
Catalans, abandonment of the, 190, 206
Chaloner (informer), 135–6
Charles II, King of England, 5 n., 6, 11, 15, 16, 28
Charles II, King of Spain, 146–7

Clarendon, Henry Hyde, second Earl of, 30 n., 50
Clement XI, Pope, and Shrewsbury, 153–4
Colbert de Croissy (French ambassador to Court of Charles II), quoted, 5
Conduct of the Allies, The (Swift's), 185
Convention Parliament of 1689, the, 32–3
Cook, Sir Samuel (Lord Mayor of Dublin), 199
Cook, Sir Thomas (Governor of the East India Company), 91
Corporation Bill, the (1690), 45
Cowper, Lady, quoted, 183 n., 184 n., 216
Cowper, William, first Earl, 162, 180

Danby, Earl of. See Leeds, Duke of
Dartmouth, George Legge, first Baron, 28
Dartmouth, William Legge, second Baron, and first Earl of, quoted or referred to, 57, 87 n., 177, 187
d'Aumont, Duc, 188, 196
Defoe, Daniel, quoted, 207
Delafaye (clerk in Secretary of State's office), 159 and n.
Delamere, Lord. See Warrington, Earl of
Delaval, Admiral Sir Ralph, 63
Devonshire, William Cavendish, fourth Earl and first Duke of, 38, 92, 110, 115, 123 and n.
Devonshire, William Cavendish, second Duke of, 180
d'Iberville (French ambassador), 208–9, 213, 214, 215
Dorset, Charles Sackville, sixth Earl of, 92
Dublin, municipal troubles in, 197, 199–200, 203

East India Company, enquiry into affairs of the, 90–1
Eugene of Savoy, Prince, 186
Evelyn, John, quoted, 6

16–2

Eyford, Shrewsbury's country seat, 66, 67, 69, 88, 116, 118–20, 131–2, 134, 137–40

Fenwick, Lady Mary, 115, 127
Fenwick, Sir John, chap. v *passim*, 135, 224
Florence, visited by Shrewsbury, 148–9
Forbas, Father, 153
Fuller, William (spy), 57

Galway, Henry de Ruvigny, Earl of, 94–5, 134, 142
Gaultier, the Abbé, 184–5, 208
Geneva, visited by Shrewsbury, 146–7, 148
Genoa, visited by Shrewsbury, 148
George I, King of England, Elector of Hanover, 209, 212–19 *passim*, 222
Gloucester, Duke of (son of Princess Anne), death of, 143
Godolphin, Sidney, Baron and later Earl of, co-operates with Shrewsbury (1691), 56; in Cabinet, 77–8; incriminated by Fenwick, 110–11, 122–4; offers Shrewsbury post of Master of the Horse, 150–1; reluctant to admit Whigs into his Ministry (1706), 162; makes terms with the Whig Junto, 166–7; decides upon impeachment of Sacheverell, 170; retires to Newmarket, 171; disgusted at Shrewsbury's appointment as Lord Chamberlain, 172–3; is persuaded that Shrewsbury is friendly, 174–5; and Sunderland's dismissal, 176–7; dismissed from Lord Treasurership, 178–9. Also mentioned, 53, 73 n., 78 n., 92, 140, 160, 168, 169, 232
Goodman, Cardell, 122–3
Görz, Baron (Swedish minister), 219–20
Grace, Act of (1690), 55
Grafton, Shrewsbury's country seat at, 132, 165
Greenwich Hospital, 87 n.

Greg, William, 166
Guise, Sir John, 29–30
Gyllenborg, Count (Swedish ambassador), 219–20

Haddock, Admiral Sir Richard, 54
Halifax, Charles Montagu, Earl of, appointed Chancellor of the Exchequer, 76; and Recoinage Bill, 97–8; attacked for share in Partition Treaties, 147–8; regards Shrewsbury as fair-weather sailor, 163. Also mentioned, 103
Halifax, George Savile, Marquis of, commends Shrewsbury to William of Orange, 24; represents James II at Hungerford, 30; accompanies James to Rochester, 31–2; recommends Shrewsbury as Secretary of State, 34 and n.; attacked in House of Commons, 42; opposes Government in House of Lords (1692), 58; and Land Tax (1692), 59; and Triennial Bill (1693), 60
Hamilton, James Douglas, fourth Duke of, 188
Hanmer, Sir Thomas, 195, 206
Harcourt, Simon, first Viscount, 165–7, 182
Harley, Robert. *See* Oxford, Earl of
Heinsius, Anthony, Grand Pensionary of Holland, 146
Heythrop (Shrewsbury's country seat in Oxfordshire), 165, 167
Hill, Richard (English resident in Turin), 156
Howe, John, 87 n.
Hungerford, negotiations at (December, 1688), 30

Indemnity Bill (1689), 37, 42
Indulgence, Declarations of (1687, 1688), 20, 22, 25
Ireland, situation of, in 1689, 36–7; Shrewsbury's Lord-Lieutenancy in (1713–14), 196–205
Islay, Archibald Campbell, Earl of (subsequently third Duke of Argyll), 218

Jacobite plots, 55, 57–8, 205 and n., 208, and chap. v *passim*
James II, issues Declaration of Indulgence, 20; tries to influence Lords-Lieutenants, 21–2; treats with William of Orange, 30; conducted to Rochester by Shrewsbury, 31–2; escapes to France, 32; claims that Shrewsbury's resignation in 1690 is due to his instructions, 50; assured that Shrewsbury's acceptance of office is in his interests, 73–4; remains at St Germain after Treaty of Ryswick, 133; Shrewsbury's relations with, 227–9. Also mentioned, 5, 15, 17, 29, 51–2, 58, 111, 145
James Edward, Prince of Wales, commonly known as the Old Pretender, 26, 145, 218
Jansen, Cardinal, 151
Jersey, Edward Villiers, first Earl of, 107
Johnson, James, 101

Kent, Henry Grey, Duke of, 171
Killigrew, Admiral H., 63
Killigrew, Henry, and his relations with the Countess of Shrewsbury, 2–5 *passim*
King, Sir Peter, afterwards Baron, 170
Kneller, Sir Godfrey, 142

La Hogue, battle of, 58
Lancashire trials, 83–4
Land Bank, failure of the, 103, 106
Landen, battle of, 63
Land Tax (1692), 59–60
Lauzun, Duc de, 144
Lechmere, Nicholas, afterwards Baron, 170
Leeds, Thomas Osborne, Duke of (previously Earl of Danby and Marquis of Carmarthen), favours joint sovereignty of William and Mary, 33; a member of the "English Junto", 43; opposes King's desire to return to Hol-
land, 45; favours the Tories, 46; Shrewsbury's jealousy of, 49, 55; suggests Shrewsbury for Lord-Lieutenancy of Ireland, 56; created Duke of Leeds, 77; his overthrow, 91–2. Also mentioned, 73 n., 78
Lely, Sir Peter, his portrait of Shrewsbury, 232
Levinz, Sir Richard, 201
Lille, capture of, 168
Locke, John, 28
Lodève, Bishop of, 146
Louis XIV, 15–17, 32, 50–1, 133, 144, 146–7, 168
Lundy, Mrs, 66–70 *passim*
Lunt, John (informer), 83–4

Macaulay, Lord, on Shrewsbury, 235
Macky, John, quoted, 223–4
Malplaquet, battle of, 168
Mar, John Erskine, sixth Earl of, 219
Marlborough, John Churchill, Earl and afterwards Duke of, intrigues of, 43, 56–8, 73; William refuses to restore him to favour, 77, 80; restored to favour, 89; incriminated by Fenwick, 110–12, 124; in power after accession of Anne, 150–1; corresponds with Shrewsbury (1704–6), 162–3; entrusted with Shrewsbury's proxy (1706), 165; makes terms with the Whig Junto, 166–7; victories of, in Flanders, 168; amazed at Shrewsbury's proceedings in 1710, 174; but trusts in his love of moderation, 175; and Sunderland's dismissal, 176–7; thinks Shrewsbury can be managed, 178; dismissed from his command, 185; his forcing of Villar's lines, 186. Also mentioned, 53, 142, 154, 159, 160–1, 171, 173, 179, 231, 232
Marlborough, Sarah, Countess and afterwards Duchess of, intrigues of, 43, 56–7; on suspicions entertained on account of Shrews-

Marlborough, Sarah, *contd.*
bury's visit to Rome, 164–5; on Shrewsbury's reputation for wisdom, 167; breach with Queen Anne, 168; Shrewsbury ceases to call upon her, 169; on Shrewsbury's appointment as Lord Chamberlain, 172–3; Shrewsbury's assurances to, 174–5; dismissed from the royal household, 183; on Shrewsbury's retirement, 215

Marsin, Marshal, 158

Mary II, Princess of Orange and Queen of England, 26, 33–4, 52–3, 86, 89

Masham, Mrs Abigail, later Lady, 168, 174

Maubuisson, Louise Hollandina, Abbess of, 10

Melfort, John Drummond, Earl of, 73–4, 178

Menzies, J. (Jacobite agent), 219–20, 223

Middleton, Charles, second Earl of, 31, 51, 111 and n., 113–14, 145 n., 194

Millington, Sir Thomas, 118

Monmouth, Earl of (formerly Viscount Mordaunt, and later Earl of Peterborough), 25, 37, 54 n., 68–9, 127–9

Montagu, Abbot Walker, 10–11

Montagu, Charles. *See* Halifax, Earl of

Montagu, Lady Mary Wortley, quoted, 216

Montgomery, Sir James, 71–2

Montpellier, visited by Shrewsbury, 146

Moore, Arthur, 207

Moore, Dudley (actor), 202

Mordaunt, Charles, Viscount. *See* Monmouth, Earl of

Morgan, James (Shrewsbury's tutor), 8–9, 13

Mulgrave, Earl of. *See* Buckinghamshire, Duke of

Namur, siege of, 95–6

Navarre College, design to educate Shrewsbury at, 9

Newfoundland fisheries, question of the, 189–90, 192

Normanby, Marquis of. *See* Buckinghamshire, Duke of

Northampton, James Compton, third Earl of, and suggested marriage of Shrewsbury to his daughter, 11–13

Nottingham, Daniel Finch, second Earl of, Shrewsbury's jealousy of, 38, 49, 63; member of "the English Junto", 43; favours the Tories, 46; becomes sole Secretary of State, 52; failure of attack upon him in Parliament, 59; dismissed, 64–5; in opposition, 75–6. Also mentioned, 56, 162, 217

Orford, Edward Russell, Earl of, his relations with William of Orange in 1687, 26; visits The Hague (September, 1688), 27; his alleged Jacobitism, 73; becomes First Lord of the Admiralty, 76, 79; sent to the Mediterranean, 80–2; serious indiscretion of (1695), 93–4; on discovery of Assassination Plot commands fleet threatening the French coast, 99–100; incriminated by Fenwick, 110–11, 121, 123–4; attacked for complicity in the Partition Treaties, 147–8. Also mentioned, 54, 64, 86, 92, 95, 176, 231

Ormonde, James Butler, second Duke of, 185, 215

Oudenarde, battle of, 168

Oxford, Robert Harley, Earl of, and the Land Bank, 103; becomes Secretary of State (1704), 162; retires (1706), 166; alliance of with Mrs Masham, 168–9, 175; forms a Ministry, 178–81; said to govern England, 182, 185; antagonism of to Bolingbroke, 195–6, 206; demands enquiry into disposal of the *Asiento* contract, 207; his moderation

Oxford, *contd.*
anathema to Bolingbroke, 209;
dismissed from Lord Treasurership, 210; impeached, 215 and n.;
finds Shrewsbury useful, 224.
Also mentioned, 84, 177, 208,
223, 233–4

Paleotti, the Marquis (the elder),
149–50
Paleotti, the Marquis (the younger),
160, 221
Paris, Shrewsbury's education in,
8–14; his visit to (1700), 144–5;
his embassy to, 188–95
Partition Treaties, the (1699, 1700),
147
Pembroke, Thomas Herbert, eighth
Earl of, 54, 92
Pepys, Samuel, quoted, 4–5
Philip V of Spain (and Duke of
Anjou), 146, 168, 189
Phipps, Sir Constantine (Lord
Chancellor of Ireland), 198, 200,
202–5
Porter, George (Jacobite con-
spirator), 108, 109 n.
Portland, William Bentinck, first
Earl of, and Shrewsbury's resig-
nation (1689), 40–1; astonished
at Shrewsbury's attitude to
Treason Bill, 98; confers with
Shrewsbury regarding financial
stringency, 104, 106; and Fen-
wick case, 112, 116, 117, 120,
131; and Treaty of Ryswick, 133;
attacked for share in Partition
Treaties, 147. Also mentioned,
138
Portmore, David Colyear, first Earl
of, 220
Poulett, John, first Earl, 179
Prendergast, Thomas, 99
Press Licensing Laws, discon-
tinued, 62–3
Pretender, the Old. *See* James
Edward, Prince of Wales
Price, Richard (informer), 135–6
Prior, Matthew, 188, 191, 194, 195

Ramillies, battle of, 168

Recoinage Bill, 97–8, 102
Regency Act (1705), 212
Reresby, Sir John, quoted, 3
Robethon, Jean de, 186, 208
Rochester, Laurence Hyde, Earl of,
76, 130 n., 143 and n., 180, 218
Rome, Shrewsbury's life in, 149–56
Rooke, Admiral Sir George, 93
Russell, Edward. *See* Orford, Earl
of

Sacheverell, Dr Henry, 170
Saint Germain, Jacobite court at,
51, 80, 109, 111, 133, 145 n., 210,
218, 220, 229
Sancroft, William, Archbishop of
Canterbury, 26 n., 58
Savoy, Victor Amadeus, Duke of,
94–5, 105, 233–4
Schism Bill, the (1714), 207
Shovell, Admiral Sir Clowdisley, 63
Shrewsbury, Adelaide, Duchess of,
her parentage, 149–50; Shrewsbury's friendship with her in
Rome, 156–7; her marriage to
him, 159–60; her eccentricities,
182–4; in Paris, 194; her influence at the court of George I,
216; sues in vain for her brother's
life, 221. Also mentioned, 164 n.,
167, 225
Shrewsbury, Anna Maria, Countess
of, her scandalous life under
Charles II, 2–7; at Pontoise, 9–
10; readmitted to Court, 11; her
marriage to G. R. Bridges, 14;
her Jacobitism, 50–1, 73, 78; her
death, 150
Shrewsbury, Charles Talbot, twelfth
Earl and only Duke of, his ancestry, 1–2; his boyhood in
France, 8–11; suggested match
for him, 11–13; enters Academy
in Paris, 13–14; his military service in Flanders (1678), 15–16;
secedes from the Church of
Rome, 17–18; enters the House
of Lords, 19; loses the sight of
one eye, 20; resigns his military
appointments, 21; dismissed from
his lord-lieutenancies, 22; his

Shrewsbury, Charles Talbot, *contd.*
negotiations with William of
Orange (1687), 23–5; joins in the
invitation to William of Orange,
26; goes over to Holland, 27;
occupies Bristol (December 1,
1688), 29; takes part in conference at Hungerford, 30; conducts James II to Rochester, 31–
2; his attitude to the Succession
question, 33; appointed Secretary of State, 34–6; his rivalry
with Nottingham, 38; anxious to
resign, 39–42; negotiates with
the Churchills, 43; dissuades
William from dissolving Parliament, 44; dissuades him from
going to Holland, 45; his rupture
with the King (April 1690), 46–7;
his resignation (June 1690), 48–
9; his offers of assistance to the
Government after battle of
Beachy Head, 53–4; opposes
Carmarthen, 55; associates with
the Marlboroughs, 56–8; and
Land Tax (1692), 59–60; intro-
duces Triennial Bill (1693), 60–
2; opposes continuance of press
censorship, 62–3; in communication with Sunderland, 64; refuses
offer of the seals (Nov. 1693), 64–
5; his negotiations with Mrs
Villiers, 66–70; his relations with
Montgomery, 71; accepts the
seals (March 1694), 72; made a
duke, 76–7; tries to restore Marlborough to favour with the King,
77, 80; tries to reconcile Russell to
wintering in the Mediterranean,
80–2; and the Lancashire Plot,
83–4; suffers from gout, 87–9;
helps to restore Marlborough to
the King's favour, 89; and enquiry into affairs of the East
India Company, 90–2; and
Russell's "indiscretion", 93–4;
on results of the defection of
Savoy, 95–6; on the Currency
problem, 97; and the Treason
Bill, 98; and the Assassination
Plot (1696), 99; and problems of

finance and currency, 102–4;
urges necessity of concluding
peace, 104–7; and Fenwick case,
chap. v *passim*; not allowed to
resign, 132; and Peace of Ryswick, 133–4; allegations made
against him by Price and Chaloner,
135–6; his resignation again refused, 136–7; negotiates with the
Whigs, 138–41; appointed Lord
Chamberlain, 141; resigns, 142;
goes abroad, 144; visits Genoa,
146–8; his life in Rome, 149–56;
his dislike of Venice, 157–8; his
marriage, 159; in Holland, 160;
his return to England, 161; his
correspondence with Marlborough
(1704–6), 162; his correspondence
with Halifax, 163; his relations
with Godolphin, 164–5; his negotiations with Buckinghamshire
(1707), 166; joins Harley, 167;
favours peace, 168–9; votes for
Sacheverell, 170; becomes Lord
Chamberlain, 171–3; his appointment causes perturbation,
173–5; and dismissal of Sunderland, 176; and dismissal of
Godolphin, 177–9; said with
Harley to govern England, 182,
185; anxious for peace but suspicious of the French, 186–8; his
mission to Paris (1713), 189–96;
his administration of Ireland,
196–205; and the Schism Bill,
207; defends Bolingbroke in
matter of the *Asiento* contract,
207–8; Bolingbroke cannot
fathom him, 208; protests his
attachment to the House of Hanover, 209–10; becomes Lord
Treasurer, 211; his power on
accession of George I, 213–14;
retires into private life, 215; sides
with Tories against the Septennial Bill, 217–18; his intrigues
with the Jacobites (1716–17), 219–
20; his death, 221

His accomplishments, 17, 149,
223–6; alleged timidity, 23, 178,
229–30; alleged Jacobitism, 50–2,

Shrewsbury, Charles Talbot, *contd.* 71–4, 111–16, 128–9, 135–6, 219–20, 226–9; conciliatory temper, 233–5; dislike of office, 35, 39–42, 101, 147–8, 151, 163, 166, 203, 213, 228, 230–2; ill-health, 39–41, 48–9, 87–9, 116–20, 125–6, 131–2, 139–41, 146–7, 157–9, 213, 221, 223; love of peace, 104–7, 134, 168–9, 184; religious opinions, 17–18, 152–7, 227; sagacity, 233

Shrewsbury, Francis, eleventh Earl of, 2–4

Sidney, Henry, Viscount (subsequently Earl of Romney), 33, 55–6

Smith, Matthew (informer), 128–31

Smyrna merchant fleet, loss of the, 63

Somers, John, Baron, appointed Lord Keeper, 63; one of the "governing men", 64–5; one of the Lords Justices, 92; and the Partition Treaties, 147–8; and rumours of Shrewsbury's reconversion to Rome, 154, 156; appointed President of the Council, 167. Also mentioned, 100 n., 120, 129, 135, 154, 156, 176, 180, 212

Somerset, Charles Seymour, sixth Duke of, 169, 211–12

Sophia, Princess, of Hanover, 37

Soranzo (Venetian envoy), 101–2

Stanley, Sir John, 141

Stillingfleet, Edward, Bishop of Worcester, 86

Strafford, Lady, quoted, 183, 216

Strafford, Thomas Wentworth, Earl of (son of the foregoing), 183, 215; quoted, 224 n., 225–6

Stratford, Dr William, 221

Sunderland, Charles Spencer, third Earl of, 176–8, 214

Sunderland, Dorothy, Dowager Countess of (widow of the first Earl), quoted, 20

Sunderland, Robert Spencer, second Earl of, advises William III to confide in the Whigs, 64, 122; appointed one of the Lords Justices and Lord Chamberlain, 132; Shrewsbury's negotiations with (1698), 139–40, 143–4. Also mentioned, 96, 120, 131, 233

Swift, Jonathan, Dean of St Patrick's, quoted or referred to, 185, 196–7, 206, 212, 230

Taaff, John (informer), 83–4, 99

Talbot, Charles. *See* Shrewsbury, Duke of

Talbot, Sir John (Shrewsbury's uncle and guardian), 8, 11–13, 15–16, 159

Talbot, William, Bishop of Oxford, 154–5, 204

Tallard, Marshal, 190

Temple, Sir William, 36

Tenison, Thomas, Archbishop of Canterbury, 88, 92, 135

Test Act, the (1673), 17

Test Act, the Parliamentary (1678), 18

Tillotson, John, Dean, and afterwards Archbishop of Canterbury, 18, 85–6

Tirol, Shrewsbury's visit to the, 158

Tollemache, General Thomas, 79

Torbay, William of Orange's landing at, 28

Torcy, Jean Baptiste Colbert, Marquis de, 185, 190, 191

Torrington, Arthur Herbert, Earl of, 53

Trelawney, Sir Jonathan, Bishop of Bristol, 29

Trenchard, Sir John, 63–5, 70, 83, 87, 89

Trials of Treason Bill, 98

Triennial Bill (Jan. 1693), 60–2, 64; (Nov. 1693), 67–8; (Dec. 1693), 68–9; (1694), 84–5, 87

Trumbull, Sir William, 90, 92, 138

Turin, visited by Shrewsbury, 148; Prince Eugene's victory at, 168

Tyrconnel, Richard Talbot, Earl of, 37

Utrecht, Peace of, 185–8

Venice, Shrewsbury's visit to, 157–8
Venier (Venetian envoy), 101–2
Vernon, James, Under-Secretary to Shrewsbury, 40, 42; and Fenwick case, 115, 116, 120, 125; appointed Secretary of State (1697), 138. Also mentioned, 140, 154–5. Quoted, 129, 134 n., 135, 147
Villars, Charles Louis Hector, Marshal de, 185–6, 190
Villeroy, Marshal, 190
Villiers, Edward. *See* Jersey, Earl of
Villiers, Elizabeth (later Countess of Orkney), 66–74 *passim*

Walpole, Sir Robert, 170, 176, 180, 218
Warrington, Henry Booth, Baron Delamere, and later Earl of, 31, 37
Wharton, Philip, fourth Baron, 48, 53, 62, 67–8
Wharton, Thomas, fifth Baron, later first Earl and Marquis of, 136, 138–9, 140–1, 143, 233
William III, Prince of Orange and King of England, negotiates with English malcontents, 23; visited by Shrewsbury (1687), 24–5; invited to cross over to England, 26; his expedition, 27–32; and the succession to the throne, 33; appoints Shrewsbury Secretary of State, 34; employs both Whigs and Tories, 37–8; refuses to allow Shrewsbury to resign, 39–42; his difficulties with the Churchills, 43; dissolves Parliament (Jan. 1690), 44–5; his rupture with Shrewsbury, 46–9; goes to Ireland, 52; disgraces Marlborough, 57; objects to the Triennial Bill, 60–2, 64–5; his indirect negotiations with Shrewsbury (Nov. 1693), 66–74; appoints Shrewsbury Secretary of State, 72; gives him a dukedom, 76–7; sends Russell to the Mediterranean, 79–82; agrees to Triennial Bill (1694), 84–5; reconciled to Marlborough, 89; and defection of the Duke of Savoy, 95–6; and need of supplies for the war, 102–6; and Fenwick case, chap. v *passim*; refuses to allow Shrewsbury to resign, 132; recognised by Louis XIV as King of England, 133; uses Shrewsbury's mediation with the Whig leaders, 139–41; allows Shrewsbury to retire, 141–2; and to leave the kingdom, 144; his forbearance with Shrewsbury, 224; Shrewsbury discontented with, 228; his fortitude, 231. Also mentioned, 35, 36, 54, 55, 75, 78, 101, 146, 164, 222, 227, 229, 233, 234
Windham, Sir William, 206, 211
Wright, Sir Nathan, 162
Wynne, Dr, 40, 42

York, James, Duke of. *See* James II
Young, Robert (informer), 58

Zuylestein, William Henry Nassau de (subsequently Earl of Rochford), 27

For EU product safety concerns, contact us at Calle de José Abascal, 56–1°, 28003 Madrid, Spain or eugpsr@cambridge.org.

www.ingramcontent.com/pod-product-compliance
Ingram Content Group UK Ltd.
Pitfield, Milton Keynes, MK11 3LW, UK
UKHW010038140625
459647UK00012BA/1470